Immigration & nationality law handbook

1992 edition

Sue Shutter

Joint Council for the Welfare of Immigrants

ISBN 1 874010 00 5

Design: Pat Kahn
Typesetting: Boldface, 17A Clerkenwell Road, London EC1M 5RD
Printing: Unwin Brothers, The Gresham Press, Old Woking, Surrey GU22 9LH

JCWI, 115 Old Street, London EC1V 9JR, tel 071 251 8706

Preface and acknowledgements

JCWI would like to thank many people for their part in the preparation of this book. The Nuffield Foundation gave us a grant for the writing and production of the book and the Gulbenkian Foundation contributed towards the additional costs.

Several people have read all or part of the manuscript in draft and have made helpful suggestions – Anne Owers (who wrote the nationality chapters and has commented in detail on successive drafts); Sue Conlan, Belayeth Hussain, Pat Kahn, Naseem Khan, Beth Lakhani, Abdul Paliwala and Erif Rison, who formed a support group for the project; Hilary Belchak, Nicholas Blake, Sophie Cowgill, Jaishree Dholakia, Roland Doven, Ann Dummett, Don Flynn, Duncan Lane, Nuala Mole and Barry Stoyle, who read and made detailed comments on particular chapters.

JCWI's knowledge and expertise is gained because of our practical experience of how the immigration system works. We have gained this because people come to us for advice, help and support and then trust us to deal with matters of vital importance in their lives. We are grateful for their confidence in us and hope that the book will be useful to them.

It cannot be overstressed that immigration law and practice are rapidly-changing and any book will immediately be out-of-date in parts. The Asylum Bill was withdrawn as the book went to press; we will publish a Supplement on asylum later in the year if any new Bill comes into force. The *Handbook* is an ongoing project and it is planned to publish annual supplements. But in order to keep abreast of general developments, we urge readers to become members of JCWI and thus receive our quarterly *Bulletins* with updated information, and other publications.

Contents

Full contents

Immigration rules and Home Office practices are frequently changed, with very little or no publicity. No book can remain up-to-date for long. JCWI plans to publish regular supplements and updates to this Handbook; write to us to ensure that you are on our subscribers' list to receive notification of updates.

Organisations and individuals can become members of JCWI and will receive our quarterly Bulletin and Annual Report and details of other JCWI publications and training courses.

1 The background to British immigration and nationality law

Immigration, nationality and the right of entry to the UK

Immigration and nationality law are often talked about together, as though they were synonymous: this causes great confusion, as people often talk about 'citizenship' when they mean 'right of residence'. In fact, immigration and nationality are two separate areas of law, each with its own major primary legislation: the Immigration Act 1971 (as amended by the Immigration Act 1988) and the British Nationality Act 1981.

Nationality simply defines the country of which people are citizens, and which usually issues them with passports. Nationality law sets out the ways in which people can become citizens (usually by being born in a country, being born abroad to parents who are citizens of the country, or taking out citizenship by naturalisation after a period of residence in a country).

Immigration is the system of laws and rules by which each country decides who shall be able to live in that country and under what conditions. Immigration law sets out the categories of people who are allowed in automatically (usually citizens of the country) and the mechanisms and officials who decide whether and on what conditions others may enter and enforce the departure of people who are not supposed to be in the country.

But in Britain this simple distinction is complicated by the fact that not all those who have British nationality are automatically able to enter Britain as citizens. There are six categories of British nationality (described in detail in chapter 17) of which only one, British citizens, has an absolute right to enter Britain. The other five are people originating from British dependencies or ex-colonies who had their right of entry to Britain taken away in 1962 or 1968, even though they travel on British passports. The **British Nationality Act 1981** (which needs to be read with the Immigration Act 1971) sets out the conditions for acquiring five of those nationalities (British citizenship, British Dependent Territories citizenship, British Overseas citizenship, British subject status and British Protected Person status). It was slightly amended, for Falklanders, by the **British Nationality (Falkland Islands) Act 1983**. The sixth kind of British nationality, British National (Overseas) status, was created for people from Hong Kong in the **Hong Kong Act 1985** and the **Hong Kong (British Nationality) Order 1986**.

At the same time, some people who do not have British nationality, but are citizens of independent Commonwealth countries, do have an automatic right of entry and are therefore free from immigration control. They are people who have the **right of abode** in the UK. Right of abode does not mean the same as the right to live in the UK, which many foreign nationals have. It is a special status, available only to Commonwealth citizens born before 1 January 1983 who had a parent born in the UK; and to women Commonwealth citizens who were married before 1 January 1983 to a man who was a British citizen or had the right of abode in the UK. Right of abode is defined in the **Immigration Act 1971** (the cut-off date of 1 January 1983 is found in the British Nationality Act 1981) and it has been slightly amended, as regards polygamous wives, by the **Immigration Act 1988**.

Nationals of other European Community countries also are not restricted by British immigration law. Their rights are found in the **Treaty of Rome** as amended by the **Single European Act** and by binding **Directives** issued by the Council of Ministers of the EC. All EC nationals who are workers or who are seeking work, or who are providing or receiving services, have an absolute right of entry. The families and dependants of such people, whether or not they themselves are EC nationals, also have an absolute right of entry (ironically, this puts the families of other EC nationals resident in the UK in a much better position than families of British citizens resident in the UK, who have no such absolute right of entry). In addition, EC students, pensioners and those without employment will have rights of entry from July 1992, provided that they can maintain themselves without needing social security.

Irish nationals are also EC nationals. But in addition, there is no immigration control between the UK and the Republic of Ireland; this territory, together with the Isle of Man and the Channel Islands, is called the Common Travel Area and is defined in the Immigration Act 1971. This means that Irish and British citizens are exempt from any immigration control when they pass between the two countries (however, nationals of other non-EC countries are not).

The structure of immigration control

Most of this book concerns people who are subject to the full requirements of immigration control: people who are not nationals of EC countries and who do not have the right of abode in the UK. The Immigration Act 1971 sets out the structure of immigration control, including the duties and powers of immigration officers, the system for appealing against decisions to refuse entry or stay in the UK and the mechanisms for deporting or removing people who are alleged to be in the UK illegally. The Asylum Bill (being debated as this book goes to press) sets up a separate system for dealing with asylum-seekers.

BRITISH IMMIGRATION CONTROL

Not subject to control	Subject to limited control	Subject to full control
British citizens	EC nationals	Aliens
Irish citizens		Other Commonwealth citizens
Commonwealth citizens with right of abode		Other types of British nationals

The Immigration Act 1971 also gives the Home Secretary the power to make **immigration rules**. The immigration rules are in practice what decide whether and how someone can enter or stay in the UK. They set out in detail the categories of people (for example, families, visitors, refugees, students) who may enter and the criteria they must fulfil. They can be made and changed without needing to change the law: they are simply presented to Parliament, which may or may not decide to have a short debate (usually one and a half hours) on them, and which cannot amend them, but can only accept or reject them in total. Immigration rules have only once been rejected within the last 12 years, when right-wing Conservatives felt the marriage rules were too lax and the opposition parties felt they were too restrictive. They were tightened up and then passed through Parliament.

When changes are made to the immigration rules (for example, new visa requirements which have become at least an annual event) the Home Office usually publishes only the amendment, and does not reissue the whole of the rules. The most recent consolidated immigration rules (called, confusingly, *Statement of Changes in Immigration Rules*) were issued on 23 March 1990 (HC 251) and came into force on 1 May 1990, but some changes have been made since then (▶see appendix for details).

As well as the published immigration rules there are also secret instructions to immigration officials on the practical details of how they should deal with applications and how they should exercise their discretion. These are classified as confidential documents and all efforts to persuade the Home Office to publish them have failed.

The immigration appeals system has its own rules, the **Immigration Appeals (Procedure) Rules**, which are now issued by the Lord Chancellor's Department. They set out the deadlines and the procedures for appealing to adjudicators and to the Immigration Appeal Tribunal. The Asylum Bill proposes a different system for asylum appeals, with its own procedure rules, under discussion at the time this book went to press.

The system of immigration control

There are three types of immigration control, which occur in different places and are run by three separate departments or groups of officials.

Before-entry control happens at British embassies, high commissions or consulates overseas when people apply for entry clearance (often called a visa) before they travel to the UK. Some people must apply for permission in this way: they are people who are visa nationals (listed in the immigration rules) who always need permission in advance, for whatever reason they are travelling; people coming intending permanent settlement (usually to join family members); or people coming for work. Other people may choose to apply for entry clearance because it will reduce problems on arrival in the UK. Before-entry control is administered by officials working for the Foreign and Commonwealth Office, although increasingly these are immigration officers working on secondment.

On-entry control happens at designated ports of entry to the UK (major airports and seaports). It is carried out by immigration officers, a separate branch of the civil service. They have the power to grant or refuse entry, to detain, to search people and their luggage, to read papers and letters and to require people to submit to medical examination (like the notorious 'virginity test' in the 1970s). They stamp passengers' passports to show how long they can stay and under what conditions.

After-entry control happens within the UK. People may want to extend their stay or change their status (for example, a student who has married a British citizen). Applications to do this are administered by Home Office civil servants working in the Immigration and Nationality Department at Lunar House, in Croydon. The second type of after-entry control is called enforcement: tracing people who are allegedly in the country illegally and enforcing their departure. This is done by immigration officers, from Isis House and Harmondsworth in London, and from major ports and airports, who work closely with the police.

The basis and history of British immigration control

Before 1905, there were no immigration laws in the UK. The entry of people who were not British subjects was technically part of the royal prerogative, and the monarch could also make decisions to expel individuals or groups of people. The **Aliens Act 1905** was passed, after two decades of intermittent agitation, in order to prevent refugees, mainly Jewish, poor and fleeing from eastern Europe, from seeking refuge in Britain. The Act only applied to boats carrying more than 20 passengers and to those travelling steerage class who could be excluded if they were 'undesirable' – defined mainly as being unable to support themselves and their dependants. The Act only applied to 'aliens' – people who were not from any part of the British empire – but it set up the first rudimentary machinery for checking entry which was later expanded and developed.

However, it was not until 1962 that any attempt was made to control the entry of people who were subjects of the British crown by being born in a country which was, or which had been, part of the British empire. The **Commonwealth Immigrants Act 1962** was passed against a background of racist agitation and pressure. The Act and the subsequent laws passed in 1968 and 1971 were designed primarily to prevent the entry of black British subjects (Commonwealth and UK citizens); hence the invention of 'right of abode' (initially called 'patriality') and of preferential treatment for Commonwealth citizens with a UK-born grandparent, in order to ensure that many Australians, New Zealanders and Canadians were not excluded by the legislation.

These laws led to some British nationals (almost all black) being excluded from Britain while some foreign nationals (mostly white) from other Commonwealth countries were free to enter at any time. Britain's entry into the Common Market on 1 January 1973 (a date which ironically coincided with the coming into force of the Immigration Act 1971) gave new rights to enter and work to hundreds of millions of EC nationals.

The Immigration Act 1971 and the British Nationality Act 1981 codified British immigration and nationality law (and perpetuated the divisions described above). Since then, new laws, rules and practices have imposed increasing restrictions on people coming from countries of the South. The only right to family reunion in UK law (for long-settled Commonwealth men) was repealed in the Immigration Act 1988; meanwhile, the primary purpose marriage rule and the support and accommodation requirements meant that, in 1990, nearly 70% of husbands from the Indian subcontinent were refused entry. Deportation was made easier and swifter by the Immigration Act 1988 and new Home Office practices which followed it. Home Office practice with regard to asylum-seekers became more restrictive after the arrival of Tamils in the mid-1980s, culminating in the **Asylum Bill 1991** and new rules. Increasing visa restrictions, and the decisions of immigration officers at ports, have made family visits more difficult for all the main ethnic minority communities in the UK.

The process of EC harmonisation, under the Single European Act, and the increasing co-operation between ministers and civil servants from different countries, is likely to add to the stringency of immigration control on non-EC citizens throughout Europe. Countries are seeking to strengthen their common external border (by increased visa controls, common visa procedures, fines on airlines and the automatic refusal of anyone refused by another member state). They are also anxious to improve internal controls (by checks on people within a country to find out whether they have the right to be there, and by linking immigration status to access to work, benefits and services). On the other hand, European harmonisation provides opportunities for co-operation between non-governmental organisations in different countries and for attempts to use EC freedom of movement legislation and the European Convention on Human Rights more creatively; but it will be hard to stop the drift towards ever tighter controls, targeted against people from poorer countries of the South.

2 Spouses and fiancé(e)s

It is often very difficult to explain the provisions and the purposes of the immigration rules on marriage. It is widely believed that being married to a British citizen gives a person a 'right' to enter or remain in the UK with his or her spouse. This is not correct; British immigration law gives no automatic rights to any family members. The spouses of certain people may be able to come to join them, but only if they satisfy the requirements of the immigration rules. This chapter covers five different sets of circumstances. These are:

- people who wish to enter the UK as spouses or fiancé(e)s of British citizens or people settled in the UK and who intend to settle permanently in the UK. They need to make applications for entry clearance before travelling to the UK (▶see page 8).

- people who came to the UK for a temporary purpose (for example, as visitors or students) and have married British citizens or people settled in the UK. They can make applications to stay in the UK on the basis of marriage, and remain in the country while they do so (▶see page 13).

- people who are accompanying, or coming to join, spouses who are in the UK for temporary purposes (for example as students, work permit holders, business people). They sometimes need to get entry clearance before they travel and sometimes can apply when they arrive (▶see page 20).

- people who want to come to, or remain in, the UK with a partner, but for whom there is no provision in the immigration rules – for example, couples who are not married or planning to marry, and gay and lesbian couples (▶see page 21).

- people whose marriages break down in the UK and any immigration consequences of this (▶see page 24).

REMEMBER:

- people abroad wanting to settle in the UK must get entry clearance before they travel
- BUT some family members may be British citizens
- AND some people may not have to fit into the immigration rules; see below

People who do not have to fit into the rules

Some people have stronger claims to enter the UK as spouses or fiancé(e)s because they can qualify under other parts of the immigration rules, or under EC law.

a) **EC citizens who are living and working in the UK** have the right under EC law to be joined by a spouse, whether or not he or she is an EC citizen and their partners do not have to meet the requirements of British immigration rules. There are full details of the procedures in chapter 6 on EC citizens. Remember Ireland is also an EC country, so foreign spouses of Irish citizens who have come to live in the UK may benefit.

b) **Commonwealth citizens with a parent born in the UK** have the right of abode (▶see glossary for definition) in the UK and are therefore not subject to immigration control at all and are free to travel to the UK.

c) **Some Commonwealth citizen women** have the right of abode and are not subject to immigration control. They are women who were Commonwealth citizens on 31 December 1982 and who were married on or before that date to British citizen men, or men with the right of abode (▶see glossary for definition; this is more than merely being settled in the UK). Such a marriage before this date meant that the woman automatically gained the right of abode in the UK herself, and therefore is no longer subject to immigration control. However, this fact needs to be proved before she travels, and she must apply to the British high commission for a 'certificate of entitlement to the right of abode'. There are special shorter queues for people with a claim to the right of abode in the Indian subcontinent countries.

In order to get the certificate, the woman will need her original marriage certificate, to show the date of the marriage, and proof that her husband was either a British citizen, or a Commonwealth citizen with the right of abode, at the time of the marriage. When the certificate of entitlement is granted, it is valid for the same length of time as the passport and she is free to travel to the UK and to return at any time during the validity of the passport. The returning resident rules (▶see page 154) do not apply to her. When the passport expires, the Home Office or the British high commission will give a new certificate of entitlement in a new passport, on production of the same evidence.

NB This provision does not apply to men, or to non-Commonwealth citizen women. Pakistani citizen women cannot benefit from this because Pakistan was not a member of the Commonwealth between 1972 and 1989 and therefore a Pakistani woman would not have been a Commonwealth citizen on 31 December 1982.

People coming to the UK as spouses or fiancé(e)s

WHAT THE RULES SAY

People coming as spouses or fiancé(e)s must hold a current entry clearance granted for that purpose.

The immigration rules state that people may come to the UK as the spouse or fiancé(e) of a person present and settled in the UK, or who is on the same occasion admitted for settlement.

The rules state that entry clearance will be refused unless the entry clearance officer is satisfied that:

- the marriage was not entered into primarily to obtain admission to the UK
- each of the parties has the intention of living permanently with the other as his or her spouse
- the parties to the marriage have met
- there will be adequate accommodation for the parties and their dependants without recourse to public funds in accommodation of their own or which they occupy themselves
- the parties will be able to maintain themselves and their dependants adequately without recourse to public funds.

The rules for fiancé(e)s are similar, but with a distinction made in the provisions for support and accommodation before and after the marriage, as the couple may not be living together until after they are married.

WHAT THE RULES MEAN

Spouse or fiancé(e)

A spouse means someone who is legally married, in a way recognised by UK law. A fiancé(e) must be someone who is legally free to marry under UK law. This excludes people under 16 even if they have been legally married, or are legally free to marry, in the countries from which they come. It also excludes people who are not yet divorced, even if divorce proceedings are under way. It can, however, include wives in polygamous marriages, as long as they were validly married in a country which permits polygamy and as long as they are the only wife in that relationship who has ever entered the UK as a spouse. If one wife of the relationship has already been admitted to join the husband, this marriage will have to be ended by divorce before another wife can qualify to enter.

Present in the UK

The other partner must be 'present and settled' in the UK or 'on the same occasion be admitted for settlement'. This applies even if the partner is a

British citizen, who cannot have conditions placed on his or her stay in the UK and therefore is always settled. It means that the British or settled spouse must be in the UK at the time the application is made, or will be travelling to the UK, for settlement, with the non-settled spouse.

Entry clearance

All spouses and fiancé(e)s must obtain entry clearance before travelling to the UK, if they are planning to remain permanently. Spouses and fiancé(e)s who are visa nationals (▶see glossary) must obtain entry clearance even if they are only planning to stay for a short time. It is possible for a spouse to plan to come simply to visit the partner in the UK, or for a fiancé(e) to come simply for the marriage ceremony, after which the couple plan to live permanently elsewhere. However, it can sometimes be difficult to persuade immigration and entry clearance officers of this. They may suspect that a spouse or fiancé(e) is trying to avoid either the queues or the more stringent requirements of the settlement rules.

The 'primary purpose rule'

* the marriage (or planned marriage) must not be entered into primarily to obtain admission to the UK

The immigration rules require officials to be satisfied that the marriage was not entered into primarily so that a person from overseas could gain settlement in the UK. This is known as the primary purpose rule. It means that the couple have to show that they did not marry mainly for immigration reasons. The immigration officials use their subjective judgement, as well as the instructions they are given, to decide if they are satisfied. It is quite clear that the procedures and practice vary enormously in different countries. In discussions with people who have come to the UK as spouses from Australia, for example, it is clear that no questions were asked on this point at all; it was simply assumed by the immigration official that this requirement was satisfied. For young men in the Indian subcontinent, eighty or ninety questions may be asked around this requirement, the questions being repeated again and again in slightly different forms to see if any 'admission' is made as to the primary purpose of the marriage. In 1990, 69% of husbands and fiancés from the countries of the subcontinent were refused under this rule.

It is therefore very important that couples should understand the reasoning behind the questioning and be prepared in advance for the kind of questions they may be asked. Often people feel that they have been tricked or browbeaten into giving answers to immigration officials which do not actually reflect their true feelings or intentions. The Annex at the end of this chapter explains this rule in more detail.

Intention to stay together permanently

The couple have to satisfy the official that they intend to stay together permanently as husband and wife. This is also impossible to prove; questions may be asked about the purpose of the marriage and about where the couple intend to live after marriage. If it appears that the couple may have competing commitments in different countries this could be a reason for refusal. If a couple have been married for some time but have not been together for much of it, this could also be a problem. Where there is inadequate accommodation in the UK, this could also be used to argue that the couple will not be staying together permanently.

The couple have met each other

The meeting does not have to take place before an application for entry clearance is made but the couple must have met before the applicant spouse or fiancé(e) is interviewed about his or her application. This requirement was intended to place an extra hurdle in the way of some arranged marriages, where the couple may not meet before the wedding day, or the wedding may be by proxy. It entails the extra cost of a journey abroad or to the UK before the marriage.

The Immigration Appeal Tribunal has held, in the case of *Meharban* (6073), that a meeting does not have to take place in the context of a marriage; it is acceptable if the couple met each other as children, as long as they both have clear recollections of the meeting and know each other as individuals. This is only likely to be a problem for fiancé(e)s, as a married couple will almost certainly have met at the wedding. Meeting can be proved by photographs of the couple together, by the recollections of both parties, by passport stamps showing that both were in the same country at the same time, by corroborative statements from relatives or friends who know of the meeting.

Support and accommodation

The immigration rules say that the couple must be able to support and accommodate themselves and any dependants without recourse to public funds (▶see box on page 124). It is possible for other family members, or friends, to show that they will support the couple; the immigration authorities require a letter to confirm the support as well as evidence such as recent pay slips or bank statements to prove ability to support. The important thing is to show that, when the spouse or fiancé(e) from abroad comes to the UK, the family will not need to have recourse to public funds.

This means that no *additional* public funds must be necessary for the spouse coming in to the UK. If the settled or British spouse is living in homeless persons' accommodation, for example, this does not prohibit a partner from abroad from coming to the UK because no additional accommodation is required. If the partner in the UK is on benefit, but the partner abroad has the offer of a job in the UK when he or she arrives, this should be sufficient. But it is important to be aware that any job offer or work plans that were made before the marriage could be used by entry clearance officers to claim that the primary purpose of the marriage was to be able to work in the UK.

It is often more difficult for British or settled women than men to show that their partners can be supported in the UK. A woman looking after young children may not be able to work and therefore may rely on benefits. If she is living with other members of her family, for example her own parents, in their accommodation, she will have to show either that this will be an adequate long-term arrangement and that the couple will be paying their own way, or that they have realistic plans and expectations of having their own home soon. A Tribunal decision in August 1991, *Kausar* (8025), suggests that it is easier to satisfy this requirement when a couple live in a separate family unit, rather than joint family living arrangements.

▶See chapter 11 for further details about evidence needed to satisfy the support and accommodation requirement.

How to apply abroad

Spouses and fiancé(e)s must apply for permission to enter at the British embassy or high commission in the country where they are living. They will all be interviewed by an official at the British post. In some countries, particularly those of the Indian subcontinent, the Philippines and Jamaica, there are substantial delays before applications will be considered. Inadequate numbers of staff have been sent to the posts and they carry out extremely long interviews and checks on people, which are very time consuming. The Home Office regularly publishes details of the waiting times in the countries of the Indian subcontinent and gives information about other countries when asked; the appendix gives details of some waiting periods near the time of writing. It is very difficult to bring forward an interview date unless there are exceptional compassionate circumstances, for example the severe illness of either partner. The fact that a couple want to be together for the birth of a child, for example, is not normally considered a strong enough reason.

Because of these delays, it is sensible to advise people to make applications well in advance of the time they hope to travel. For example, if a man in the UK seeks advice about his proposed marriage in India and is planning to travel for the wedding in several months' time, it is sensible for his fiancée to apply straight away to the British high commission, explaining when her wedding is planned and when her fiancé will be in India, to ask that an interview for them both can be fixed after the wedding while he is in India. The more notice that is given, the higher the chance that the high commission will be able to arrange this. It may be helpful for the British or settled spouse to be present, so that he or she can also be interviewed if the British authorities want to check anything about the situation in the UK.

Documents needed for an interview

At the interview, the official will need evidence of the legal status of the spouse in the UK and of the support and accommodation available. ▶Chapter 11 gives details of the documents which may be required by the entry clearance officer.

Information needed specifically for spouses and fiancé(e)s

- **proof of the marriage**. If the original marriage certificate is in the UK, it should be sent to the spouse abroad to take to the British high commission or embassy for interview, with a certified copy being kept by the partner in the UK. If there is no such certificate in existence, the spouse abroad should explain this. In India, for example, if there is no marriage certificate there may be a declaration under the Hindu Marriage Act that the wedding has taken place. If it is a customary marriage, for example in West Africa, the British post may require statutory declarations from members of the family of both sides to confirm that the correct procedures took place.
- **proof that the couple were or are free to marry**. If either party has been married before, the British post will need to see evidence that the previous marriage(s) have ended, by death, divorce or annulment. The evidence could be original divorce certificates or statutory declarations to prove a customary divorce, or the original death certificate of a previous spouse who has died.
- **proof that the couple are over 16**.

When an application is successful

If the application is successful, the spouse or fiancé(e) will be given entry clearance, which will confirm that the person is coming for marriage. The person must travel within six months; if people are unable to travel within this time, they should apply to the British high commission or embassy to explain the reasons for the delay and ask for the entry clearance to be extended.

Fiancé(e)s will be admitted for six months, with a prohibition on employment and business, on arrival at a British port or airport. They are expected to get married within that six months and should then apply to the Home Office for permission to remain for a year as a spouse. While the application is under consideration, the prohibition on work and business continues. If there are reasons why the marriage has to be delayed, the fiancé(e) should still apply to the Home Office, within the six months' leave granted, for an extension of the time, explaining why the marriage has not yet taken place.

Spouses will be admitted for one year. The stamp placed on their passports states 'given leave to enter the UK for twelve months', with no other restriction, which means that they are free to take employment, run a business or do anything else (see chapter 13 for example of this passport stamp). They are not normally given any further information about their rights and status by the immigration officers. Shortly before the year is over, they should apply to the Home Office for permission to remain permanently; see below for details of making this application.

When an application is refused

If an application for entry clearance is refused, the British embassy or high commission has to give the spouse or fiancé(e) a formal letter stating that the application has been refused, with brief reasons for the refusal and information about the right to appeal against the refusal, and a form to fill in to appeal. Any appeal has to reach the British high commission or embassy within three months of the date of refusal. There are more details about the appeals processes in chapter 16.

If the appeal is lost, the couple can make representations to the Home Office to reconsider the case. Unless there is new information which was not available at the appeal, it is unlikely that representations will be successful. The person abroad may make a fresh application to come to the UK; if the couple are married, events since the marriage will be considered. When one of the couple is a British citizen, EC law may also be helpful; see chapter 6 for more information.

People who marry or become engaged in the UK

People already in the UK, for example as visitors or students, may apply to the Home Office to remain because they have married a British citizen or a person settled in the UK. They do not need to leave the UK in order to apply.

People who are in the UK illegally or whose leave to remain has already run out may also apply to stay on the basis of marriage, but this may be problematic. The rules state that the person applying to remain must not have been in the UK without authority before the marriage. Thus an overstayer applying to remain with a spouse is making an application for exceptional treatment, outside the immigration rules.

People who apply when they are legally in the UK

WHAT THE RULES SAY

The rules state that where a person with limited leave seeks an extension of stay on the basis of marriage to a person settled here, an extension of stay will not be granted unless the Secretary of State is satisfied:

- that the marriage was not entered into primarily to obtain settlement in the UK
- that the parties to the marriage have met
- that the marriage has not been terminated
- that each of the parties has the intention of living permanently with the other as his or her spouse
- that there will be adequate accommodation for the parties and their dependants without recourse to public funds in accommodation of their own or which they occupy themselves
- that the parties will be able to maintain themselves and their dependants adequately without recourse to public funds.

WHAT THE RULES MEAN

A person with limited leave married to a person settled here

This phrase means that the person applying to remain on the grounds of marriage must have valid immigration leave to remain, for example as a visitor, a student or a work permit holder, and must apply to the Home Office before the end of the time limit on that leave (▶see chapter 11 on how to apply). The person whom she or he is marrying must be a British citizen or have indefinite leave to remain in the UK. The rules and the way in which the application is considered are different if one partner is in the UK without permission (in breach of the immigration laws); ▶see page 15.

Tests of the marriage

- 'primarily to obtain settlement'
- the couple have met
- intention to live together permanently

▶see discussion of these points on pages 9–10

- Support and accommodation ▶see pages 144–145.

How to apply

Applications may be made in writing or in person at the Home Office, before the person's leave to remain runs out. There are no application forms. The person is legally in the UK while the application is being considered and the conditions attached to the original leave to remain, for example a prohibition on working, are still valid until the application is decided. The application may take a long time; for more information about the situation while applications are pending, see chapter 11.

The Home Office does not often subject such couples to the detailed questioning which happens in some countries abroad. If the person is legally in the UK at the time of marriage and at the time of application, and if the couple are able to support and accommodate themselves without recourse to public funds, there is a good chance that the application to remain will be granted.

Some problems which may arise

The Home Office may be suspicious of people who marry soon after gaining entry for another purpose. For example, if a person gained a visa as a visitor stating that he would be going back to his job in India after three weeks and then gets married after being in Britain for a fortnight and applies to stay as a spouse, the Home Office may suspect that this was his intention from the beginning, but that he wanted to avoid the queues in applying for a fiancé entry clearance. The Home Office may therefore treat the person as an illegal entrant who entered the UK by deception; ▶see chapter 14 for further details on illegal entry. It is therefore important to explain in such applications how and why the person's plans changed after arrival in the UK, as well as showing how he or she fits into the rest of the immigration rules on marriage.

The Home Office may also be suspicious of people who marry very shortly before their leave to remain runs out, and may believe that the marriage was entered into primarily to enable the person to stay in the UK. Evidence of the length of relationship and of the reasons why the marriage was planned for that particular date may be helpful in this situation.

There are no provisions in the immigration rules for people who have been allowed into the country on some other basis to apply to remain as fiancé(e)s. However, if a person who is in the UK for a temporary purpose has plans to marry which cannot be achieved while his or her leave to remain is still current, for example because the British or settled partner is awaiting a divorce, it is worth making an application as a fiancé(e) outside the rules, at the discretion of the Home Office. The application should explain the reasons for the delay in marrying. As the Home Office is often very slow in replying to applications, the couple may well be able to marry while waiting for the Home Office to respond. After the marriage, they should continue the application for leave to remain to the Home Office with the evidence of their marriage and ask for leave to remain as a spouse.

People who apply when they are in the UK without permission

WHAT THE RULES SAY

The immigration rules state that the Secretary of State must be satisfied that:

- the applicant has not remained in the UK in breach of the immigration laws
- the marriage has not taken place after a decision has been made to deport him or he has been recommended for deportation or been given notice under section 6(2) of the Immigration Act 1971.

WHAT THE RULES MEAN

Any application from a spouse who is an overstayer, or who has already been refused permission to stay on other grounds but is still in the country appealing against the refusal, is made outside the immigration rules, at the discretion of the Home Office. It is therefore possible for an application to be refused solely on the grounds that a person was in the UK without leave; it is not necessary for the Home Office to interview the couple or even to look into all the circumstances of their case.

How to apply

When an overstayer or someone who has been treated as an illegal entrant gets married and wants to apply for leave to remain with his or her spouse, it is important that the couple should seek detailed advice before deciding when or whether to make an application to the Home Office. The Home Office always has the discretion to consider an application; so when there are strong family or compassionate reasons it is often worth making out a case for people who do not fit into the immigration rules.

It is usually best to make the application to the Home Office in writing and to put forward as full and detailed case as possible at the outset. There are no application forms. In general, once the couple have decided that they want to make an application, it is best to do so while they both remain in the UK. If the person who has been in the country without permission leaves in order to make an entry clearance application abroad, the previous immigration history will still be considered, the application is still discretionary and the couple will be separated for the months that will be taken in considering the case.

There may be practical problems in getting married for people who are unwilling to produce their passports. The marriage registrar must by law be satisfied as to the identity, age and freedom to marry of couples requesting marriage. If the registrar is satisfied by what couples say, no further evidence may be requested. If not, instructions to registrars from the General Register Office state that the best evidence from a person from abroad is a passport. When people have lost their passports, or do not wish to show them, they may have difficulty in fixing a wedding. Birth certificates may be acceptable, but will not show whether people have been married, or whether they still hold their nationality of birth. Registrars state that a passport, issued more recently and which will have a photograph of its holder, is more useful, and the passports issued by many countries state whether the holder is married or single.

Other evidence, such as driving licences, may be acceptable at the discretion of the registrar. There have been reports of people being unable to book a wedding because the registrar has not accepted other evidence of their identity. There have also been cases where a registrar, suspicious about a particular person, has alerted the immigration authorities to the date fixed for a wedding, or the immigration authorities have requested information from the registrar, and people have been arrested as overstayers before they are able to marry.

Some important points to consider

- **how long the person has been in the UK**. If this is less than seven years, there will be no full right of appeal against deportation, should the Home Office refuse the application (▶see chapter 16 for more details). If the person has been in the UK for nearly seven years, it may be worth waiting before making the application.

- **how long the relationship has subsisted** and any evidence to show this, for example, children of the relationship, joint purchase of property, evidence the couple have been together for a long time. The European Court of Human Rights, in the case of *Berrehab* (1988 11 EHRR 322), has held that to deport a father away from his young child was an infringement of the child's right to respect for family life. When there is a child or children involved, it is worth reminding the Home Office of this case.

- **the person's previous immigration history** and any problems he or she has had with the Home Office in the past. When a marriage takes place at the end of a long series of applications or other immigration problems the Home Office will be particularly suspicious of the intentions of the person from abroad.

- **whether a deportation decision has already been made**. If so, it is important to urge that the decision be reversed or the deportation order be revoked. ▶See chapter 14 for details of the factors the Home Office must consider in deciding to deport a person and of how to counter them.

The Home Office may interview couples when the partner applying to remain is an overstayer or has had other immigration problems. They may be asked to go to the Home Office or to an immigration office, where they will be interviewed separately, but both may be asked the same questions about their meeting and relationship, to see if they give the same answers. Occasionally, the immigration service may come to a couple's home, unannounced, in order to see whether they are living together and whether there is any evidence that a couple live at that address.

In general, it is easier to get permission to stay as spouses outside the rules for women, and for people who come from countries other than those where the Home Office considers there is 'pressure to emigrate' (for example, the Indian subcontinent or North or West Africa). There is little point in an overstayer making an application to remain as a fiancé(e) unless there are very strong reasons why the marriage cannot take place before making an application to the Home Office.

When an application is successful

If an application is successful, a spouse will be given permission to remain for twelve months initially, without any restrictions on employment (see chapter 13 for example of this passport stamp). The Home Office sends a standard, detailed two-page letter explaining other rights in the UK (▶see copy in appendix). During this year the person is free to do any kind of work or business without needing any permission. Shortly before the end of the twelve-month period, the person should apply to the Home Office for settlement; see below for the procedure.

When an application is refused

If the application was made while the spouse or fiancé(e) from abroad had leave to remain, there is the right to appeal against a refusal. The Home Office must give the person a letter explaining the reason for refusal and the right to appeal, and forms to fill in to appeal. The forms must be returned to the Home Office within fourteen days of the date of refusal. The spouse may remain legally in the UK while the appeal is going on. There is more information about appealing in chapter 16.

If the application was made when the spouse or fiancé(e) from abroad did not have leave to remain, there is no formal right of appeal against refusal. The refusal letter states that the person should leave the UK without delay. It is still possible to make further representations to the Home Office on the person's behalf, explaining or reiterating any compassionate or other circumstances why an exception to the rules should be made.

People admitted or given leave to remain as spouses
The initial twelve-month period

Claiming benefits

It is expected that the couple will not have recourse to public funds (▶see box on page 124) but if this is financially necessary it is possible to claim certain benefits. See chapter 10 for more details about claiming.

The Home Office has stated that if a couple need to claim public funds for a short period during the twelve-month period, but are mainly able to support themselves, this will not automatically lead to a refusal. 'We would not use this power [to refuse] if a person had become dependent on public funds for a short time through no fault of his own. Moreover, if a sponsor here is dependent on public funds the relevant question will be whether extra funds were necessary to support the applicant.' (letter from David Waddington MP to Max Madden MP, December 1985) Thus the British or settled partner may claim for his or her individual needs, but not for the spouse from abroad.

A couple asking about entitlements to benefit during this first year should therefore be informed of their entitlement to claim (if appropriate) but told of the possible immigration consequences should they need to claim for a prolonged period, or should they still be claiming at the time of the settlement application, which could lead to a refusal. If a refusal is made solely on the grounds that a couple cannot show that they can support themselves, there is a right of appeal provided the application is made in time. During the appeal period, the spouse from abroad is allowed to work, so if one of them could then find work and they no longer needed to claim benefits, a fresh application to the Home Office could be made, which would be granted.

Travelling into and out of the UK

During the initial twelve-month period, the spouse from abroad is free to travel into and out of the UK and will be allowed in again until the end of the twelve months previously given. Visa nationals do not need visas to re-enter. When they return, leave to enter to the same date will be granted, usually with a stamp stating 'given leave to enter, section 3(3)(b) until [date]'. This refers to section 3(3)(b) of the Immigration Act 1971, which provides for people to be readmitted within a period of leave granted.

Applying for settlement (indefinite leave to remain)

WHAT THE RULES SAY

The immigration rules state that:

- a person who was admitted for a limited period, or given an extension of stay, as the spouse of a person settled here may have the time limit on their stay removed at the end of the period if

- the Secretary of State is satisfied that the marriage has not been terminated and that each of the parties has the intention of living permanently with the other as his or her spouse.

- there is a general power to refuse applications if the person has failed to maintain and accommodate himself and any dependants without recourse to public funds.

Making the application

Before the one year's permission has expired, the spouse from abroad must apply to the Home Office for settlement (indefinite leave to remain). The spouse who is British or settled should be in the UK at the time the application is made. If he or she is temporarily abroad, this should be explained to the Home Office and it should be informed when he or she returns.

Documents required for the application

- applicant's passport
- husband's or wife's passport
- original marriage certificate
- a letter from the settled or British spouse confirming that he or she supports the application. This can be handwritten and does not have to be in any particular form of words. Couples may wish to give the Home Office extensive details about their relationship, but a simple statement like 'I confirm that I am still married to [name of spouse] and we intend to remain together permanently as husband and wife' is sufficient.
- evidence of financial support, for example recent bank statements or pay slips, to show that the couple can be supported without recourse to public funds.

It is usual for this application to be granted routinely if the Home Office has no reason to suspect any problems. If the Home Office has been informed, either by the couple or anyone else, that they have separated or there have been marital problems, or if they have claimed public funds during the year, it is likely that the Home Office may want to interview the couple to be sure that the immigration rules are met.

Spouses coming to the UK for temporary purposes

Workers and business people

The immigration rules state that:

- spouses of workers, business people, self-employed people, persons of independent means, writers and artists should be given leave to enter for the period of the person's authorised stay, if they hold a current entry clearance. Entry clearance will be refused unless the entry clearance officer is satisfied that there will be adequate accommodation for the person admitted and that person's spouse and children without recourse to public funds in accommodation of their own or which they occupy themselves and that they will be able to maintain themselves adequately without recourse to public funds.

Proof of their identity, and having adequate support and accommodation without recourse to public funds (▶see box on page 124) are the only requirements that these spouses have to fulfil. The 'primary purpose rule', the intention to stay together permanently and the requirement that the couple must have met do not apply. Spouses must apply for entry clearance at the British embassy or high commission in the country in which they are living. The British post will require evidence of identity and of the status of the spouse in the UK, usually attested photocopies of the passport to show his or her immigration leave. There is more information about making entry clearance applications in chapter 11 and in chapter 7 on workers and business people.

People in the UK for some other temporary purpose who marry people who are in the UK as workers or business people may apply to the Home Office for leave to remain with their spouse. They need to show only that they are married and that they can be supported and accommodated without recourse to public funds.

If the applications are successful, the spouses will be granted leave to remain for the same length of time as the spouse who is a worker or business person. Spouses of persons of independent means are prohibited from working; others are free to work.

Students

Wives of male overseas students may be allowed to join them. If the wife is a visa national, she must apply for entry clearance before travelling. If she is not, she may apply for leave to enter at a British port or airport. She has to prove that she is the wife of the student and that there is adequate support and accommodation for her in the UK. If she is allowed in, she is given leave for the same length of time as her husband. If he is prohibited from working, she will be too; if he has a restriction on working, she will be free to work. ▶Chapter 9 on students gives more information.

There are no provisions in the rules for husbands of female overseas students to join them in the UK. The Home Office sometimes makes exceptions to allow husbands to come if there are exceptional reasons and if the husband can show that he can be supported and accommodated. Husbands will not be allowed to work.

Other partnerships

Non-marital relationships

There is no provision in the immigration rules for couples to be together in the UK if they are not married and not planning to marry. The formal provision for common-law wives was abolished in the 1985 immigration rule changes, on the grounds that it was sex discriminatory. However, in practice, permission may be granted to couples who have had a stable relationship and are from a culture where marriage is less important. There is a standard letter produced by the British high commission in Australia implying that there is a set procedure for Australians. If the couple is abroad, the partner who is not British or settled in the UK should apply for entry clearance, explaining the length and importance of the relationship and why they should be treated exceptionally. If entry clearance is granted, the partner will normally be granted leave to enter for a year and may apply to the Home Office to extend this.

If the couple have been living together in the UK while one of them was allowed entry on a temporary basis and one is British or settled, the non-settled partner can apply to the Home Office for permission to remain on the basis of the relationship. The Home Office may consider the application on the basis of the length and stability of the relationship and the reasons for not marrying. The Home Office also considers whether the other parts of the immigration rules on marriage are satisfied, particularly the couple's long-term commitment to each other. If leave to remain is granted, it is likely to be on a yearly basis, not for settlement.

Entry clearance as a fiancé(e) is not granted to anyone when both parties are not free to marry. Thus when people live in a country where divorce is very difficult, or impossible, for example the Philippines, there is no provision for them to come to the UK as fiancé(e)s in order to continue with divorce proceedings. They may be treated exceptionally, outside the rules, if the relationship is long-standing or if there are children involved, but an individual, detailed case will have to be made out in each instance. If people married abroad are already in the UK, living in a common-law relationship, it may be possible to apply for an extension of stay in order for the divorce to take place. Even if the application is not successful, people may be able to remain long enough to get divorced, and then remarried, because of Home Office delays in dealing with applications.

Gay and lesbian relationships

There is no provision in the rules for a gay or lesbian couple to remain together in the UK. Applications are entirely at the discretion of the Home Office and they are very rarely granted. The only couple to try to argue their case through the courts were a Swedish man, Lars Olaf Wirdestedt, and his British partner; they were unsuccessful but after their case had been heard by the Court of Appeal the Home Office decided to give in. The case was heard in 1984 but is reported in the 1990 Immigration Appeals reports, page 20. It is possible to ask that discretion should be exercised for a lesbian or gay couple, by stressing the length of the relationship, the difficulties there would be for the couple in living in the other person's country, or the particular reasons why it is necessary for the settled partner to remain in the UK. The Home Office has stated, in a conversation with JCWI, that discretion is less likely to be exercised in favour of a gay or lesbian couple than for an unmarried heterosexual couple, and that this reflects the fact that a common-law heterosexual relationship is recognised in English family law but a gay or lesbian one is not.

EC law may be helpful to gay and lesbian couples. Gay and lesbian marriages may be recognised in the Netherlands and Denmark so a partner from abroad may be able to remain there. As EC law gives free movement rights to 'spouses' of EC citizens it may be possible to try to extend this to gay and lesbian marriages. For example, a British and

Ghanaian gay couple might travel to Denmark, marry and live together there if the British man is engaged in any economic activity there. JCWI does not know of any couples who have been able to do this successfully.

Polygamous marriages

Since the Immigration Act 1988 came into force on 1 August 1988, it has not been possible for a woman who is a partner in a polygamous marriage and whose husband has previously brought another woman to the UK as his wife to come here on this basis. This applies irrespective of the legality of the marriage or of whether the wife concerned is the first wife of the marriage; if one wife has come to the UK as a wife, a second polygamous wife will not be recognised under British immigration law. This applies also to Commonwealth women who have gained the right of abode through marriage; a woman who has the right of abode because of a polygamous marriage cannot exercise that right if another wife has already come to the UK on that basis. Clause 2 of the Immigration Act 1988 is the most tortuous clause in the immigration law, drafted in order to try to express the concept of a right of abode which cannot be exercised.

Even if a polygamous marriage is not recognised for immigration purposes, it may be recognised for nationality purposes. The children from a legally contracted polygamous marriage are British citizens by descent from a British father, even if the marriage will not allow their mother to come to the UK (▶see chapter 3 for more details on children).

Marriages and divorces in other countries

There is often confusion with regard to marriages which took place abroad, in countries with very different marriage laws. Many people believe that, for example, a Ghanaian customary marriage is 'not recognised' in the UK, or that after seven years' separation, a marriage in the Philippines is 'automatically' ended. Couples may then marry, in the UK or abroad, in good faith, but then the Home Office may investigate past statements and allege that the marriage is bigamous. The police may be asked to investigate with a view to prosecution for bigamy. The whole subject is very complicated, as it involves the relationship between different countries' laws which may be constructed on entirely different bases. It is not proposed to go into all the details here.

Broadly, however, if a marriage is legally recognised and valid in the country in which it took place, it will be recognised as a valid marriage under UK marriage law. The validity of certain forms of marriage may depend on the country in which they took place and the domicile (which means more than simple residence in a country; ▶see glossary) of both parties involved. For example, a Nigerian customary marriage, where there is no documentation and the ceremony is an exchange of gifts between the families, will be valid if it takes place in Nigeria and both parties were domiciled in Nigeria at the time of the marriage. It will not be valid if it takes place in Britain or any other country which does not recognise this form of marriage.

Similarly, a customary divorce will also be valid if it took place in the prescribed forms in a country which recognises customary divorce and in which both parties were domiciled. When a person living in the UK performs a customary divorce, and then marries again, the Home Office may argue that a divorce should take place in the UK before the person is free to marry again in a way that is valid in the UK.

Immigration status and nationality do not affect people's ability to divorce in the UK; the process is the same as for anyone else wishing to divorce. There may be extra delays in that papers may have to be sent to a spouse abroad, who may be difficult to contact and unwilling to co-operate, particularly when divorce is more difficult, or impossible, in that country, but there is no need for specialist information about the divorce laws of the country in which the marriage took place.

If a person has gained entry to the UK on the basis of a marriage which is later found to be invalid, the person can be treated as an illegal entrant. For example, a Filipino woman married a British man in Hong Kong when they were both working there. She had believed that because she had been separated from her husband in the Philippines (where divorce did not exist) for more than seven years, she was free to marry again, and later came to Britain. She was treated as an illegal entrant when she later tried to bring children from her first marriage from the Philippines to join her, and it was discovered that there had been no divorce. She was able to obtain a divorce in the UK and then marry her British husband again, in order to secure her status.

Marriage breakdown and immigration consequences

Since 1 August 1988, both men and women entering the UK as spouses are given a year's initial stay. If marriages break down during that year, for whatever reason, and couples are no longer living together at the end of it, the partners from abroad no longer have any claim under the immigration rules to remain because of the marriage. Either they will have to show that they fit into some other part of the immigration rules, for example as students, or that there are strong exceptional compassionate reasons to permit them to stay. It is unusual for this to be granted.

This provision is seen at its worst when there is violence within the marriage. A woman may have to decide whether to remain in a violent and dangerous relationship for a longer period, and be granted settlement in the UK after a year, or whether to leave the marital home for her and her children's safety, and risk being refused permission to stay, deportation and possible family disgrace. Advice can only depend on the individual situation and the priorities for the person concerned.

If a marriage has broken down, an application outside the rules may be made to the Home Office and all the compassionate features can be argued. This is certainly worth doing, if the person wants to, and there have been several successful immigration campaigns for women threatened with deportation after leaving violent husbands. Since the Immigration Act 1988, however, there has been no effective right of appeal against a decision to deport someone in these circumstances, as compassionate aspects can no longer be raised at an appeal against deportation for a person who has been in the UK less than seven years.

If a marriage breaks down after the person has been granted settlement, this does not affect his or her immigration position. The person remains settled even if she or he is divorced or separated from his or her partner. When the separation has been difficult, it is not uncommon for the spouse who is British or was settled first to threaten the other partner with deportation. This is an idle threat if settlement has already been granted. The only exception to this is when the Home Office believes, and can prove, that settlement was granted through deception – that a couple had already separated at the time settlement was granted but had agreed at that stage not to inform the Home Office, or that the couple had never intended to remain together. It is theoretically possible then for the Home Office to initiate deportation proceedings on the grounds that the person's deportation would be conducive to the public good, because of the deception practised, but this is very rare.

ANNEX: THE PRIMARY PURPOSE RULE

The 'primary purpose rule' is the basis for many refusals of couples, mainly from the Indian subcontinent and other Asian countries. It is worth considering it in detail, to advise people whose partners are applying abroad to come to join them, so that they understand the rule and its implications and are therefore able to satisfy officials about their primary purpose in marrying. It is important that people reply truthfully to questions; an understanding of the process will help them to do so.

There are various areas of questioning which entry clearance officials use to try to establish people's motives in marrying. However, the main problem with the primary purpose rule is that, if rigidly applied, it is almost impossible for an applicant to *prove* a negative intention – that a marriage did not take place primarily for immigration reasons – when the foreign spouse is in fact applying to enter the UK and comes from a country with a lower per capita income than the UK, or a community with a history of emigration to the UK. This means the majority of people from Britain's black and ethnic minority communities.

Criteria used in primary purpose refusals

Religious or cultural traditions

Entry clearance officers may use their views or (often limited) knowledge about different religions and cultures. For example, a Pakistani Muslim man may be asked if he believes in Islamic traditions and follows them, and if he says he does, he may then be asked why he will be joining his wife, rather than she joining him, as this is contrary to 'Muslim tradition'. Officials may use such a statement to attempt to show that the primary purpose of the marriage is immigration since it goes against their views of the person's normal activities and plans.

Previous migration

Entry clearance officers may believe that people's past history shows that immigration is the primary purpose of marriage. For example, a man who has worked on contract in the Middle East, returned to Bangladesh when the contract came to an end and married a women resident in the UK may be assumed to have married in order to help him to work abroad again, his first venture having ended or been unsuccessful. The intention to work abroad may also be considered a strong motive for a man who is unemployed at home, or who has been unable to find work commensurate with his educational qualifications, who may be assumed to be seeking greater opportunities elsewhere. Although the Immigration Appeal Tribunal has stated that these should not be relevant considerations, they still appear to be so for entry clearance officers.

Discussion between the couple

Questions may be asked about what discussion the couple had before marriage as to where they would live. If it is alleged that the partner abroad did not know that the spouse came from the UK, or that no discussion took place, this is unlikely to be believed and officials will think that there is deliberate evasion. Often there are very strong reasons why the partner in Britain does not want to leave the country and it can be important for all these to be spelled out: not wanting to leave family or friends or job (although it must then be explained why the partner from abroad is more ready to do this), having family responsibilities in the UK (for example, having children from a previous marriage whose education should not be disrupted, or other dependent relatives who need physical care) or other reasons why it would be difficult. The authorities are becoming suspicious of UK-based women who say that the heat of a country in the subcontinent makes them ill, particularly when they or their family have come from a country with a similar climate.

Previous marital status

The position of the partner in the UK is also considered. If a woman in the UK has previously been married and divorced, and has then chosen a new husband from abroad, crude stereotypes about the prejudices against women who have been previously married may be brought into play. It may be suggested, directly or indirectly, that a pay-off for a man in getting married to a previously-married woman was that the marriage would enable him to go to the UK. This may also be used when the woman has a child or children from a previous marriage.

Depth of relationship

Entry clearance officers can demand any evidence they wish to show further details of the relationship. The case of *Arun Kumar* decided that if a couple who have been kept apart for some time can show there is 'intervening devotion' between them, this may show that the primary purpose of the marriage is no longer immigration. Often couples will show their letters to each other, in the hope that this will show an ongoing and genuine relationship. Officials are mainly interested in letters that were exchanged before the application to come to the UK was made, or any other evidence of a relationship continuing for some time. This may also lead to insinuations about a woman's physical attractiveness. If the woman has a physical disability, is older than the man or suffers from ill-health, entry clearance officers may insinuate that she was chosen because she lives in the UK.

Women applying to come to the UK

The primary purpose rule is also increasingly being used against women applying to join husbands and fiancés. This has been seen both in the Indian subcontinent and in other Asian countries, particularly Thailand and the Philippines. It is often assumed that women who have married British men who were on short holidays in those countries have done so because of the closing of doors on immigration to work in many Western countries and that the primary motivation for the marriage was to be able to work abroad and to support existing family members. This is particularly so if the couple had not known each other for long, or had been introduced by a marriage agency. In the Indian subcontinent, entry clearance officers have expressed surprise at the readiness with which young girls state that their families arranged their marriage in order for them to have a better life overseas.

Questioning by British officials

When a husband or wife is refused entry clearance and appeals against the refusal, it is now the practice of officials at the British post to give a full question-and-answer record of the interview as part of their statement of their reasons for refusal. The following questions come from an explanatory statement and show how officials build up their case.

Did you meet Himat by prior arrangement?
Did you meet him specifically with a view to marriage?
Why did Mr P pick on you to show to the young man?
Did he invite other girls to see the man also?
So then why did he pick on you?
Yes, but of all the other single girls in the village, why you?
But how could your husband know he likes you if he hasn't met you yet?
But why did Mr P show you in the first place? Was it possibly because your father had asked him to find someone suitable for you?
What requirements did your father have in a future son-in-law?
What do you mean, working out?
Do you mean your father wanted someone from London?
Why did your father want that?
Why was that important to your father?
Had your father or Mr P asked you to look at any other young men?
Was it essential to your father that he find someone from London for you?
Why was it essential from your father's point of view?
Just now you said it was important to your father that you live there so that you would be happy. Does that mean you would not be happy marrying someone and staying here?
Would you have even looked at this boy if he had not been from London?
Did you agree to marry him so that you could go to London like your brother?
Did you agree to marry him straight away after that five-minute meeting?
Did anyone tell you anything about the boy before you met other than that he was from London?
Other than the fact that he's from London I can't see any other convincing reason for you agreeing to marry him. Can you suggest any?
I've asked you at least twice but you haven't been able to tell me what you liked about him. Do you want to suggest anything now?
Anything else?
I'm sorry, I'm left with the overall impression that this marriage was arranged and undertaken by you and your family to enable you to go to the UK. I don't think it would have been contemplated if your husband had been resident here.

These questions are taken from a report of 86 questions a British high commission asked a 21-year-old Indian village woman who had recently married. She repeatedly stressed that she liked her husband and that the marriage would have been considered if he had been resident in India. She was refused entry clearance to join him.

Case law

A large body of case law, in the Immigration Appeal Tribunal and the courts, has now grown up around the interpretation of the primary purpose rule. In December 1991 the most frequently cited cases were *Arun Kumar, Hoque and Singh, Shameem Wali, Najma Rafique, Kandiya and Khan, Choudhury* and *Surinder Singh*. Most of these cases are reported in the quarterly Immigration Appeals Reports (Imm AR), known as the 'green books'; ▶see chapter 16 for more details on the appeals system.

Arun Kumar (1986 Imm AR 446) established that entry clearance officers should differentiate between applications from husbands and from fiancés. In the case of a fiancé, the motives of the parties at the time of application have to be considered, while in the case of a husband, events since the marriage may be considered to show what its primary purpose is. Evidence of the 'intervening devotion' of the couple to each other in the period since the marriage, for example, time spent together outside the UK, is important. Although the primary purpose of the marriage and the couple's intention to stay together permanently are separate points, if the second is proved, this will 'often cast a flood of light' on the first.

Hoque and Singh (1988 Imm AR 216) provided a list of ten propositions which should be considered in marriage cases. These include a reminder that the burden of proof is on the person applying to come to the UK to show that the primary purpose of the marriage is not immigration; that the official dealing with the case may make his or her own inquiries into the marriage and is not limited to information given by the applicants; and that the reasons of anyone involved in organising the marriage may be relevant as to its primary purpose. It also stressed that the fact that the marriage is an arranged marriage 'though a circumstance which the entry clearance officer is entitled to take into consideration, does not show that its purpose is or was to obtain admission to the UK'.

Shameem Wali (1989 Imm AR 86) decided that it was reasonable for a woman living in the UK to make it a condition of her marriage that she and her husband should continue to live in the UK, and that this in itself was not enough to show that the primary purpose was immigration.

Najma Rafique (1990 Imm AR 235) decided that where an applicant had appeared uncertain as to whether he was coming to the UK permanently or temporarily for marriage, the application should be treated as one for settlement, because this, unlike a visit application, could encompass a person who was undecided as to his or her long-term intentions. Najma Rafique's fiancé, Abid Hussain, had applied to come to the UK to marry her, but had said it would depend on discussions with her after marriage whether they would settle in the UK or Pakistan.

Kandiya and Khan (1990 Imm AR 377) confirmed that it was generally helpful, though not necessary, that the entry clearance officer should make a decision on whether the couple intend to stay together permanently as well as on the primary purpose of the marriage. It is also important to give some reasons why the officer believes that the primary purpose is immigration, and the officer's understanding of customs and tradition may be used.

Choudhury (1990 Imm AR 211) decided that, although a marriage had existed for four years and a child had been born, a refusal on primary purpose grounds was justified because a man had told lies when he visited the UK and when he later applied for entry clearance to join his wife. The couple had claimed that theirs was a love match, when the marriage had been arranged by their families

Surinder Singh (6639), a case heard by the Immigration Appeal Tribunal, decided that when a person from abroad is married to an EC citizen who has exercised his or her EC Treaty rights to free movement, the Home Office must consider any EC law aspects of the case. Mr Singh was an Indian citizen married to a British woman; they had lived and worked together in Germany before coming to the UK, but their marriage had broken down soon after they came to the UK. Because his wife had exercised her EC free movement rights, this gave Mr Singh rights under EC law, so it was decided that the British immigration rules could not be applied to him. The Home Office has taken the case to the European Court of Justice for a final ruling, but no decision had been made there at the time of writing. Although the case was not specifically about primary purpose, it is important for advising couples who have been kept apart by the primary purpose rule. If they are able to live together for some time in another EC country, with the British partner working there, they may then be able to return together to the UK.

Points to consider

- **is the marriage an arranged marriage or a 'love' marriage?** It is important for the couple to be clear and straightforward about the circumstances of the marriage. The fact that a marriage was arranged, that is, discussed and agreed by other members of the families concerned as well as, or largely instead of, the couple themselves, does not mean that the primary purpose was immigration.

- **customs and tradition:** entry clearance officers may have an out-of-date view of the customs and traditions of a particular area; the couple can explain how things have developed.

- **living together:** the fact that couples have spent prolonged periods together, outside the UK, and have proved their 'intervening devotion' is important in showing that the primary purpose is to be together, not to be in the UK.

- **children of the relationship:** although the birth of children does not affect the purpose at the time of the marriage, their existence may mean that further arguments from decisions of the European courts may be used about the child's right to be in contact with both parents and to live in the country of his or her nationality.

3   Children

This chapter covers the immigration rules about children coming to the UK to join adults, usually their parents. It also covers children who may qualify to come to the UK in their own right, for example as students. There are three main sets of circumstances in which children may come to join their parents, or other guardian, in the UK. These are:

- children coming to join parents who are British or settled in the country, or accompanying parents coming for settlement. They must obtain entry clearance from the British embassy or high commission before travelling.

- children who are accompanying, or coming to join, parents who are in the UK for temporary purposes, for example students or work permit holders. They sometimes need to have entry clearance before they travel and sometimes can apply at the port of entry. The rules about this are also discussed in the chapters which relate to their parents' status.

- children who are already in the UK for a temporary purpose, for example as visitors, and who then apply to remain in the UK with their parents or guardians. They can make applications to the Home Office while they are in the UK, and remain in the country while they do so.

▶There are also provisions for children to join a lone parent in the UK (see page 37), or join a relative other than a parent (see page 39), for adopted children (see page 43), for some children over 18 (see page 41) and for children born in the UK but not born British citizens (see page 50) to come to or remain in the UK, but these are generally more restrictive and it is more difficult to convince the immigration officers that children qualify.

REMEMBER:

- people abroad wanting to settle in the UK must get entry clearance before they travel

- BUT some family members may be British citizens

- AND some people may not have to fit into the immigration rules; see below.

People who do not have to fit into the rules

Some people have stronger claims to come to the UK in their own right and therefore do not have to fit into the rules.

a) **Children who are British citizens:** all children born in the UK before 1 January 1983 are British citizens and have the right of abode in the UK. Most children born abroad before 1983 to British citizen fathers are automatically British citizens and are not subject to immigration control. Children born in the UK from 1 January 1983 onwards are automatically British citizens if either parent was a British citizen or was settled in the UK at the time of the child's birth. Most children born abroad from 1 January 1983 onwards are automatically British citizens if at the time of the birth either parent was a British citizen who was born, adopted, registered or naturalised in the UK. In all cases, the father's status counts only if the parents are married. See chapter 17 on nationality to check on the nationality status of children born in the UK or children with British parents.

b) **Other children with the right of abode:** a child who is a Commonwealth citizen and who was born before 1 January 1983 to a parent who was born in the UK has the right of abode in the UK and does not have to prove anything more than these facts. If the parent is the father, the parents have to be married (which would normally make the child a British citizen as well).

The children need to have their position confirmed abroad before travelling by applying to the British high commission or embassy. If they are British citizens they may obtain British passports. If they are Commonwealth citizens they have to obtain a certificate of entitlement to the right of abode (see chapter 13 for example). They will need the birth certificate of the parent born in the UK, the marriage certificate of their parents if the parent concerned is their father, and their own birth certificate, to show that they are descended from that person. If these certificates are not available, or not accepted as genuine, it may be difficult to satisfy the British authorities about the relationship (see below).

c) **Children of EC workers:** nationals of any EC country other than the UK who are engaged in any kind of economic activity in the UK have the right under EC law to be joined by their children and grandchildren, automatically up to the age of 21, and beyond that age if the children are still dependent. There is no further definition of 'dependent', so it may mean emotionally or physically dependent as well as financially. If the children are visa nationals they have to obtain visas in advance but must not be charged for these visas and the authorities must not delay the applications. Nothing other than the relationship and the economic activities of the EC citizen parent have to be proved. See chapter 6 on EC citizens for more details.

Children under 18 joining both parents

WHAT THE RULES SAY

The rules about children coming to join parents who are British citizens or who are settled in the UK state that:

- the children must be under 18 and unmarried
- both parents, if they are both still alive, must be settled in the UK or must be coming for settlement with the child
- the parents must show they can support and accommodate the children in the UK without recourse to public funds.
- If both parents are alive but one parent is not living in the UK and does not intend to live there, more tests must be satisfied; ▶see page 37 for further information. If the children have passed the age of 18, entry is much more difficult; ▶see page 41.

WHAT THE RULES MEAN

Parents

In the immigration rules, the word 'parent' includes the stepfather of a child whose father is dead; the stepmother of a child whose mother is dead; and the father as well as the mother of a non-marital child. It can also include an adoptive parent, but there are other restrictions on the entry of adopted children, discussed further on pages 43–47.

Under 18 and unmarried

Children must be under 18 on the date of application to come to or remain in the UK. An application from abroad is considered to be made on the day the application forms and the fee are received by the British post. An application in the UK is made on the date it is posted. It is therefore very important that this is done before the child is 18; it does not matter if the child becomes 18 while the application, or any appeal against refusal, is pending, as long as he or she was still under 18 when it was made.

A child who is married is not eligible for permission to come to or remain in the UK to join parents, even if he or she is still under 18. Marriage means that the child has formed a closer family link with his or her spouse and no longer qualifies to join his or her parent(s).

Both parents are settled in the UK

This means that at the time the application is decided the child's parents must be in the UK and be either British citizens or have indefinite leave to remain, or have British citizenship or indefinite leave to remain and intend to travel with the child back to the UK when the child's entry clearance is granted. If only one parent is British or has indefinite leave to remain and the child is applying with the other parent to come to join the settled parent, the child's status will depend on the parent he or she is accompanying. If the parent is granted entry clearance or leave to remain, the child will be granted permission in line with this parent. If the child travels to the UK ahead of the parent, he or she will not be granted permission to enter unless the parent comes to the UK for settlement.

Support and accommodation

▶See details of this general requirement in chapter 11.

Children applying overseas to join their parents

▶See chapter 11 for general details of entry clearance applications.

The children have to satisfy the entry clearance officers at the British embassy or high commission that they qualify. They will be interviewed (unless they are under 10) and the person who has been caring for them abroad will be interviewed. In a letter to JCWI of 8 July 1991, the Home Office confirmed that instructions to entry clearance officers state that 'children aged between 10 and 14 should be interviewed only in the presence of an adult who is associated with the case and questions should be confined to simple matters and details of the immediate family.' Older children may be questioned on their own and in more depth. They will need to show evidence about their relationship to their parent(s) and of the support and accommodation available in the UK.

Up-to-date evidence to support the application will be necessary when the child and/or guardians are interviewed. The interview may take place immediately, but long queues have built up in some British posts (see appendix for some of the delays near the time of writing). Where there is a long delay before interview, this evidence is not needed at the time of application but should be available at the interview.

Evidence that may be required

- **proof of the child's relationship to the parents**. If the child has a birth certificate showing the names of both the parents, this is very helpful. However registration of births is not universal or compulsory in some countries and a birth certificate may not exist. Also British officials are often suspicious of documents that are produced by third world governments, refusing to rely on them. If the document does not exist, it is much safer to explain this and to provide any alternative evidence.

Examples of alternative evidence which could be helpful, if there is no birth certificate, include:

- records from the school the child is attending to show what that institution has been told about the child's age and parentage

DNA FINGERPRINTING

DNA fingerprinting techniques, first used commercially in 1985, can prove conclusively that children are related to their parents. The test involves taking a small blood sample from the child and the parents and testing this for the DNA in the blood, to see that all the child's DNA corresponds to that of the parents. This is a much higher standard of proof than asking family members detailed questions. However it can show that, for example, a father is not the father of a child whom he has always accepted and believed to be his.

In January 1991 the immigration authorities set up a system for providing DNA tests for families applying to come to the UK *for the first time* 'where the relevant relationships cannot be demonstrated easily by other means' to the entry clearance officer, who would otherwise be likely to refuse the application. If families agree to take the test, arrangements will be made by the immigration authorities, at no extra cost to the family. If they refuse, this should not be a reason in itself for refusal of the application.

The scheme does not apply to reapplicants: people who have been refused once and who are applying again. Families not included in the scheme may still have tests done privately. They must get in touch with one of the companies which the Home Office has approved to carry out DNA testing and follow the company's procedures. The Home Office has approved only two companies, Cellmark Diagnostics and University Diagnostics (▶see chapter 19 for addresses), to do the tests. There are standard charges; ▶see appendix for details. If the family want the test done before application or refusal, they will have to pay. If the application has been refused and there is an immigration appeal pending, and the family qualifies for legal aid for advice and assistance (green form), it is possible for the expenses of the test to be met under a green form extension.

- records from the hospital where the child was born
- information from the midwife or anyone else who knows about the birth
- affidavits from people, preferably not related to the child and parents, confirming their knowledge of the birth and relationship
- a scientific report of a DNA fingerprinting test (▶see box above)
- **proof of the parent(s)' status in the UK** e.g. certified photocopies of his, her or their passports (▶see information on applying for entry clearance in chapter 11)
- **the parents' birth certificates** if either of them was born in the UK
- **evidence of financial support** available to the children (▶see information on applying for entry clearance in chapter 11)

- **evidence of accommodation** available to the children (▶see information on applying for entry clearance in chapter 11)

If the application is successful

If the entry clearance officers are satisfied, they will grant entry clearance to the children. This is a stamp or a sticker in the passport (see chapter 13 for example) and will usually state 'settlement – to join parents, valid for presentation at a UK port within six months of date of issue'. This means that the child must travel to the UK within six months of being granted entry clearance. If travel is delayed, the child has to apply again for the validity of the entry clearance to be extended, explaining the reasons for the delay in travelling.

When the child arrives at a UK port or airport he or she will be admitted for a year if either parent is only allowed to stay for a year, or for an indefinite period if both parents already have this settled status. If the child is coming to join a lone parent in the UK, he or she will be given the same length of time to stay as the parent, which may be an indefinite period (settlement) (see chapter 13 for examples of these passport stamps). The child is free to remain for the period given and is immediately entitled to state education, National Health Service medical treatment and all non-contributory benefits. The parents can claim child benefit as soon as the child or one of the parents has been in the UK for six months, or immediately if a parent is working.

When a child has been admitted only for a year, because the parent who he or she was accompanying or joining was only allowed to remain for a year, welfare benefits can be claimed on his or her behalf. However, if these are any of the benefits that count as public funds for immigration purposes, (income support, housing benefit, family credit, being rehoused as homeless) this claim could be used against the child when an application is made for settlement at the end of the year (▶see chapter 10 for further details).

Applying for settlement after one year

If the child has been granted admission only for a year, it is important that an application is made to the Home Office before the year finishes, for permission to stay permanently. There is likely to be a parent applying for settlement at the same time, and the Home Office will need the passports of the parents and the child and can require evidence that the family is able to support and accommodate itself without recourse to public funds, before settlement is granted. It is extremely rare for a child to be refused at this stage, unless the parent he or she accompanied to the UK has been refused.

If the application overseas is refused

The British embassy or high commission has to give a letter explaining why the application was refused, stating the child's right to appeal against the refusal, and sending forms to fill in to appeal. The appeal forms have to be returned to the British post which refused within three months of the date of refusal. It does not matter if a child becomes 18 while the appeal is pending; the important date is the date of application. If the appeal is successful two years later, when a child is 19 or 20, he or she will be granted entry clearance. However, if the appeal fails, but a child later produces fresh evidence, for example a DNA test result, and applies again, the application is considered to be made on the date of the second application.

Children joining lone parents in the UK

WHAT THE RULES SAY

If the other parent is dead, there are no other specific requirements the child has to meet apart from proving the death. If the other parent is still alive but will not be coming to the UK, the immigration authorities must be satisfied that either:

- the parent settled in the UK or on the same occasion admitted for settlement has had the *sole responsibility* for the child's upbringing; or

- the parent or a relative other than a parent is settled or accepted for settlement in the UK and there are serious and compelling family or other considerations which make the child's *exclusion undesirable* – for example, where the other parent is physically or mentally incapable of looking after the child – and suitable arrangements have been made for the child's care.

WHAT THE RULES MEAN

A substantial amount of case law has grown up around these definitions. The first cannot ever be wholly true when a parent has been living in a different country from the child and the second is difficult to quantify. The immigration authorities consider each case in detail, to weigh up where responsibility for the child's upbringing lies or the difficulties of his or her circumstances abroad. It is therefore important that full details of the child's circumstances, and any evidence showing the continued support, direction and concern of the parent in the UK should be provided at the time of application.

The 'sole responsibility' rule

The 'sole responsibility' rule was first promulgated in 1969. The government's stated intention was to prevent the growth of all-male Pakistani families, where men who had come to work in the UK were sending for their sons, but not their wives and daughters, and it was felt that this was not in the best interests of the children. The result was that whole families then applied to come.

The communities which have suffered most from the sole responsibility rule are people from the Caribbean and West Africa. Many women migrated in search of work, leaving young children in the care of an older relative, commonly a grandmother, for what was intended to be a short period until they could make a home for them in the UK. Money was sent for their support and close contact was maintained, but it was not possible to say that the 'sole' responsibility was with the mother. British high commissions also asked the children many questions about contact with their fathers, who may well have remained abroad but separated from partners and children. It was clearly hard for children or grandparents to admit that they had been abandoned – but if the father's contact had been kept up, even sporadically or at a very low level, this could be a reason for refusing entry clearance for the child.

The Immigration Appeal Tribunal decided in the case of *Rudolph* (1984 Imm AR 84) what should be proved in order for a child to qualify under the 'sole responsibility' rule. In this case, the parents were separated and the child had been brought up in a convent in Sri Lanka while her mother was in the UK. It stated 'we need therefore to be satisfied not only that essential financial support was provided by Mrs Rudolph but also that she was regularly consulted about and expressed 'a continuing and positive concern' for Dilkish. We agree . . . we should not necessarily rule out 'sole responsibility' if for a limited time during childhood it cannot be proved. It is a matter of looking at the childhood as a whole and all the actions of the mother.'

Another case, *Ramos* (1989 Imm AR 148), gave a further definition of 'sole responsibility'. A Filipino mother, abandoned by her husband, had left her daughter with her own mother when she came to the UK to work to support them; the child's aunt and uncle lived nearby. 'Obviously there are matters of day-to-day decision in the upbringing of a child which are bound to be decided on the spot by whoever is looking after the child in the absence of the parents settled here, such as getting the child to school safely and on time, or putting the child to bed . . . and so forth. In the present case it is not in doubt that money was provided by the mother here to support the child, and indeed the grandmother, but that again is not *per se* conclusive of sole responsibility . . . The suggestion is of course not that the father has had any responsibility or that the mother has abandoned all responsibility, but that the true conclusion on the facts is that responsibility has been shared between the mother and the grandmother and possibly also the uncle and aunt'. The girl was not allowed to come to join her mother.

'Exclusion undesirable'

In general, proving that a child qualifies under any part of this rule can be very hard, and detailed representations have to be made to the relevant British high commission or the Home Office or in representing an appeal against refusal. It has been decided that the considerations making the child's exclusion undesirable are to do with the child's situation in the country of origin, and this must be exceptionally hard. For example, in one case where it was accepted that a father in Trinidad had sexually abused his daughter, but there was no evidence he had done anything other than beat his twin sons, the girl's appeal was allowed but her brothers' dismissed. In the case of *Rudolph*, the Tribunal stated, 'we are of the opinion that such [family and other] considerations must be applied to the country in which the appellant lives and not to those pertaining in the UK . . . The specific example of when the general requirements will be met [is] the inability of the parent in the foreign country to look after the child. It is strongly arguable that once we have found as a fact that Mr Rudolph is incapable of looking after Dilkish the appellant's case is made.' It has to be shown that the other parent is incapable of, as well as unwilling to, look after the child. The girl was allowed to join her mother.

The 'under-12 concession'

If children are under 12 at the time of application, they may satisfy this second criterion of the rule, that there are family or other considerations making their exclusion (from their mother) undesirable. Because of the very great difficulty of satisfying the sole responsibility rule, and because of the complaints and campaigning against it, the Home Office stated in 1975 that the full rigours of the rule would not be used against children who were under 11 when they applied to join a lone parent. They would 'fairly freely' be allowed to join a parent settled in the UK 'provided there is suitable accommodation and, if the parent is the father, there is a female relative resident in the household who is willing to look after the child and is capable of doing so'. This assurance was given in reply to a Parliamentary question from Helene Hayman MP on 28 July 1975, and the terms of the concession were repeated on several subsequent occasions. In 1976 it was extended to children under 12 at the time of application. However the Home Office has refused to write it into the immigration rules and has made little attempt to publicise it. Officials at British high commissions overseas do not always carry it out unless reminded about it.

Joining a relative who is not a parent

Children may be able to join an older relative who is not a parent, if they are living in extremely difficult circumstances overseas. This is usually only possible if the child's parents are dead and if it can be shown that there are no other relatives in the country of the child's origin who could look after him or her instead. An adult sibling, for example, married and settled in the UK, might be the only relative to care for a child after their parents had died. Grandparents settled in the UK might wish to care for a grandchild abandoned by his or her parents. Any application for a child to join a relative other than a parent should be made in great detail, explaining the exceptional circumstances why the child needs to come to, or remain in, the UK and why no other arrangements could be made in the country of origin.

Children applying to join parents in the UK for temporary purposes

Children may be given permission to come to join their parents when the parents are not settled in the UK or British citizens. If they are allowed to come, they are given permission to stay for the same length of time as their parent(s). If the parent is prohibited from working (as, for example, persons of independent means are prohibited) the child will be as well. If the parent is restricted to working only with the consent of the Employment Department, the child will be free to work.

Children of workers and business people

They must apply for entry clearance abroad. The immigration rules state that the children under 18 of people admitted as work permit holders, for permit-free employment, as business people, writers and artists and as self-employed people should be granted entry clearance to come to join them. They have to prove that there will be adequate support and accommodation, without recourse to public funds, for them. If only one parent is in the UK and the other is still alive, the more restrictive rules about children joining lone parents apply to them; see above for details.

Children who have come into the UK as visitors or students and whose parent(s) later come in to work may apply to the Home Office for permission to vary their leave to remain so that they can stay with their parents.

When the parents apply to extend their permission to remain, they should also apply on behalf of the children. This application will automatically be granted if the parents' is, but if the children are not formally mentioned in the application to the Home Office they may become overstayers while the parents' application is under consideration. When the parents apply for settlement, they must apply for the children as well. It does not matter if the children have become 18 during the years they have been living here; they will still be granted settlement in line with their parent(s).

Children of students

Children of students may be allowed to come to join them. If they are visa nationals, they must obtain a visa from the British post overseas. If they are not, they do not need entry clearance and can apply for leave to enter at a sea- or airport. In other respects, the rules are similar to those for the children of workers. In practice, it may be more difficult for a female student to have her children with her, because her husband has no claim under the rules to join her while she studies so she will have to fulfil the very restrictive requirements of the sole responsibility rule; see above for details.

Applying in the UK

If a child has already come to the UK for some other purpose, for example as a visitor, it is possible for an application to be made on his or her behalf to the Home Office for permission to remain permanently or in line with the parent(s)' stay (▶see chapter 11 on making applications to the Home Office). The same requirements of the rules, apart from the need for entry clearance, have to be satisfied by convincing the Home Office, rather than officials at the British post abroad, that the child qualifies. Because it is possible for such applications to be made in the UK, entry clearance officers are often loath to grant entry clearance to children to visit their parent or parents in the UK. It can be very hard to satisfy them that the child intends to leave the UK at the end of the visit.

When children who are in the UK apply to the Home Office to settle or to remain temporarily with their parents it is important that the application should explain why the decision for them to settle was made. Any changes in their circumstances – for example, the death or incapacity of the relative who had been caring for them, the parent in the UK finding out from the child about the shortcomings of care abroad, the parent obtaining adequate accommodation in the UK – should be explained to the Home Office to show why a decision was made during the child's visit that he or she should settle. It is also important that both parents intend to settle in the UK. If, for example, one parent has brought the child in and intends to leave him or her with the other parent and return abroad, the child may not qualify to stay unless the parent in the UK can show that the rules for children joining lone parents are satisfied.

Children over 18

WHAT THE RULES SAY

The immigration rules provide that unmarried daughters between the ages of 18 and 21 may be given 'special consideration' in coming to the UK to join their parents for settlement. They have to show:

- they are financially dependent on their parents
- they formed part of the family unit overseas

- they would be left entirely on their own in the country in which they are living, without any other close relatives to turn to for help
- they can be supported and accommodated in the UK without recourse to public funds

WHAT THE RULES MEAN

When a family is applying to join a parent in the UK and the eldest daughter is over 18, it may be possible for her to accompany the rest of the family. However it is likely that entry clearance officers will ask more questions about her than other members of the family and more checks will be made to be sure that she has needed to remain financially dependent, rather than has done so for immigration purposes. There is no provision in the rules for sons over 18 or daughters over 21 to accompany their families to the UK. They would normally have to qualify in their own right under some other part of the rules, for example in the extremely unlikely event that they were able to obtain work permits.

'Over-age children'

There is a particular controversy about children, mainly from Pakistan and Bangladesh, who applied to come to join their parents before they were 18 but who were refused as the authorities were not then satisfied that they were related to their parents as they claimed to be. They were later able to use the DNA fingerprinting technique (▶see box on page 35) as conclusive proof of those disputed relationships but do not now fit into the immigration rules as children as they are over 18.

The only provision in the rules for such people is that for 'other relatives'. The rules state that they have to show they are financially dependent on the relatives in the UK, that they are living on their own with no other close relatives to whom they could turn for support, that they can be supported and accommodated in the UK without recourse to public funds and also that people under 65 should not be able to qualify unless they are living in the most exceptional compassionate circumstances.

The Home Office has stated that it will consider these people's cases individually to see if there are any exceptional compassionate circumstances involved. These have to be over and above the basic injustice of wrongly separating a family for many years. The young people also have to show that they have remained 'necessarily' dependent on their parents rather than dependent 'by choice' and that they are unmarried. It seems that there is no chance of people over 23 being allowed to come. The refusal rate is very high. By July 1991, 570 young people's cases had been decided; only 116 had been allowed to come and 454 refused.

Another common situation where children over 18 apply to settle with their parents is if the parents are granted settlement after the child has become an adult. If a family has come to the UK together as a family, for example if either parent was given a work permit, its members will all have been granted initial permission to stay for the same period. If a child becomes 18 during the four-year period, it is usual practice for that child to be granted settlement in line with the rest of the family. When a child has been in the UK in his or her own right, for example as a student, and the rest of the family has come later, it may be more difficult to show that the child has remained part of this family unit and therefore should be allowed to settle, but it is still worth making the application.

Special quota voucher scheme

An exception to the rules is usually made for children aged up to 25 of special quota voucher applicants, if they are not themselves British nationals and therefore will not qualify for vouchers in their own right. ▶See chapter 17 for an explanation of the special quota voucher scheme, which permits some British nationals who are not British citizens and who have a connection with East Africa to come to the UK. Because of the long waiting period for people applying in India, which has reached eight years in the past, and which means that many children will become adults while they and their parents are waiting in the queue, children up to the age of 25 have been considered as dependants.

Such people have to show that they have remained financially dependent on their parents, have not been working and are not married. These requirements have led to detailed inquiries being made, particularly into young women in their early twenties, as to whether they are married and therefore would not qualify as dependants. The British authorities appear to be particularly worried about allowing in young women who may get married soon after their arrival and then try to bring in their husbands to join them in the UK. If a woman gets married shortly after coming to the UK for settlement, it is likely that her husband's entry clearance interview will concentrate on his intentions in getting married. He will stand a high chance of refusal under the primary purpose rule.

Adopted children

Children who have already been adopted

WHAT THE RULES SAY

The immigration rules do not provide for adopted children to be treated in the same way as other children, even though British law provides for this in nearly all other circumstances. The rules state that adopted children will only be allowed to come to join their adoptive parents if it can be shown:

* that an adoption has taken place, either in law or in fact

- that the adoption entailed a genuine transfer of parental responsibility on the ground of the original parents' inability to care for the child
- the adoption was not arranged in order to facilitate the admission of the child to the UK
- the child can be supported and accommodated in the UK without recourse to public funds

WHAT THE RULES MEAN

Legal adoptions

Adoption laws are very different in different countries. An adoption that takes place overseas is only recognised in the UK as a valid adoption under the Adoption (Designation of Overseas Adoptions) Order if it takes place in one of a specified list of countries whose laws are considered to have similar safeguards for the child's welfare as British laws.

These countries are: Anguilla, Australia, Austria, Bahamas, Barbados, Belgium, Belize, Bermuda, Botswana, British Virgin Islands, Canada, Cayman Islands, Cyprus, Denmark, Dominica, Fiji, Finland, France, Germany, Ghana, Gibraltar, Greece, Guyana, Hong Kong, Iceland, Ireland, Israel, Italy, Jamaica, Kenya, Lesotho, Luxembourg, Malawi, Malaysia, Malta, Mauritius, Montserrat, Namibia, the Netherlands, New Zealand, Nigeria, Norway, Pitcairn Island, Portugal, St Kitts and Nevis, St Vincent, Seychelles, Singapore, South Africa, Spain, Sri Lanka, Surinam, Swaziland, Sweden, Switzerland, Tanzania, Tonga, Trinidad and Tobago, Turkey, Uganda, United States of America, Yugoslavia, Zambia and Zimbabwe.

If an adoption takes place in one of these countries, the child may apply for entry clearance to come to the UK to join his or her adoptive parents. If the other requirements of the immigration rules are met (see above), the child is recognised as an adopted child and will be granted entry clearance for settlement. It is not necessary for the parents to arrange a further adoption under British law.

If an adoption takes place in a country not on this list, it can still be recognised for immigration purposes, provided it was valid under the law of the country in which it took place. This will depend both on the procedures carried out and whether the adopter was domiciled (see glossary for definition) in the country where the adoption took place. In countries where adoption is not recognised as a legal change of status, but where informal adoptions take place, often within the family, the facts of each case will be considered in deciding if the adoption can be recognised.

Thus when a child applies for entry clearance to join adoptive parents, the first consideration is whether the adoption can be recognised as valid. Even when it is, this does not qualify a child for admission unless the reasons for the adoption and the circumstances of the child's birth family are those stated in the immigration rules.

Reasons for adoption

The rules state that there must be a 'genuine transfer' of parental responsibility for the adopted child, and that the adoption must not have taken place to 'facilitate' the child's entry to the UK. When an adoption takes place mainly because a couple in the UK are unable to have children, this in itself is not a reason which will permit the child to enter. If the natural parents abroad are still physically able to care for the child, or are still caring for their other children, the child will not qualify under the immigration rules. It is quite common for a childless couple to wish to adopt a relative's child, for example a nephew or niece, and for this to be agreed within the family while other siblings of the adopted child remain abroad, but it is very hard to bring a child to the UK in these circumstances. The debate in the UK about inter-familial adoption may also make it less likely that an adoption order will be granted in a UK court.

The adopted child needs to apply for entry clearance to come to join the adopted parents; if at that stage the child is living with its natural parents, they will be involved in the application and therefore will show that they are still concerned about the child and may still be caring for it. It will then be necessary to show why these arrangements cannot continue and why coming to the UK is the only solution for the child's care.

Poverty of the family abroad is not normally accepted as an adequate reason as entry clearance officers may allege that family in the UK can send financial support which would enable the child to continue to stay with its natural family. Entry clearance officers may also claim that arrangements have been made within a family to send a child to the UK for educational or other purposes, rather than for a genuine adoption and may refuse entry clearance.

If it is impossible for the natural parents to care for the child, for example if the parent(s) are physically or mentally ill, medical evidence should be obtained to show that they cannot take responsibility for the child. If a child has been adopted from an orphanage or other agency caring for children, the entry clearance officers will require evidence that the child was genuinely available for adoption.

Adopted children also have to prove that there is adequate support and accommodation for them in the UK, without recourse to public funds. ▶See chapter 11 for details of these requirements and how to meet them.

Children adopted in countries where the adoption is not recognised in the UK will be granted entry clearance for adoption. They will probably be admitted for six months initially and must apply to the Home Office for an extension of this time. During the six months, the parents can begin the process of adoption under British law. They should keep the Home Office informed of its progress; if it is very slow, the Home Office may grant a further extension of stay. When the adoption is granted, this gives the child the right to settle in the UK and British citizenship if either adoptive parent is a British citizen.

Nationality of adopted children

An adoption which takes place outside the UK does not affect the nationality of the adopted child. An adoption which takes place in the UK, when either adoptive parent is a British citizen, automatically gives the child British citizenship. An adoption which takes place in the UK when neither parent is a British citizen, but either parent is settled in the UK automatically gives the child settlement. See chapter 18 for further information about applying to register children to become British citizens.

Children coming to the UK for adoption

No immigration rule deals with this situation. Therefore, if no adoption has taken place abroad, an application must be made outside the immigration rules to bring a child to the UK for adoption, to join its adoptive parents. Applications are dealt with exceptionally outside the rules.

The Home Office has worked out a long and complicated process which must be gone through in order that detailed checks can be made on the child's and the prospective adoptive parents' circumstances to see whether it is likely that the proposed adoption would be approved by a British court. The Home Office sends a detailed standard letter, RON 117, to inquirers, which gives full information about the process. This includes obtaining detailed medical and social reports on the child and on the prospective adoptive parents from official sources such as the Department of Health. The whole process can be very slow. Some local social services departments refuse to cooperate because of their own policies discouraging inter-country adoption. In practice therefore it is very difficult to bring a child to the UK for adoption.

In May 1991 the Department of Health announced that new procedures would be set up to facilitate bringing adoptive children to the UK. A lengthy review of adoption procedures has been taking place but it was expedited in view of public concern about difficulties in adopting children from Romanian orphanages. In fact the vast majority of applications to bring children from Romania for adoption were successful; by December 1991, 330 children had been allowed to come and 12 refused. The new procedures were not finalised at the time of writing.

If entry clearance is granted for the child to come to the UK for adoption the child must travel within six months. He or she will be admitted initially for a year. During that time it should be possible to begin the legal process of adoption in the UK and to apply to the Home Office, before the end of the year, to extend the child's permitted stay while the process goes on. If a child is legally adopted in the UK, the adoption automatically gives him or her the right to remain indefinitely; if either of the adopters is a British citizen, the child automatically gains British citizenship.

Because of the delays and complications of this procedure, British or settled parents have sometimes circumvented it, by travelling abroad and bringing babies or young children back with them, without entry clearance. The Home Office and adoption agencies discourage this practice, because it is effectively impossible to refuse entry to young children and to return them abroad on their own and because the detailed checks necessary to ensure the suitability of the adoption have not been done. However, in some inter-family adoptions (see above), adoptive parents may see this as the only way of being able to bring in an adoptive child. Visa national children cannot normally be brought in in this way, as most airlines will not carry them without visas.

If children do arrive without prior permission, they may be admitted for six months on arrival. The adoptive parents are then expected to begin the process of a British adoption and to apply to the Home Office, before the child's leave to enter has expired, for permission for the child to remain while the adoption takes place.

It is also possible for prospective adoptive parents to apply to adopt children admitted for another purpose, for example as visitors or students, and to apply to the Home Office for an extension of their stay while the adoption takes place. When the adoption case is heard in court, the court has to consider, among other things, whether the main purpose of the adoption was to keep a child in the UK, if he or she would not qualify to remain in any other way, rather than the lack of other arrangements for his or her care. If so, the application for adoption can be refused.

Children in the UK without their parents

Fostering of children/children in care

Families from abroad may want to make arrangements for their children's care in the UK, even if they themselves are unable to be in the country. A comparatively common situation is for a couple to come to the UK to study and to decide that they are unable adequately to concentrate on their studies with the children to care for and therefore to make private fostering arrangements for them. The children of overseas students are able to be with them in the UK under the immigration rules so there is no reason to inform the Home Office about these arrangements while the whole family is still in the UK.

There are no provisions in the immigration rules for the children to stay if the parents leave and want the child to remain with the foster parents, so as not to disrupt their education, for example. If an application is made to the Home Office for the child to remain exceptionally, it should be done with great care and the plans for the child to rejoin his or her parents abroad should be explained.

In some cases, the foster parents are unaware of any immigration implications and the children may inadvertently become overstayers. Specialist independent advice should be sought for any attempt to regularise the child's position.

If there are problems with the fostering, or if for any other reason the care for a child from abroad is inadequate or the child is in danger, the local social services department has the same statutory responsibility to care for the welfare of the children as for others in their jurisdiction. It is therefore possible for a child who is not settled in the UK to be taken into the care of the local authority. The local authority is then *in loco parentis* and will have to make arrangements for the child. This may be attempting to trace the parents in order to return the child to them abroad, or it may be applying to the Home Office for permission for the child to remain here exceptionally when there seems to be no prospect of the family being reunited abroad, or of the parents returning.

There is no authoritative statement about the immigration consequences of a child being taken into the care of the local authority. For a child who is not a British citizen, being taken into care does not in itself alter the child's immigration status. However, the local authority then has responsibility for the child and it is important that it should receive correct legal advice before making any approach to the Home Office. If it appears clear that there will not be further contact with the family and that the child's long-term future will be in the UK, and the authority applies to the Home Office for settlement on behalf of the child, with full details of the circumstances, it is likely that the application will be granted.

Children at school

The only way in which children are likely to be allowed to remain in the UK in their own right (that is, without being British citizens or without their parents living in the UK with them) is as students. This means that the child must be going to a private, fee-paying school, must have the money to pay the school fees and to live here and, if it is not a boarding-school, there must be adequate arrangements for looking after the child. The Home Office must also be satisfied that the intention is for the child to leave at the end of the studies.

There is no provision in the rules for a child to stay in the UK in order to attend, or to continue to attend, a state school. This can create problems when the child has been in the UK with the family for a short-term purpose, for example if the parents are students, or diplomats posted to the UK for a term of duty, who then have to take up another post when the child is at a critical stage of education. An application to the Home Office may be made, exceptionally, for permission to continue in these studies and because of the delays in response and the right to appeal against any refusal the child may be able to complete the relevant academic year while the application is pending. ▶See chapter 11 for more information on making applications to the Home Office.

Children over 16 are no longer required by law to attend school but they may be able to remain as students by going to full-time studies (at least 15 hours' daytime classes per week) at a college of further or higher education, or a private college. See chapter 9 for information on grants and fees for further education.

Children born in the UK

Children born in the UK before 1 January 1983

Except for the children of diplomats, any person born in the UK before 1983 is automatically a British citizen by birth. This gives the child full rights to remain in the UK and to return at any time as an adult, even if he or she was taken abroad as a baby. There have been instances of people, mainly in West Africa, who have had difficulty convincing the British high commissions that they are the babies who were born in the UK. Others travelling on British passports have had difficulty in satisfying immigration officers that they are in fact British citizens. People have also been arrested in the UK and alleged to be illegal entrants. Although they have claimed that they were born in Britain, the immigration authorities have not believed them. In general however, people born in the UK before 1983 are able to return to the UK to live on production of their full birth certificate (the one which has details of both parents so that it can be seen that the father was not a diplomat). If the birth certificate is a recent copy obtained from St Catherine's House further evidence may be requested to connect the applying adult with the child who was born in the UK and left at a very young age.

Children whose parents are forced to leave the UK

The fact that a child is British through birth in the UK does not affect the parent's immigration status in any way. Thus parents who were students, for example, do not have any claim to stay on after their studies because of the birth of a child; overstayers do not gain any right to remain because their children can do so. The British-born children of such families cannot, of course, be deported, even if their parents and siblings are. But in practice the deportation of the rest of the family usually means that the British child was forced to leave as well.

However, the European Commission of Human Rights, in the case of *Fadele*, has recognised that British children do in some circumstances have rights and expectations that they will be able to live in the UK and this may mean that their families should be allowed to remain with them. In that case, three British children were able to show that their travel to Nigeria and living there with their father, who had not been permitted to stay with them in the UK after their mother's death in a car crash, had caused them great hardship. The European Commission held that the father's removal from the UK was wrong and the Home Office had to pay for the family to return.

A European Court of Human Rights case, *Berrehab* (1988 11 EHRR 322), in addition provides a precedent to seek the return of a deported parent of a British-born child. The decision confirmed the right of a child to continuing contact with both her parents following the breakdown of their marriage (▶see page 17 for further details).

Children born in the UK in or after 1983: immigration status

Since 1 January 1983, not all children born in the UK have been born British citizens (▶see chapter 17). Only a child with a British or a settled parent is automatically born British in the UK. When the parents are not married, only the mother's status counts. Other children born in the UK have no claim to British nationality by birth and are subject to British immigration control. There is a special section in the immigration rules to cover children born in the UK.

Technically, a child born in the UK and not born British does not have, or need, an immigration leave to remain in the UK. These children are not illegal entrants or overstayers just because of their parents' status. They may therefore remain in the UK indefinitely, so long as they do not leave the country. A child who has never been granted an immigration leave cannot be deported, unless his or her parents are deported, in which case the child can in law be deported as part of the family unit. If the parents leave voluntarily, there is nothing illegal in leaving the child in the care of other relatives or foster parents living in the UK. However, if the children leave the UK and their parents have also left, they will not be given permission to return unless they fit in to another category of the immigration rules. If children born in the UK remain until they are 10 years old, they gain the right to register as British citizens (▶see chapter 18).

If parents wish to obtain an immigration leave for their non-British children born in the UK, the Home Office will grant this if the parent has leave to enter or remain. The child will be given the same length of time as the parents. If the parents have a different length of stay, the child will be given the longer. If the parents are living separately, the child will be given the length of time that the parent with day-to-day care for him or her has. If one parent is settled, the child can be granted settlement. This would be relevant, for example, for a child whose parents were not married, whose mother was an overseas student so the child would not be born British but whose father was a British citizen. If the parents applied to the Home Office for settlement for the child, this would be granted. The Home Office will only require evidence that the child is the child of the parent(s) and of the parent's length of stay; it does not have to be shown that the child can be supported and accommodated.

If children travel overseas at a time when they have not yet been granted leave to remain in the UK, they will need to convince immigration officers on their return that there is a reason for admitting them to the UK under the immigration rules. If they are returning with their parents, or while their parents are still in the UK, they will normally be given the same immigration leave as the parents are given, or as the parents have. If children have already been granted leave to remain, they are free to travel and are likely to be readmitted for the same length of time. They do not have to prove that there is support and accommodation available to them in the UK. Children who are not visa nationals do not need entry clearance. Children who are visa nationals do not need visas if they are returning within a period of leave to remain of more than six months but do require visas in all other circumstances. Once leave to enter or remain has been granted, it is important to apply to extend it in time, as children can become overstayers if this is not done.

4 Relatives other than children and spouses

Apart from children and spouses there are many other relatives who may need or want to come to stay permanently with family members settled in the UK. The immigration rules about this are very restrictive and only make provision for a limited number of relationships. There are similar rules for parents and grandparents, and then more restrictive ones for aunts, uncles, sisters and brothers. More distant relatives are not mentioned at all and their entry is therefore always at the discretion of the Home Office.

REMEMBER:

- people abroad wanting to settle in the UK must get entry clearance before they travel
- BUT some family members may be British citizens
- AND some people may not have to fit into the immigration rules; see below

People who may not have to fit into the rules

People who want to come to the UK because they have relatives settled in the country may qualify under some other parts of the immigration rules. They might, for example, qualify as persons of independent means, or only intend to visit their relatives.

a) **EC citizens:** EC law gives the right to 'relatives in the ascending line' to join an EC citizen who has travelled to another EC country and is engaged in economic activity there. Thus it does not apply to British citizens, as they have not travelled between countries to work, but may apply to Irish citizens, if they have travelled between the Republic of Ireland and the UK. Relatives in the ascending line means parents, grandparents and great-grandparents, who may be the relatives of a non-EC spouse of an EC citizen. The relatives themselves do not have to be EC citizens. Thus, for example, the Colombian parents of a Colombian woman married to a German man working in the UK would qualify under this provision. Support and accommodation has to be available but the other requirements of the British immigration rules do not apply. EC citizens may also qualify in their own right under any other part of EC law, irrespective of the presence of their relatives in the UK.

b) **Commonwealth citizens with the right of abode:** Commonwealth citizens with British-born parents, and Commonwealth citizen women married before 1 January 1983 to a man with the right of abode, have the right of abode (▶see glossary) in the UK. Commonwealth citizens with a grandparent born in the UK may qualify to come because of that relationship. ▶See chapter 7 for more details.

c) **People with capital of at least £200,000**, and with close relatives living in the UK, may qualify as persons of independent means. ▶See chapter 7 for more details.

d) **Visitors:** people may not want to stay permanently but may want to be able to visit relatives frequently. It may therefore be better to apply as visitors and not to give the immigration authorities any reason to think that more than a visit is intended.

Parents and grandparents

WHAT THE RULES SAY

Parents or grandparents who are coming to the UK in order to live with their adult children or grandchildren have to satisfy the entry clearance officer:

- if they are a couple travelling together, that one of them is over 65; a widowed father must also be over 65 but a widowed mother may be of any age
- that they have been wholly or mainly financially dependent on their children settled in the UK
- that they have no other close relatives in their country of origin to whom they can turn for support
- that they can be supported and accommodated in the UK without recourse to public funds.

WHAT THE RULES MEAN

Age requirement

This is interpreted strictly and it is important to show the age of the applicants, by a birth certificate if possible. There can be serious problems in countries where there was not a system of registration of births when the parents or grandparents were born. Elderly people may not know exactly when they were born and may date their age from some local events, also unrecorded. When they obtained their passports, they may have given an approximate age for this purpose. The British authorities may take this as the only definite proof of age and it may be very difficult for the parents or grandparents to satisfy them at the time of any application for settlement that any different date of birth is more correct.

The rules only exempt widowed mothers and grandmothers from the age requirement. Mothers who are divorced or separated or who have never been married do not qualify and have to be 65 before their applications will be considered under the rules relating to parents. They may still apply to join their children but will have to fit into the more restrictive rules for other relatives (see below for more details).

Previous financial support

This means that *before* coming to the UK the parents or grandparents must have been financially dependent on their children in the UK. If they are visiting the UK at the time of the application, and have been financially dependent during the visit but were not before, this requirement will not be satisfied. It is demeaning for elderly people to have to show that they cannot maintain themselves.

It can also be difficult to prove, as many people do not keep records of all the money they have sent to their families abroad. If money has been sent through postal orders, people may have kept at least some of the counterfoils; if it has been sent through a bank account, the bank may have records. Registered letter slips, showing at least that something valuable was sent, can be useful. So are letters from the parents, mentioning money sent, from as far back as possible.

If money was taken in cash by visiting relatives or friends, it may be more difficult to do anything more than assert this fact. It may be helpful to have letters from the couriers, confirming when and how much money they took, or letters from the parents confirming they received the money. When parents or grandparents have other means of support, for example an occupational pension, it has to be shown that the money they receive from their children is more than the pension, so that they can show they are mainly, if not wholly, dependent on the children.

This requirement discriminates against people who have been thrifty, or people who live in a country where an adequate old-age pension is paid. Retired people in the United States, for example, are unlikely to be financially dependent on their children rather than on any pension or insurance. It also means that parents or grandparents who own property, for example their own home, may not be considered dependent, even though they intend to leave the home to their children and do not wish to keep it themselves.

No other relatives to turn to

This requirement is also difficult to meet, if there is more than one adult child in the family and they do not all live in the UK. It does not take adequate account of cultural differences; in the Indian subcontinent, for example, it is generally accepted that it is the sons' responsibility to care for their aged parents, not the daughters', who, when married, have a corresponding responsibility to their husband's parents. Thus when the sons are in the UK but the daughters are in India, it has to be argued that they cannot usually be expected to care for their parents and that the parents themselves, as well as the son-in-law's family, would not feel that it was right. If there is another son still in India immigration officials will expect that he should care for his parents, even if he lives a long way away and the care he would provide would not be acceptable to the parents. In all cases when there are other relatives living in the same country as the parents it is therefore important to show why they are not able to care for the parents.

It can also be argued that the children abroad do not have the resources to look after their parents adequately. This has sometimes been successful, for example in Filipino cases, when although there have been several children in the Philippines it has been shown that their economic circumstances are such that they cannot manage to look after their parents, or even their own families, without the financial support they receive from the UK.

If other close relatives with whom the parents previously lived have died, their death certificates should be produced. If circumstances have changed, making other relatives no longer able to care for the parents, this should be explained.

Emotional dependence

The concept of emotional closeness to a particular child has also been argued, with some degree of success. It is necessary to spell this out, to show why living with one particular child would be the best solution for the parents. The parents may have to show they attempted to live with other relatives, or other relatives may have to explain why they are unable or unwilling to look after them, before they will be allowed to come to the UK.

The cases of *Bastiampillai* (1983 Imm AR 1) and *Dadibhai* (October 1983, unreported) have confirmed that the other relatives must have both the ability and the willingness to provide all the support needed by the parent. This includes all the financial and emotional support necessary. It may be useful to quote these cases to entry clearance officers who may attempt to refuse merely because there are other relatives living in the same country. However, emotional dependence will not overcome the primary need for *financial* dependence to be shown.

Support and accommodation

The requirements for this are similar to those for spouses and children, and similar evidence should be provided; ▶see chapter 11 for more details. The main difference is that because there is no other legal liability in British law for an adult to maintain his or her parents or grandparents (unlike a spouse or children) it is more likely that entry clearance officers will request an undertaking to support them.

This means that as well as providing evidence of ability to support the parents, the sponsor may be required to sign a formal undertaking to do so, which also confirms his or her understanding that this undertaking may be made available to the DSS. The undertaking gives the DSS the power under the Social Security Act 1980 to reclaim from the person who signed the undertaking any income support that the sponsored person may claim. It does not mean that the sponsored person is debarred from claiming, but that the sponsor can be treated as a liable relative.

There have been instances of the Benefits Agency of the DSS attempting to secure repayment, or to discourage claims, from sponsored parents. The pressure put on families by the Benefits Agency has certainly led to people abandoning claims for benefit to which they are entitled and this seems to be an important element in DSS policy.

If parents or grandparents have arrived in the UK but the family is later unable to continue to support them the parents may claim benefit. If the Benefits Agency then takes the case up with the sponsor the children may show that their circumstances have changed since they signed the undertakings, so that they are no longer able to carry out what they promised to do. The DSS normally decides not to press for repayment. JCWI knows of only one instance of the DSS successfully taking a sponsor to court, in September 1990, for failure to maintain his sponsored mother.

For more details on sponsorship and undertakings, see chapter 10 on benefits.

How to apply

It is important to remember that if the parent or grandparent's application for settlement fails, this will have other consequences. It will be more difficult in the future for the person to make visits to the UK, because it will be more difficult to convince the immigration authorities that he or she intends to leave the UK at the end of the visit. Thus the long-term as well as the short-term plans of the person and the family should be considered before making an application which does not precisely fit into the rules.

Applying abroad

Parents or grandparents abroad need to apply for entry clearance at the British embassy or high commission nearest to where they live; they cannot get permission to enter to settle with their children at a port of entry. ▶See chapter 11 for details of the entry clearance application process and the documents and evidence required.

In the countries of the Indian subcontinent, people over 70 years old applying for settlement are considered in a priority queue, so they should not have to wait long for an interview. There are no special provisions made for the elderly in other countries. Parents or grandparents will need to provide evidence that they satisfy all the requirements of the rules and may also be asked detailed family questions.

Applying in the UK

If the parents or grandparents are already in the UK, for example as visitors, they may apply to the Home Office for permission to stay with their children. However, there is the danger that people could be treated as illegal entrants, if it is thought that they came to the UK claiming to be visitors when in fact they intended to stay. It is rare for elderly people applying to stay with their children to be treated in this way. However this possibility makes entry clearance officials overseas more reluctant to grant visit visas to elderly parents or grandparents who appear to be alone or in need of care overseas.

It is important to make the application to the Home Office before the person's leave to remain has expired; ▶see chapter 11 for information about making the application. As long as the application is made in time, the person is legally in the UK while it is under consideration and will have a formal right of appeal if the application is refused. It is also important to remember that the Home Office will look at the parent's situation in the country of origin, before coming for the visit. Although, for example, parents visiting children in the UK are likely to be financially supported in the UK during the visit the important consideration for the Home Office is how they were supported in their country of origin before they travelled for the visit. It is therefore important to provide evidence of funds sent abroad as well as how the people are being supported at the time of the application.

Parents joining young children

There are no provisions in the immigration rules for adults to come to, or remain in, the UK because they have children born or living in the country who need their care. However, two cases considered by the European Commission and Court of Human Rights, *Berrehab* and *Fadele*, have confirmed that children's rights may be infringed if they are separated from their parents. This is discussed more fully in chapter 3.

Relatives other than parents and grandparents

WHAT THE RULES SAY

The rules are even more strict about 'other relatives'. Uncles, aunts, brothers and sisters may apply to join their relatives here. They have to show:

- that they are related as claimed to the person they wish to join
- that they are financially dependent on the person here
- that they have no other close relatives to turn to in the country in which they are living
- that they are living alone in the most exceptional compassionate circumstances
- that they are over 65 (the rule states that it should be particularly exceptional for someone under 65 to be allowed to come in this category)
- that they can be supported and accommodated in the UK without recourse to public funds.

WHAT THE RULES MEAN

Statistics are not kept to show how many people are allowed to come or to stay in the UK as 'other relatives' but all casework experience shows there are very few – partly because few people apply once they have seen the strict nature of the rule. This is the rule under which parents who are not yet 65, or mothers who are separated or divorced or have never been married, may also apply. Although there may well be compassionate circumstances involved there is no objective definition of 'exceptional compassionate circumstances' which will be decided by the immigration official dealing with the case.

The case of *Manshoora Begum* (1986 Imm AR 385) struck out a previous requirement of this rule, that the relative had to have a standard of living lower than the average in his or her own country. The Divisional Court agreed that this requirement was unreasonable, since the fact of receiving money from abroad at all, another requirement of the rule, could bring people above the average standard of living in several countries. Applications will still be decided on a case by case basis, because of the necessity of proving that there are exceptional compassionate circumstances. It is therefore important that the relatives applying give the fullest possible details of their circumstances to the immigration official dealing with the case, with any evidence they can produce, as discussed above.

More distant relatives

In exceptional circumstances it may be necessary for more distant relatives to apply to come to, or remain in, the UK with other family members. Applications for this can still be made, outside the immigration rules. There are no provisions in the rules for any other relatives to come to the UK: cousins, half-brothers, 'de facto' mothers of adopted children or step-mothers all apply outside the rules, at the discretion of the immigration authorities, and would be asking for special treatment because of their special circumstances. The Home Office can grant applications outside the rules, so it may be worth trying if there are exceptional circumstances.

It is important to show the immigration authorities what the strong exceptional compassionate reasons for the application are, for example when there was a close emotional relationship between the relative and the person settled in the UK. A person who had been brought up by a great-aunt or a cousin, and who had a quasi-parental relationship with that person, will need to explain this family background, why it had happened and why there were no other closer relatives who could support the person in the country of origin. If the person is elderly, it is more likely that exceptional compassionate reasons will be accepted. If the person has physical or mental disabilities, medical evidence to show this is important.

However, it is important to remember that if the application for settlement fails, this will have other consequences. It will be more difficult in the future for the person to make visits to the UK, because it will be more difficult to convince the immigration authorities that he or she intends to leave the UK at the end of the visit. Thus the long-term as well as the short-term plans of the person and the family should be considered before making an application outside the rules.

5   Refugees and asylum-seekers

On 1 November 1991 the government published its Asylum Bill and draft immigration and asylum appeals procedure rules. The Bill passed through the House of Commons unaltered but widespread dissent in the House of Lords led to its postponement. Some of the proposed changes are indicated below. JCWI will produce a refugee supplement to this handbook after any new legislation and rules are confirmed.

WHAT THE RULES SAY

The present immigration rules mention refugees almost as an afterthought after listing other ways in which people may qualify to come to the UK. The rules state:

- Special considerations apply where a person seeking entry claims asylum in the UK, or where it appears to the immigration officer as a result of information given by that person that he may be eligible for asylum in the UK. Every such case is to be referred by the immigration officer to the Home Office for decision regardless of any grounds set out in any provision of these rules which may appear to justify refusal of leave to enter.

- The Home Office will then consider the case in accordance with the provisions of the Convention and Protocol relating to the Status of Refugees. Asylum will not be refused if the only country to which the person could be removed is one to which he is unwilling to go owing to a well-founded fear of being persecuted for reasons of race, religion, nationality, membership of a particular social group or political opinion.

WHAT THE RULES MEAN

All asylum decisions are made by the Home Office. If people apply for asylum at a port of entry, immigration officers take the details but refer the case to the Home Office for decision. It considers each case in detail. If it is satisfied that people meet the criteria of the UN Convention, they will be granted **refugee status** or **asylum** (the terms are synonymous). If it does not believe that the people meet these criteria but that there are strong reasons why they should not have to return to their country of origin at that time, they will be granted **exceptional leave to remain**, outside the immigration rules. If the Home Office does not accept either of these, the application will be refused.

The Home Office is planning to introduce new and more restrictive rules when the proposed Asylum Act 1992 becomes law. The new rules are likely to make it easier to return people immediately to allegedly safe countries and to make it more difficult for people who are part of a group suffering discrimination or ill-treatment, or who have arrived under false identities or without disclosing their true intentions, or who do not apply immediately, to be granted asylum.

The UN Convention relating to the Status of Refugees

The immigration rules include part of the definition of a refugee in the UN Convention relating to the Status of Refugees. Under the Convention, a person who has a well-founded fear of persecution for reasons of race, religion, nationality, membership of a particular social group or political opinion must also be someone who is

* outside the country of his nationality and is unable or, owing to such fear, is unwilling to avail himself of the protection of that country; or who, not having a nationality and being outside the country of his former habitual residence . . . is unable or, owing to such fear, is unwilling to return to it.

The Convention was signed in 1951 and was prepared and debated in the aftermath of the Second World War, mainly in the context of the thousands of displaced people in Europe. In 1967 a Protocol was added to it, extending the definition of refugees to non-Europeans and to people forced to seek refuge because of events that took place after 1945.

Interpretation of the Convention and Protocol

There are no internationally agreed procedures or standards in deciding who falls within the UN definition. Governments which have signed the Convention and Protocol choose the criteria they will use to decide whether people qualify and what standard of proof is necessary. This varies between countries of refuge and according to the countries from which people are fleeing.

The UN has prepared a *Handbook on procedures and criteria for determining refugee status* on the interpretation of all the phrases in its definition. This is very helpful in preparing an asylum case, as its principles are accepted by the Home Office.

It is important to consider all the individual phrases in the UN Convention definition in deciding whether someone has a claim to asylum.

Well-founded fear

There is no internationally agreed definition but it has been accepted that 'well-founded' means 'serious possibility' or 'reasonable degree of likelihood'. But it is up to the Home Office to decide, using both subjective and objective criteria, whether this has been shown. This was decided by the House of Lords in the case of *Sivakumaran* (1988 Imm AR 147), which concerned six Sri Lankan Tamils who had been refused asylum and returned to Sri Lanka. The Home Office considers applications in the light of the detailed information it has about the situation in different countries and how the person's history fits in with this. Refugees must satisfy the Home Office that they have a genuine fear for their safety. Often there is no proof or evidence to substantiate that fear and the decision may depend on the Home Office's assessment of the person's credibility.

Persecution

There is no internationally accepted definition of persecution, apart from it constituting a threat to life or freedom, or other serious violations of human rights. The Convention has been interpreted to mean that there must be a danger to the person individually, though the reason for this may be membership of a particular group. It is not usually held to cover people who are living in a generally unstable or dangerous situation, for example because there is a civil war in the country of origin. It is also possible that discrimination against a person in many and persistent ways, combined with other factors such as an atmosphere of insecurity, can amount cumulatively to persecution.

Persecution is also not synonymous with prosecution, though the two can be connected. People who are fleeing their country because they are facing criminal charges cannot normally claim this to be persecution. However, when the criminal penalties for a certain action in a particular country are disproportionate to those in most other countries, or when it is alleged that the real reason for the prosecution is because of the person's political or other opinions, this may show persecution.

Reason for fear of persecution

Refugees have to show that the persecution they face is for one of the reasons listed in the UN definition: race, religion, nationality, membership of a particular social group or political opinion. It is up to the people seeking asylum to satisfy the Home Office about their views and the danger in which these would place them. The part of this definition where there is most development in the law and which may be most difficult to establish is the membership of a social group. The UN *Handbook* (see above) defines this as 'persons of similar background, habits or social status' and states that fear of persecution on these grounds may often overlap with others. People who have argued that their fear of persecution stems from membership of a social group include westernised women from Iran and gay men and lesbians from several countries. The Home Office has not yet accepted these arguments but has occasionally granted exceptional leave to remain to gay men from such countries as Iran and Argentina. However, a man from the Turkish Federated State of Cyprus lost his court case, *ex parte Z* (QBD 25.7.89), because it was not accepted that if returned he had to 'practise' his homosexuality.

People who have a well-founded fear of returning for other reasons not listed in the UN definition, for example family pressure, danger of criminal attacks, or the bombardment of their town or village by military units, do not fit into the terms of the Convention. However it is often still worthwhile to make an application for leave to remain on these grounds, as the Home Office may decide to grant exceptional leave to remain. People do not have to have suffered persecution in the past, though any evidence to show that they had would be helpful. If it is likely that persecution would be suffered in the future, any evidence about the general situation in the country, or of what has happened to people of that racial, religious or other group would be helpful.

Outside the country of nationality

Under the Convention, people cannot be refugees while still in the country in which they fear persecution. They must leave that country before claiming asylum in a safe country. It is therefore theoretically impossible for people to apply for visas to come to a country for asylum, but the Home Office has stated that such applications may, exceptionally, be considered at British embassies and high commissions. It is rare for them to succeed.

Criminal convictions

People may be excluded from the definition of a refugee if they have committed 'a crime against peace, a war crime, a crime against humanity or a serious non-political crime or have been guilty of acts contrary to the purpose and principles of the United Nations' and can be refused asylum on these grounds. A 'serious non-political crime' is not closely defined because of the differences in countries' criminal laws, but would have to be a crime for which death, or a very serious penalty, could be imposed. This clause would not automatically exclude people whose prosecution had been initiated for political or other reasons and could therefore be considered to be part of the persecution from which they were attempting to flee.

Deciding if people qualify for asylum

It may be useful for an adviser to go through the following points, and to decide whether people qualify under them, to check whether they are likely to fit in to the narrow definition of a refugee.

1 Is the person afraid to return?

2 Is what she or he fears 'persecution'?

3 Is the reason for the fear a 'Convention reason', that is, because of the person's race, religion, nationality, membership of a particular social group or political opinion?

4 Is the fear well-founded?

5 Is the person excluded?

Visas and carriers' liability

Home Office policy for a long time has been to attempt to discourage people from coming to the UK to seek asylum. The Home Office has initiated new processes and legislative changes in order to avoid taking responsibility for asylum-seekers and refugees. Citizens of certain countries were made into visa nationals – people who always need to obtain entry clearance in advance of travelling – in order to make it harder for them to reach the UK. Iranians were made visa nationals in 1980, Sri Lankans in 1985, Turks in 1989 and Ugandans in 1991, for this reason.

People without visas still managed to board planes in order to seek asylum. The Home Office next enlisted the airlines in immigration control, through the Immigration (Carriers' Liability) Act 1987. This provided for fines on airlines for each passenger they bring to the UK who does not have the correct documents; in July 1991 the fine was doubled to £2000 per passenger. The airline is still liable to be fined even if the incorrectly-documented person is granted asylum. This means that airlines may be reluctant to allow passengers to board planes.

Immigration officials may be stationed at airports abroad, to 'advise' airlines whether passports and visas are genuine. This is very dangerous for people not permitted to travel, as the national authorities may be alerted to their attempts to leave. There is evidence that people have been turned back from check-in desks and not allowed to fly to the UK. There have also been instances when airlines refused to let people off planes in the UK, on some occasions with the connivance of immigration officers, so that they could not make applications for entry and therefore the airline would not be fined.

Asylum-seekers by definition are often not able to approach the authorities of their own country to obtain passports, or the authorities of another country to obtain visas, without putting themselves in greater danger. They are also outside the immigration rules, because they cannot be considered as refugees until they have left their country of origin. Thus visa requirements and sanctions on airlines do not produce the result of fewer people needing and seeking asylum but of asylum-seekers having to resort to forged documents and visas in order to be able to escape. The UN Convention makes it quite clear that this should not affect the person's application, stating that a country 'shall not impose penalties, on account of their illegal entry or presence, on refugees . . .'

The Home Office has also been in discussions and has signed conventions with other EC countries to create a Europe-wide policy on asylum-seekers (▶see chapter 6 for more information). As most European countries are also attempting to cut down the number of people granted asylum, this policy is extremely dangerous for asylum-seekers and may result in lowering of standards of dealing with applications in all EC countries.

Applying overseas

In very rare cases, refugees may apply for entry clearance to come to the UK. There have been limited government programmes for refugees from particular countries, for Chileans in the 1970s and for some Vietnamese during the 1980s, for example. This is a government decision to accept a quota of people who are already recognised as refugees. They will normally be given permission to enter for four years and granted settlement at the end of that time. People who have come in this way may be referred to as 'programme refugees'.

If asylum-seekers are applying in their own country, they do not fall within the terms of the UN Convention if they are applying for entry clearance. Applications cannot succeed under the immigration rules, as there are no such provisions. The British authorities have to decide whether to make an exception to the rules to consider the application of such people.

If asylum-seekers are applying in another country, where they have managed to escape temporarily, the immediate presumption is that the application for asylum should be made to the authorities of the country in question, unless it can be shown that that country also is not safe. It is unlikely that an application will succeed unless the person already has very close ties with the UK, for example a spouse or young children already settled or granted refugee status. These applications are known as 'third country applications'.

The families of people granted leave to remain in the UK may apply for entry clearance to join them. If refugee status has been granted, spouses and children under 18 have the right to join the refugee and will be granted visas, for which they do not have to pay. If exceptional leave to remain has been granted, any application from family members is outside the immigration rules, at the discretion of the Home Office; it is unlikely to be granted until the person has had exceptional leave for four years. The Home Office first stated that such applications would be considered when

Sri Lanka was made into a visa country in 1985. People who could prove 'severe hardship' through being separated from family members could apply in Colombo but very few visas have been granted on this basis. The families of people whose applications for refugee status have not yet been decided have no claim to be allowed to join them.

Applying on entry to the UK

People seeking asylum at an air- or sea port should apply to the immigration officer for asylum, explaining the danger they would be in if they had to return. People may feel able to do this but equally may not want or dare to give full details to an official, having been persecuted by officials until then. People also may not know the correct procedure for applying for asylum, and may believe it would be safer or better to gain entry to the UK in some other category, for example as a visitor, and later apply for asylum once in the UK.

When people apply for asylum at a port of entry, a decision on the application is not made immediately. Immigration officers may not even ask many detailed questions, except to establish whether the person has come directly from the country of danger. While the application is under consideration (which has been taking an average of 16 months and in many cases two or three years) the applicant may either be detained in a prison or immigration detention centre or be given temporary admission to live at a named address (▶see chapter 12).

The usual procedure is then for the asylum-seekers to complete a long questionnaire giving details of their claim. These are known as 'political asylum questionnaires' or PAQs. If people are detained, they will be interviewed in more detail by the immigration service. The immigration officer will fill in the questionnaire at the interview and will send the completed questionnaire to the Home Office for consideration. People given temporary admission will be given the questionnaires to complete themselves within a given period, normally twelve weeks. They may be asked to return to the airport for a further interview before a decision is made.

At Heathrow airport, an advice service, the Refugee Arrivals Project, (▶see chapter 19 for address) exists in order to advise and help asylum-seekers to find accommodation and financial support, and to seek release of those initially detained. It also refers asylum-seekers to sources of legal advice on their cases.

'Third country cases'

If people have not come directly from their country of origin, but have spent some time in any other country on the way to the UK, immigration officers question them in detail to see whether that country would be a more appropriate one in which to seek asylum. Under the UN Convention, people seeking asylum are assumed to have come direct from the country where they were in danger, and should apply for asylum in the first safe country they reach. It is therefore possible for asylum-seekers to be refused entry to the UK and to be returned to the country from which they have immediately come, in order to seek asylum there. Immigration officers are obliged to be satisfied that the country to which they are returning people will not send them back to the country in which they were in danger without first considering their asylum claim.

EC governments signed a Convention on asylum-seekers in Dublin in June 1990. The text of the Convention is printed at the end of the 1990 Immigration Appeals reports. This confirmed that asylum-seekers in any country in the EC should have their applications considered in the first EC country they reached and that it would not be considered in any other country. This Convention had been signed but not yet ratified by all EC governments at the time of writing, so was not yet in force. However it is partially operated in practice: asylum-seekers are returned to other EC countries for their applications to be considered. The Home Office states that if asylum-seekers have close relatives in the UK, their applications may be considered in this country even if they have come through another. 'Close relative' normally means a spouse, a child under 18, or a parent if the applicant is a child under 18. Others who have travelled through another country which is considered 'safe' are likely to be returned there and it is unlikely that this can be delayed or contested.

Applying after entry to the UK

People may apply for asylum after being allowed into the country for any other purpose, for example as visitors or students. They should then apply to the Home Office for a change of status. The Home Office usually sends out a questionnaire and asks them to fill it in themselves and return it within twelve weeks. While a decision is pending (which may take many months) an asylum-seeker is not liable to detention, provided that the application was made while he or she was legally in the UK. The Home Office may then grant asylum or exceptional leave to remain on the basis of the response to the questionnaire. It has stated that it will not normally refuse an application without interviewing the asylum-seeker to give him or her a chance to put forward any other information and evidence. In practice, applications have been refused on the basis of questionnaires alone; for example, Pakistani citizens who had applied for asylum on the basis of their membership of the Pakistan People's Party but whose applications were not decided until after that party had been returned to power.

The process of decision-making

All asylum decisions are made by officials in the Immigration and Nationality Department of the Home Office, not by immigration officers. This is the case even for people who arrive at an air- or sea port to seek asylum; although immigration officers initially deal with the application, they have to pass all the information to the Home Office to make the decision. They then communicate the Home Office's decision to the asylum-seeker and implement it.

Asylum-seekers are normally sent a detailed questionnaire to fill in, which asks for personal details about themselves and their families, about their travel to the UK, about their past education and employment history and about the reasons for their claim to asylum. It is important that people should have help and advice in filling these in, to ensure that all relevant information and any supporting evidence is sent to the Home Office in order that a decision on whether a person has a well-founded fear of persecution for any of the reasons listed in the UN Convention may be made.

If the Home Office is not satisfied from the information in the questionnaire that the person qualifies for refugee status or exceptional leave to remain, it is usual for an interview to be arranged with the asylum-seeker. In view of the seriousness of the issues involved and the possibility of misunderstandings, it is important that a representative should accompany an asylum-seeker at any interview at the port or at the Home Office and make a full written record of the interview. Many asylum-seekers do not speak English and their interviews will therefore be carried out through an interpreter. If the representative or clerk at the interview is not fluent in both languages, an independent interpreter should also be present at the interview, to note any difficulties in interpretation. The Home Office has agreed that this is permissible.

Sources of information

The Home Office relies on the detailed information given by the asylum-seeker as the basis for the claim for asylum. Thus filling in the questionnaire and responding at interview are of paramount importance. It is necessary to explain in detail exactly what has happened to the person, what activities he or she has engaged in which could result in persecution, what has happened to members of the family or the particular group to which the asylum-seeker belongs. It may be simplest for an adviser to go through this chronologically, in order to prepare a clear statement either on the questionnaire or as a separate letter, explaining what has happened and why the person qualifies for asylum.

It is also helpful to have other corroborative evidence.

Amnesty International has detailed information about most countries of the world and its researchers may be able to provide references or information to support what the asylum-seeker has said. It publishes a yearly review, with brief details about each country and many detailed briefings and bulletins, which are invaluable.

The Minority Rights Group publishes in-depth studies of particular groups which are very helpful.

The UK Immigrants Advisory Service Refugee Unit may have up-to-date information about the Home Office's current practice with regard to particular countries or know what statements will require particular supporting evidence.

The Medical Foundation for the Care of Victims of Torture is able to provide medical reports, prepared by doctors and psychiatrists, on their assessment of physical and mental scars, to confirm information given by asylum-seekers.

The United Nations High Commission for Refugees may offer support in particular cases or its views on the situation in particular countries.

The addresses of all these organisations are in ▶chapter 19.

Connections with another country

If an asylum-seeker has close connections with another country as well as the one from which she or he is claiming asylum, the Home Office may suggest that asylum is not necessary because there is another country to which he or she could go. People who are dual nationals are always expected to go to the safe country of nationality. This has been used, for example, for people of Jewish origin, who have been told that they could go to Israel. The Court of Appeal agreed with this view, in the case of *Miller v IAT* (1988 Imm AR 358).

Pending applications, benefits and work

The Home Office is very slow in considering asylum applications, on average taking over a year and frequently much longer. While an application for asylum is being considered, the person is eligible to claim income support and this will be paid at the urgent cases rate. This means that an asylum-seeker is expected to survive on 90% of income support, although full income support premiums and full housing costs are paid, as well as full benefit for any children. The Benefits Agency requires evidence that the person has claimed asylum before paying out benefit. This is becoming more difficult to prove; in general, the Benefits Agency has accepted standard Home Office letters, in original, written to individuals, which confirm that the application under consideration is for asylum, but no longer accepts letters from lawyers or other representatives.

From November 1991, the Home Office has started using a standard letter of acknowledgement of an asylum application, to which a photograph of the asylum-seeker is attached, which will be acceptable as proof of identity. The Asylum Bill proposes that fingerprint evidence will also be used.

The Home Office has stated that if an asylum application has not been decided after six months, it will give the asylum-seeker permission to work while waiting for the decision. This permission is not automatic; the asylum-seeker or his or her representative should write a letter to the Home Office stating the date on which the asylum application was made and that no decision has yet been reached, requesting permission for the asylum-seeker and his or her spouse, if any, to work. This permission will normally be granted on request. The Home Office has also said that if an asylum-seeker is offered a specific job, permission to work may be given before six months have elapsed.

If refugee status is granted

If the Home Office gives refugee status, it will state this on a standard letter and refugees will be given permission to remain in the UK for four years. The letter explains that they have been given refugee status under the UN Convention, that they have full rights to live and work and to claim benefits in the UK, that they are entitled to grants and to home fees as students, and gives details of the Refugee Council and World University Service as organisations giving advice on benefits and education respectively. Near the end of that four-year period they may apply for settlement, and this is always granted.

A person recognised as a refugee is also entitled to a travel document from the authorities of the country which has granted asylum; this is known as a 'Convention travel document' or CTD and has a pale blue cover. The Home Office will issue one on request. It is valid for all countries except the one from which the person needed asylum and entitles the refugee to travel and to return to the UK within the period of leave given, without needing a visa. Refugees may also be required to register with the police (▶see page 174) and the Refugee Council will pay the police registration fee for refugees who are on benefits.

Exceptional leave to remain

If refugee status is not granted but the Home Office believes it would be wrong to force the person to return at the time, a lesser status called 'exceptional leave to remain' may be granted (▶see appendix for copy letter). It is given either because of the general situation in a country, or on an individual basis, normally for a year at first and then for two periods of three years. The person may apply for settlement after seven years' exceptional leave and this is normally granted.

The Home Office sometimes makes statements that a whole group of people will be covered by a policy of granting exceptional leave to remain. This was granted, for example, to Poles who were in the UK before March 1983, Tamils from Sri Lanka who arrived before May 1985, Lebanese people who had a fear of returning during the civil war, Kuwaiti citizens after the Iraqi invasion (but not automatically to people of other nationalities who had been resident in Kuwait), Chinese citizens who were in the UK before 4 June 1989 and Liberians during the 1990 civil war.

When such an exceptional leave policy has been announced, it is not normally necessary for a person who falls within its remit to make a detailed application for asylum to the Home Office. A statement that he or she qualifies under the policy, with a brief outline of the reasons, should suffice. However, if the person might in fact qualify for refugee status and wants to attempt to obtain this, full details should be sent.

Exceptional leave may also be given for personal or compassionate reasons. This status is granted entirely at the discretion of the Home Office and there is no provision for it in the immigration law or rules, or in international conventions.

The Home Office expects people granted exceptional leave to remain to continue to use their national passports. If the country of origin of a person granted exceptional leave will not issue or renew a passport, the Home Office may issue a travel document, similar to those issued to stateless people. It will normally require written confirmation from the authorities of the country concerned, usually its embassy in the UK, that a passport will not be issued and may ask for details of the reason and urgency of the travel, before issuing a document. The travel documents are brown-covered and are valid for all countries except the person's country of origin and for the same length of time as the exceptional leave to remain. People are entitled to re-enter the UK without visas within the time granted to stay.

Refusal of applications

There is at present a two-stage process for refusing on-entry asylum applications. After considering all the information submitted and deciding that the person does not qualify for leave to enter, the Home Office writes a statement that it is 'minded to refuse' the application and gives reasons, which may be very detailed. The asylum-seeker then has an opportunity to put forward further evidence or further reasons why the refusal is wrong, which the Home Office then has to consider. This process is the result of a court case called *Thirukumar* (1989 Imm AR 402). This concerned four Sri Lankan Tamil men who had sought asylum in the UK and whose cases had been under consideration for varying periods, some for over a year, when they were suddenly called to the airport and told that the applications had been refused and removal arrangements had been made, without giving them the chance to tell the immigration service of any new developments or further evidence collected during this waiting period. The court decided that the Home Office must give an asylum-seeker the chance to put forward any further information before the application is finally decided. It is possible for full refugee status to be granted after the Home Office has been 'minded to refuse' a person, as often evidence and information take a long time to collect.

If the Home Office is not satisfied with the further information given, it will refuse asylum. Rights of appeal depend on the person's immigration status at the time of refusal.

Rights of appeal

The law as at January 1992 is as follows:

If an application for entry clearance has been made abroad at a British embassy or high commission, there is a right of appeal within three months of the refusal date. The appeal will be heard in the UK even though the person appealing has to remain abroad.

If the application was made on entry to the UK, and the person did not have entry clearance before travelling to the UK, there is no right of appeal under the immigration appeals system before being sent back. The only way to try to contest the decision while the person is still in the UK is by seeking judicial review and referring the person to a solicitor experienced in these matters. If the person had entry clearance, there is a right of appeal while he or she is still in the UK, but only on the basis of the application made to the immigration officers before refusal.

Thus, for example, people who travelled to the UK with entry clearance as visitors, applied to enter as visitors and were refused entry have the right to appeal against that refusal and to remain in the UK while the appeal is pending. If, after the refusal, they apply for asylum and this also is refused, the appeal would only be against the visitor refusal, not the asylum claim because it would have been made after the refusal date. People who travel to the UK with entry clearance as visitors and who apply for asylum immediately on arrival and are refused will have the right of appeal against the asylum refusal, because the application was made before refusal.

If the application was made after the person had been granted leave to enter the UK in another capacity, for example as a visitor or student, there will be a right of appeal under the immigration appeals system as long as the application was made to the Home Office before any previous leave to remain ran out. If the application was made late, there will only be a formal right of appeal against any later Home Office decision to deport the person. See chapter 16 for more details about appeals.

However, the Asylum Bill, in progress through Parliament at the time of writing, will mean that all asylum-seekers in the UK have the same, limited, appeal rights. It proposes that anyone in the UK refused asylum must apply, within a very limited period, to a special adjudicator for leave to appeal. The special adjudicator will decide very quickly, without an oral hearing, whether to grant leave. The full appeal will be heard within a few weeks of that decision.

Transfer of asylum

People who have been granted asylum in one country may wish to transfer their asylum to another country. If they have obtained asylum in the first country to which they went but have many relatives in another country, or if there is a much larger community of their nationality or religion in another country, they may wish to change their country of asylum. Transfer of asylum is always difficult, as most countries do not wish to add to their refugee population. People have to make a very convincing case to show that they are having difficulties in their country of first asylum or have very strong connections, usually close family, in the second country.

Family reunion

The spouse and the children under 18 of a person granted **refugee status** may have travelled to the UK together with the refugee, in which case they will be granted permission to stay for the same period as the refugee. If they apply to join the refugee later, they have the right to do so. If they require visas, these should be granted simply on establishing the relationship; there is no visa fee. It is not necessary for a refugee to prove that she or he can support and accommodate the spouse and children. There is no right for any other members of the family to come and they normally have to wait until they fit into the immigration rules. Elderly parents, for example, can only come to join their adult children once the son or daughter has gained settlement, normally after four years as a refugee.

There is no right for a person granted **exceptional leave to remain** to be joined by any family members. If the whole family has travelled to the UK together and one member has been granted exceptional leave, it is usual for the spouse and children to be granted this too. However, if the other family members have remained outside the UK they are unlikely to be granted entry clearance. The Home Office has stated that family reunion will not normally be allowed until the person with exceptional leave has been in the UK for four years, and the other criteria of the immigration rules on families, most importantly that there is adequate support and accommodation for the family, are met.

Families may make applications for entry clearance to join someone with exceptional leave earlier than this, but the Home Office will only grant the application if it can be shown that there are 'compelling compassionate circumstances'. The Home Office did not, for example, consider the case of a Kurdish child who had cerebral palsy compelling enough; neither was his death considered compelling enough to allow his brothers and sisters to join their parents afterwards until the family's solicitors had begun a judicial review application. This rigid operation of the policy creates a very difficult situation both for families abroad and for the person here. Refugee community groups and others have been campaigning against this.

The families of **asylum-seekers**, that is, people whose asylum applications have not yet been decided, have no right to come to the UK to join them. If families manage to arrive, and explain at the port that they are coming to join an asylum-seeker, it is probable that they will be given temporary admission to remain until the main applicant's case has been decided. They will then be granted leave in line with him or her if the application is granted. However, there is no automatic right for them to be allowed in and they can be refused entry at a port or airport. In that case, they may wish to apply for asylum in their own right, even if the danger they would face is mainly because of their connection with the relative they are coming to join, so that this application can be considered too.

Other rights connected with asylum

People granted either refugee status or exceptional leave to remain are entitled to claim any welfare benefits in the UK, on the same basis as other residents. This does not affect their immigration status. They will be treated as home students for the purposes of assessment for fees for studies. Asylum-seekers however will be treated as overseas students until their applications are granted. Refugees and people granted exceptional leave to remain are both free to work without needing work permits.

Loss of asylum

Once a government has granted a person refugee status, this status is permanent and is unaffected by any change in the country of origin which may later make it safe for the person to return. Under the UN Convention, a person may lose asylum after it has been granted only if he or she is convicted of any crime which would have excluded him or her from being granted refugee status, but this is very rare. The Home Office standard letter to people granted refugee status makes mention of this possibility, particularly in relation to political activities, but this seems designed to discourage refugees from political activities rather than because any action will be taken.

Refugees can themselves renounce their asylum if they wish to return to their country of origin or again use their national passports. When refugee status is granted, the Home Office will normally keep the person's passport, if it was available at the time of decision, and will issue a refugee travel document, which is valid for every country except the one from which asylum was granted. By requesting the return of a passport, or going back to the country, the person shows that he or she is again seeking the protection of that country and has therefore lost refugee status. However, the status under British immigration law remains the same. A refugee who was settled in the UK but who returned to his or her own country remains settled and is subject to the normal returning resident rules (▶see chapter 11).

People with exceptional leave to remain normally still use the passport of their original country. It is then theoretically possible for them to return to that country, if they wish, and they will probably be readmitted to the UK if they return within the time limit of their original permission to enter or remain. It may however be more difficult for them to gain an extension of their stay in the future. It will be clear from their passport that they have travelled back to the country they said they could not return to, and the Home Office may ask more questions to determine whether it is now safe for them to return permanently. If the country is one for which there is a blanket policy, and if there was an emergency reason for travel there, such as the serious illness or death of a close relative, further leave will probably be granted.

Green form legal aid

The Home Office proposed in July 1991 that legal aid for advice and assistance (green form) would be abolished for all immigration and asylum matters, and that increased funding would be given to the UK Immigrants Advisory Service in order to cope with the increased demand for advice. This proposal was opposed by almost all organisations dealing with immigration advice, as it is against the principle of access to justice being available for all and would rob a particularly vulnerable group of choice of legal representative. On 10 February 1992, the government announced that the proposal would be shelved.

6 The European Community

European Community (EC) law and British immigration law are not always compatible. This is not surprising, because they are based on completely different premises. One of the aims of the EC is to minimise barriers for EC citizens travelling between EC countries for what are defined as economic purposes. On the other hand, the aim of British immigration law is principally to deter economic migration for people who are not EC nationals.

The countries of the EC are Belgium, Denmark, France, Germany, Greece, Ireland, Italy, Luxembourg, the Netherlands, Portugal, Spain and the UK. There are applications for membership from several other countries, including Austria, Hungary and Turkey, but joining is usually a long-drawn-out process which has to be agreed by all existing members. Citizens of EC countries are, by and large, able to move freely between all other EC countries and the individual national immigration laws do not apply to them. Citizens of Portugal and Spain obtained full free movement rights on 1 January 1992.

How the EC works

The EC was set up in 1957 by the Treaty of Rome, which provided for the gradual reduction of barriers to free movement of workers, capital, goods and services between EC countries. An amendment to the Treaty, the Single European Act, came into force from 1986. The intention of this Act was to create a single internal market in goods and services and the free movement of people within the whole EC area, by harmonising the laws of the individual countries in specific areas. There are several Europe-wide institutions that debate proposed change within the EC and provide for its implementation.

The European Parliament, which sits in Brussels and Strasbourg, has directly-elected members from each EC country and debates proposals for change in EC laws and resolutions on particular areas. It can investigate particular areas and produce reports. In practice, it has very little power other than to recommend changes, although it has the theoretical power to dismiss all the Commissioners and to veto the whole EC budget.

76   **The European Commission**, based in Brussels, is the executive cum

civil service of the EC. It has 17 appointed members, representing all the EC countries, and drafts legislation for the EC. It has its own supporting bureaucracy, also recruited from all the different EC countries.

The Council of Ministers is the legislative body. It consists of Ministers from the twelve EC countries and takes the final decisions, having taken account of the views of the European Parliament.

EC policies are changed through **EC regulations and directives**, which are provided for by the Treaty of Rome, produced by the European Commission, debated and amended in the European Parliament and agreed by the Council of Ministers. Directives are 'binding in their entirety and take direct effect in each member state'. This means that each country has to take immediate measures to bring them into force. There are directives on the freedom of movement of workers, on establishment and provision of services, for example. Regulations are 'binding as to the result to be achieved', meaning that countries may use different means to bring them into force. There are regulations on employment and workers' families, and on trade union rights, for example.

The European Court of Justice, in Luxembourg, decides on legal cases brought under EC law. Its interpretation of EC law has to be followed by individual countries.

All these institutions decide matters of EC law. However member countries still keep their own individual laws for areas which are not covered by the Community. This includes laws which relate to non-EC citizens, including therefore migration and asylum laws and procedures. The governments consult with one another regularly through a number of **official and semi-official coordination groups**. On migration issues, these are the Trevi Group of ministers responsible for border controls and the Ad Hoc Group on Immigration, which meet every six months. Though the agendas for each of these groups and fora are slightly different, each is contributing to the process of making immigration laws more uniform throughout the EC and the process of harmonisation of laws between the countries is a continuous one. These groups are not directly responsible to any democratically accountable forum, and their deliberations are secret. They are discussed further on page 83.

Freedom of movement

The EC Treaty provides for the freedom of movement of goods, services, capital and workers between EC countries. The definition of workers includes only EC citizens and not other people living in any EC country. People holding valid passports as citizens of any individual EC country are EC citizens; each EC country has its own citizenship law establishing who are its citizens. In other respects it is a broad definition, as it includes:

• people who have a job to come to

- people who are involuntarily unemployed and are looking for work in another EC country
- people who have worked in the UK but are unemployed by reason of permanent disability through illness or injury, or who have reached retirement age
- people who wish to set up a business in another EC country
- people who wish to be self-employed
- people who are coming to provide services.

Some other people, although not strictly classified as workers, may also benefit from free movement rights:

- people who are coming to receive services
- people who are coming to study, provided they are paying for their studies
- people who are retired but have adequate means to live on.

There are three recent EC directives on the freedom of movement of students, retired people and others, which were decided in June 1990 and are expected to come into force on 30 June 1992. These will mean that EC citizens who are self-supporting are free to travel within the EC for almost any purpose and do not have to fit into individual countries' immigration laws.

EC citizens do not require permission to enter the UK and no formal time limit can be put on their stay. When they enter the UK, their passports are not stamped though they may be given a form explaining their status and the process for applying for a residence permit should they wish to do so. They are free to remain in the UK, to work or to study and do not need to apply for any further permission to stay, as this is an automatic right under EC law. They are eligible to claim benefits on a similar basis to people settled in the UK. The European Court of Justice has agreed in the case of *Antonissen* (February 1991) that UK legislation giving the power to require an EC national to leave if he or she is not working within six months and is not genuinely seeking work is not contrary to the EC Treaty, but it is not clear how this would be enforced.

Individual countries do have the right to restrict some jobs to their own nationals, but these areas are defined by EC law. Some public service jobs, for example, may be restricted, but only those which involve the official in some exercise of discretion.

Residence permits

EC citizens may find it useful to have a document to show to anyone who has the right to request proof of identity or of status in the UK, for example a Benefits Agency official when the person is claiming benefit. A residence permit is not compulsory and does not in itself give permission to the EC national to remain. It is merely a document confirming the right that the person already has through the operation of EC law.

EC citizens carrying out any kind of economic activity may obtain residence permits from the Home Office. The permits of people who are self-employed or carrying out business are confusingly known as right of abode certificates. Application forms EEC1 can be obtained from any Jobcentre or from the Home Office. If the person is in employment, the employer needs to confirm this fact, or if studying, the college. If the person is self-employed, evidence of the financial state of the business will be required. The Home Office also requires two passport-size photos and evidence that the person is an EC citizen (normally a valid passport) and then issues a residence permit. Residence permits are normally valid for five years. If the person's job is a temporary one, or if the Home Office believes that a check should be made on the person sooner, for example if a business is being set up but there is no evidence it will succeed, the permit may be granted for one year only.

After four years holding a residence permit, EC nationals may apply for settlement. This will be granted if they have been working or doing business for most of the four-year period. Absences for up to six months do not constitute a break in this period and part-time employment also counts.

Appeals for EC citizens

EC law provides that EC citizens have the right of appeal against any decisions made against them in the exercise of their free movement rights. This gives them more rights than others under British immigration law.

All EC citizens refused entry to the UK have the right of appeal against refusal and can remain in the UK while the appeal is pending. This is because they are appealing against the immigration officer's decision that they require leave to enter the UK. EC citizens exercising their free movement rights do not require leave; the Immigration Act 1971 provides that people claiming that they do not require leave to enter have a right of appeal before removal, even when they do not have entry clearance.

EC citizens also have a right of appeal against being refused a residence permit or the curtailment of a residence permit. Under the Immigration Act 1971 people only have a right of appeal against refusal if they had leave to remain at the time they made the application that was refused. As EC citizens do not have or need leave to remain, the Home Office has insti-tuted a special review procedure for EC nationals, who can apply direct to the Immigration Appeal Tribunal if they are refused a residence permit or if their permit is curtailed.

Deportation of EC citizens

EC citizens who are exercising EC rights can only be deported for reasons of public policy, public security and public health. They cannot be deported for remaining in the UK without leave, because they do not require leave, or for claiming benefit. They will always have a right of appeal against deportation. Section 5(1) of the Immigration Act 1988, which restricts rights of appeal for people who have been in the UK less than seven years, does not apply because the deportation is not on the grounds of overstaying or breaking conditions of stay. 'Public policy' has been defined very tightly by the European Court of Justice, in the case of *Bouchereau* (1981 2 All ER 924). This decided that an EC citizen cannot be recommended for deportation solely because of a criminal conviction, for example, but only if the person's continued presence in the UK can be shown to be detrimental to the UK.

Family members

Under EC law, the families of EC citizens who have travelled to another EC country for any purpose provided for in EC law are entitled to go to that country and to remain on the same basis as the EC citizen. This applies to family members whether or not they themselves are EC citizens. Family members who are visa nationals can be required to have visas before entry, but they must not be charged a fee for them and the issuing of the visa must be expedited. If the EC national in the UK has a residence permit, the Home Office will grant family members residence permits for the same length of time.

UK citizens living in the UK do not count as EC citizens for this purpose because they have not moved to the UK to work and therefore are not exercising free movement rights.

The family of an EC national is defined as:

- a spouse
- children and grandchildren up to the age of 21 automatically; children over 21 if still dependent
- dependent parents, grandparents and great-grandparents
- other relatives who had been living 'under the same roof' if dependent (this has not been more closely defined).

These people have the right under EC law to travel with, or to come to join, an EC national who is engaged in any economic activity in any other EC state. They do not have to fit into any requirements of British immigration law to do so; the primary purpose rule, for example, does not apply to spouses of EC nationals. They will be allowed to enter or to remain for the same length of time as the EC citizen. The only evidence the Home Office will need is evidence of identity, of the relationship and of the economic activity of the EC national. Thus, for example, if a Polish overstayer marries an EC national who is working in the UK and applies to remain with her, the Home Office has no right to ask further questions about the relationship but will grant leave to remain for the same length of time as the EC national.

Irish citizens are also EC citizens. Anyone born in Ireland, whether in the Republic or in Northern Ireland, is under Irish law an Irish citizen; people born in Northern Ireland are British citizens as well. An Irish citizen who travelled from the Republic of Ireland to the UK after 1 January 1973 (when Ireland joined the EC) and who is working has EC rights. Irish citizens are allowed to remain in the UK permanently; thus anyone who marries such an Irish citizen will also be granted indefinite leave to remain, with no further inquiry. However, because people born in Northern Ireland are British citizens too, if they travel to mainland Britain without any connection with the Republic this does not count as movement between EC countries.

British immigration rules regarding family members are more restrictive than the EC rules; for example, a British citizen living in France and engaged in any economic activity there has the right to be joined there by her husband, even if he was refused permission to join her in the UK under the primary purpose rule. After the couple have lived and worked in another EC country for some time, preferably at least a year, it should be possible for them to return together to the UK under EC law, because the wife has exercised her rights of free movement. Some British women have attempted to benefit from this provision after spending only a few days or weeks in another EC country with their husbands but the husbands have been refused. On current evidence, it would seem that the period of work must be at least several months. This is an area of law which is being tested before the European Court of Justice in the case of *Surinder Singh* (▶see Annex to chapter 2). If this case is successful, it will undermine the operation of the primary purpose marriage rule by giving British women this option of bringing in their husbands.

Public funds

EC citizens are not required to satisfy immigration officers that they can support themselves without recourse to public funds. They are therefore eligible to claim any benefit, at any time, if they meet the qualifying conditions for the benefit. EC citizens who are signing on and genuinely looking for work are entitled to income support whether or not they have a residence permit. The Social Security Commissioners have accepted that EC citizens do not require leave to remain and that their entitlement to benefit is unaffected by whether the initial six months of their stay is over or whether they have applied to the Home Office for a residence permit, or been granted one. However, benefits offices have instructions to inform the Home Office after two weeks' claiming. If the person does not have a residence permit, the Home Office may then write threatening letters, suggesting that the person should be supporting him or herself in order to qualify under EC law to remain.

The point of these letters is to scare the claimant; there are no effective practical sanctions that the Home Office can take. Although the person's stay may be formally curtailed, there is a right of appeal against this curtailment. If the person appeals and remains in the UK pending the appeal, as soon as he or she becomes engaged in any economic activity and applies for a residence permit it will be granted.

Once a residence permit has been granted, this is convenient evidence for the Benefits Agency of people's status and their eligibility to claim, but the fact of their nationality makes them eligible to claim. EC citizens cannot be deported solely for claiming, although they must be exercising their treaty rights, that is, they must be genuinely seeking work. Thus it is safe for EC citizens to claim income support between jobs when necessary as long as they are not voluntarily unemployed or to claim benefits, such as family credit, as well as working.

The main danger for EC citizens who have lived on income support is that if they leave the UK, they may be refused re-entry. It is possible for an EC citizen to be refused entry if the immigration officers are not satisfied that he or she can be supported without recourse to public funds. If there is evidence that a person has claimed benefits for a substantial period, more questions can be asked or evidence demanded to show that this is unlikely to happen again. However if the person is returning with a substantial amount of money, or with a reliable promise of a job, it is probable that he or she will be admitted. It is now rare for EC citizens to be examined in detail when they enter the UK; usually immigration officers check only whether they hold an EC passport.

EC nationals: the UK's definition

Each EC country has the right to determine who are its nationals for EC purposes, within common parameters. The UK's definition is:

- **British citizens (excluding those from the Channel Islands and the Isle of Man)**
- **British subjects with the right of abode (▶see glossary)**
- **British Dependent Territories citizens connected with Gibraltar; it was decided that as Gibraltar is a territory in Europe its people should have free movement rights.**

All other British nationals (▶see chapter 17) are *not* EC citizens.

Many people living in the UK are *not* EC nationals. They include:

- people from the Isle of Man and the Channel Islands, because these islands have their own immigration and citizenship laws; other EC nationals are not able to go to live there either

- other kinds of British nationals
- Commonwealth citizens with the right of abode in the UK who are not British
- other people settled in the UK who are not British.

All these people are not EC nationals and do not have freedom of movement rights. They have no rights in the other countries of the EC. They need to fit in to the individual countries' immigration laws in order to travel there.

Other EC countries with overseas responsibilities have also defined their nationals for EC purposes. France, for example, has defined people from Guadeloupe and Martinique as EC citizens but not people from other overseas areas. Portuguese citizens from Macau are EC citizens.

Future developments

EC law is being developed constantly, through directives issued by the Council of Ministers on particular subjects and through decisions of the European Court of Justice. Directives are binding on each EC government and national laws should provide for them to be incorporated. Britain has not yet done so; although section 7(1) of the Immigration Act 1988 provided the means for this to be done, it has not yet come into force. It appears that the Home Office has not yet worked out how to carry it out in a way that remains compatible with the rest of British immigration law. In spite of this delay in formal incorporation, decisions about many aspects of British immigration law and policy in the future will not be made in Britain but in transnational informal groups within the EC, such as the Trevi Group and the Ad Hoc Group on Immigration.

There are three ways in which these groups' decisions affect immigration policy and legislation:

a) they can agree to sign Conventions, binding them to common policies and procedures. The Dublin Convention on asylum-seekers has already been signed. A convention on the crossing of external frontiers is expected to be signed during 1992.

b) they can agree to take action in their national Parliaments for a common purpose, for example to impose visas on nationals of a certain country, or to propose carriers' liability legislation

c) they can exchange information about fears of numbers of people arriving or about new procedures which informally influence policy-making and development at a national level.

The '1992 process' and the 'Schengen process'

The single internal market is intended to be an area without internal frontiers, so that there can be free movement of goods, capital, workers and services between the twelve EC countries. 1 January 1993 is the target date for harmonising many of the different laws and regulations in different countries. Much of this work has already taken place since the Single European Act came into force in 1986. It will probably not be completed during 1992. There will be no sudden change in laws and practices after 1992 but the process of bringing down barriers between EC countries and erecting higher ones around the external EC frontiers will continue.

Eight EC countries have already completed the negotiations for an internal market and barrier-free zone between them. They are known as the 'Schengen group' because the original treaty was signed in the Luxembourg town of Schengen. They are France, Luxembourg, Belgium, the Netherlands, Germany, Italy, Spain and Portugal. The Schengen supplementary agreement was agreed by the end of 1988 but its implementation was delayed firstly because of the destruction of the Berlin wall and the end of the border between East and West Germany and latterly because of a dispute between the Dutch Council of State and the Dutch government about its provisions, which may be in conflict with the Netherlands' obligations under other international treaties. The provisions of Schengen are seen as a possible blueprint for decisions to be made by the whole EC in connection with the 1992 process.

Third country nationals

The measures for the free movement of workers apply only to EC citizens, so the movements of non-citizens living in EC countries, known as 'third country nationals', will still be controlled. Governments are considering ways of checking whether people are EC citizens as they travel over internal borders or by means of internal controls within each country. People who are not EC citizens will not benefit in any way from the reduction of internal barriers. If they are resident in one EC country, they will have no right to move to another but will still be subject to the immigration laws of the country they wish to move to.

Refugees and asylum-seekers are likely to face even greater problems. The Dublin Convention, agreed in June 1990 and now signed but not ratified by most EC countries, provides that if one EC country refuses an asylum application no other EC country could then consider the person's case. People will therefore have only one chance of gaining asylum in all twelve EC countries. It is therefore likely that countries with more liberal policies will become more restrictive so that they will not have larger numbers of asylum-seekers arriving, and because of pressure from countries with harder-line policies.

Immigration laws of individual countries will be harmonised so that there are similar requirements for entry to all countries. There may be a single visit visa which will entitle people who are not EC nationals to enter all EC countries for a visit; it is expected that this will be for three, rather than the present six, months.

7 Workers and business people

The following groups of people do not need specific permission to work in the UK:

- people who are settled (allowed to stay permanently)
- people who have been allowed to enter or remain to join close relatives settled in the UK, for example husbands and wives, and have been allowed in for a year initially
- people granted refugee status or exceptional leave to remain
- Commonwealth citizens who have been allowed in as working holiday-makers or because they had a grandparent born in the UK
- other people who have no restriction or prohibition on working stamped on their passports

These are all people who have been able to come to the UK for some other reason but, following on from this, are able to work.

It is very hard for non-EC nationals to be allowed to come to the UK *in order to* take up work. British immigration law and rules on coming to work are designed mainly to protect jobs in the UK for people already allowed to live and work in this country, and to encourage investment in businesses only from people with a very substantial amount of money to offer. The work permit scheme is not designed to help people to come to work in the UK. It ensures that employers will only go through all the paperwork and delays involved if the worker is essential. People may only come to set up a business or to live off their capital if their means are substantial; there are no provisions for people from abroad to set up small businesses.

Workers

The work permit scheme

Work permits are granted to employers by the Employment Department, not the Home Office. In May 1989 the Employment Department published a discussion paper on possible changes in the scheme, in order to stream-line it and to make it easier for transnational companies and large employers to transfer workers. The results were announced in February

1991 and most of the new scheme came into effect on 1 October 1991. The main proposed change that had not come into force at the time of writing was charging employers fees for work permits; in March 1991 the Employment Department suggested that this should not be more than £100.

How the work permit scheme operates

Work permits are issued to employers, not to workers, to enable them to employ a named worker in a particular job at a particular rate of pay. They thus give extremely specific permission and if the worker changes jobs, even within the same company, a new permit is necessary. Permits are issued by the Employment Department Overseas Labour Section, not by the Home Office. The possession of a work permit means that the immigration authorities should allow the person to enter the UK, or to remain, in order to do the job.

Employers have to apply to the Employment Department for a work permit. They obtain application forms from the local Jobcentre but return them to the Employment Department Overseas Labour Section, Caxton House, Tothill Street, London SW1H 9NF. The application form for most work permits is form WP1, which comes with an explanatory leaflet WP1/5; the form for training and work experience permits is at present OW22 but is to be changed to WP2. There is a specific form for entertainers, sportspersons and models (WP3) and an extra one for footballers (WP4). The forms come with explanatory leaflets about the scheme and it is important that employers do their best to comply with the requirements or the application may be rejected out of hand.

From 1 October 1991, there has been a two-tier system, making it easier for employers to obtain permits to employ workers in high-level posts. Tier 1 includes transfers within transnational companies, board level posts with a salary of £50,000 or more, posts involving substantial financial investment in the UK and 'posts where the occupation is recognised as being in acute short supply'. Where jobs come within the first tier, permits will be granted 'with the minimum of checks' and the jobs will not have to be advertised within the UK.

Tier 2 covers all other jobs. It includes a new category of 'keyworker', to allow for recognition of language and cultural skills as well as the specific professional skills for the job. Previous work experience or qualifications gained in the UK may be taken into consideration.

The main requirements of the scheme in general are:

- the worker from abroad will not be taking a job which could be done by anyone already permitted to work in the UK or by an EC national. Employers are required to sign a declaration confirming that no other worker has been displaced by the worker from abroad.

- the person must usually have had at least two years work experience, normally abroad, in a similar job to that for which a permit is now being requested. The Employment Department will need to see proof of these jobs from previous employers. The employer's word is usually accepted when the application is for an inter-company transfer. People in the UK as students will not normally be permitted to change to employment and cannot generally use their UK qualification to justify their suitability for the job.
- the person must have all the skills and qualifications necessary for the job. Permits are normally only given for highly skilled professional jobs, so evidence of studies and qualifications may be very important.
- there must be a genuine vacancy
- for jobs in Tier 1, the employer has to confirm either that the job is one at board level, with a salary of over £50,000, or essential to new foreign investment and creation of jobs in the UK or must give details of the high levels of skills and qualifications needed
- for jobs in Tier 2, the job must normally have been advertised in all the places and papers where such a job would usually be advertised for at least four weeks and the employer must explain why no other applicants were suitable.

This may be a problem when a person is in the UK already and doing the job, or has been offered the job before the fact of needing a work permit was known. The form requires evidence of all the attempts made to find someone already allowed to work, including copies of the advertisements, details of the response to them and explanations of why the other applicants were not suitable.

Applying when the worker is abroad

People coming to work need entry clearance. A work permit counts as prior entry clearance for non-visa nationals; visa nationals need visas as well. Normally people have to be outside the UK while the employer is applying for the work permit. If the Employment Department Overseas Labour Section grants the permit, it sends it to the employer, who sends it to the worker abroad.

Applying in the UK

Since 1 October 1991, any application for a work permit or for an extension of a work permit holder's permitted stay is made direct to the Employment Department, not to the Home Office. It is therefore very important that the application is made while the person's leave to remain is still valid, so that he or she remains legally in the country while the application is pending and does not become an overstayer.

It is rare for a person in the UK for some other purpose to be granted leave to remain as a work permit holder. The immigration rules do not permit people who entered as visitors, for example, to remain as workers and it is very difficult for people who entered for any other purpose to be allowed to stay for work. If an employer applies for a permit for a person who is in the UK at the time, without a work permit, the Employment Department may grant a permit but the case then must be referred to the Home Office to decide whether to grant the person leave to remain. The Home Office can refuse to grant leave to remain to take up the job even if the Employment Department has granted a permit.

When a permit is granted

If the worker is not a visa national he or she needs no further documents except a passport in order to come to the UK. A visa national needs a visa as well, but will be given it on application to the British embassy or high commission, provided the job is still available. Work permit holders arriving in the country can only be refused entry by immigration officers if it is believed that false representations were employed in order to get the permit (even if they did not know that this had been done) or that the job is no longer available.

The worker will be admitted for a period of four years, unless the permit is limited to a shorter period, when the worker will be admitted for the period of the permit. During this time, it is possible for the person to stop working and to remain in the UK legally, but only to change jobs if the new employer first obtains a new permit. The same criteria apply to the new application, except that the worker does not need to be outside the country while the application is pending, having already obtained entry clearance for the purpose of work. Because of the requirement of previous experience abroad, changes of employment will usually only be allowed within the same type of occupation. The Employment Department may insist that the person leaves his or her original job before it will consider an application from a new employer.

Extending a permit

Work permit application forms require the employers to specify the period of employment. They are not able to state 'indefinitely'; if the period is for more than four years they are required to justify this. The Employment Department assumes that most permits will be required for a short, finite period and employers will have to make out a special case for a permit for permanent employment. The 1991 regulations state that only 'in exceptional circumstances will permits be granted or extended for the four year period which can qualify the overseas national to apply for indefinite leave to remain in the UK'. If a permit is granted for a limited period and the employers want to continue to employ the worker there is a specific form, WP5, to apply for an extension. The employers must again show why this is necessary, for how long and why it has been impossible to train, transfer or recruit a local replacement for the job.

Families of work permit holders

The wife or husband of a work permit holder qualifies under the immigration rules to come to live with the permit holder in the UK. So do the children under 18 of work permit holders, provided both parents are living, or coming to live, in the UK. Family members must also obtain entry clearance from the British embassy or high commission before travelling. They will have to prove their relationship to the work permit holder and that there is adequate support and accommodation for them in the UK without recourse to public funds (▶see box on page 124 for definition). There are more details about the procedures in the chapters on spouses and on children. No other relatives will be allowed to join a work permit holder before he or she is granted settlement.

Work permit holders' passport stamps will usually state that they cannot take employment paid or unpaid without the consent of the Secretary of State for Employment and that they cannot do business without the consent of the Home Office. Their families' passports will usually just be stamped with a time limit, in line with the work permit holder's, with no restrictions on taking employment. The spouse of a work permit holder is therefore free to work without needing a permit in his or her own right. The children are entitled to state education and to child benefit. The permit holder and any family members are entitled to National Health Service medical treatment immediately on arrival.

Rights of work permit holders

Work permit holders pay national insurance contributions and tax. They are therefore entitled to any benefits for which they qualify as a result of their contributions. They also have the same rights under employment law as any other workers; the work permit does not alter any contract of employment or remove any trade union, employment or negotiating rights. However, workers who wish to continue to live in the UK may be deterred from making complaints by the fact that the permit depends on the employer and their chance of remaining in the UK depends on keeping a work permit.

Because the purpose of work permit holders being allowed into the UK is to work, the immigration rules do not specifically state that they must be able to support and accommodate themselves without recourse to public funds. Work permit holders (as distinct from their spouses and children) are therefore not listed as 'persons from abroad' for income support purposes (▶see chapter 10) and are not ineligible to receive income support for this reason. If they need to claim income support between jobs they can do so without this jeopardising their immigration status in any way. It is possible, however, that they could be refused income support on the grounds that they are not 'available for work' under the income support regulations. This is because they cannot legally take up another job until the new employer has obtained a new work permit for them and this would only be granted for a very specific job. If they are exempt from the availability for work requirement, for example through illness, they may receive income support.

Settlement

After four years working in a job or jobs for which permits have been granted, the worker will qualify to settle. Near the end of the four years the worker must make an application to the Home Office for permission to settle, enclosing his or her passport and confirmation from the employer that the job is still continuing. If there have been periods of unemployment, or periods when the person was working without a permit, these do not count towards the four years; the person will have to continue working until he or she has accumulated four years in approved employment. Any other family members who have been admitted to be with the work permit holder will also be granted settlement in line with him or her if they apply. If the children of work permit holders have become 18 during the four years of the permit, they will be allowed to settle with the rest of the family, provided they are still unmarried and financially dependent.

Permit-free employment

The immigration rules list a number of occupations for which work permits are not necessary, and the immigration authorities deal with applications for people to come to do them. These jobs are known as 'permit-free employment' and are normally jobs for which it is unlikely that someone already resident in the UK will qualify. People coming for any of these jobs need to obtain entry clearance from the British high commission or embassy in their country of origin, but the employers do not need to apply to the Employment Department. The person will need confirmation of the job offer and should then fill in the application forms IM2A and IM2D at the British embassy or high commission and pay the fee (see appendix). The entry clearance officer may refer the application back to the Home Office to confirm details of the job or the employers before making a decision about granting entry clearance.

The occupations which can be considered for permit-free employment are:

- **ministers of religion and missionaries**. They have to show that they will be working full-time as ministers and that they are capable of filling the position required by the religious group requesting them to come. They will be asked for evidence of any formal qualifications and of past experience of religious work as well as for details about the job and pay offered. Pay or fringe benefits such as accommodation must be sufficient to show that they and their dependants can be supported and accommodated by the religious community or denomination which will employ them. The community needs to show that there is a genuine need for the person to come to work there. The entry clearance officer will require a letter from the religious group giving full details of the position offered.

Although the immigration rules specify that entry clearance is necessary, the Home Office has stated that it may, exceptionally, consider applications made on behalf of ministers of religion who are already in the UK as visitors. Congregations may have invited priests from abroad to visit, to see if they are mutually compatible, and then decided to offer them a post. It is possible for this application to be considered in the UK without the visitor having to leave and for permission to remain as a minister of religion to be granted, provided the other criteria of the rules are satisfied. In practice, it may be more difficult for people from non-Christian churches and non-mainstream Christian churches to convince entry clearance officers or the Home Office of their status.

- **members of religious orders**. They may come to live in a monastery or nunnery and be part of its life, or to teach in a school run by the order and part of it. If they are teaching in an outside school, the school must obtain a work permit to employ them. It is assumed that the religious order will be providing board and lodging for its members.
- **representatives of overseas newspapers, news agencies and broadcasting organisations** on long-term assignments to the UK. Their permanent employment will be with the organisation abroad but their place of work will be the UK for prolonged periods.
- **representatives of overseas firms which have no branch or subsidiary in the UK**. The firm must be based overseas but the representative may spend many months in the UK, perhaps preparatory to setting up a branch or carrying out particular business activities.
- **people employed by an overseas government or a United Nations organisation or other international body**. These are people who are not formally diplomats, but are based overseas and have formal contracts of employment with the international body or overseas government, not with the embassy or high commission in the UK.

Most of these people will be admitted for a year at first, except representatives of overseas firms who may be admitted for up to four years. The spouse and children under 18 of all these people may also be allowed in, provided that they obtain entry clearance and can be maintained and accommodated without recourse to public funds. They will usually not be restricted from working themselves. After four years in the category, the person and spouse and children can be allowed to settle.

Short-term workers

Some people may be admitted to work for short and clearly-limited periods. The following categories of short-term worker do not need work permits.

- **teachers and language assistants** coming to schools in the UK under approved official exchange schemes. Two years is the maximum period they will be permitted to stay.
- **seafarers under contract to join a ship in British waters**. They will normally remain only a few days or weeks before the ship sails.
- **operational ground staff of overseas-owned airlines**.
- **seasonal workers at agricultural camps under approved schemes**. These are mainly people coming to help with harvests and they are never allowed to remain beyond 30 November of any year.
- **private servants of diplomats**. They must be at least 16 years old and be working within a diplomatic household, for example as a housemaid or a chauffeur. They are not exempt from immigration control (see below) because they are employed by an individual diplomat, not by the embassy. Their permission to work is limited to working for a single employer; they will not be allowed to change employment. Although they may work for a long period in the UK, they will never qualify to settle on the grounds of their work.

People allowed to work outside the immigration rules

Academic work

After students have completed higher degrees, universities may want to continue to benefit from their research and knowledge. It may be possible for the university to obtain work permits for students to stay on as lecturers/ demonstrators and to be paid for this work, because of the very specialised knowledge and experience required. They do not need to be outside the UK while the application is made, and it is possible for an overseas student's status to be changed in this way.

Visiting academics may also be allowed to work in the UK but without needing work permits. These would normally be people employed and paid by a foreign university, coming to do academic work or research for an academic year and allowed to do this exceptionally, outside the immigration rules.

Domestic workers

There is no provision in the immigration rules for domestic workers to come to the UK, other than those working for diplomatic families. Work permits for this type of work have not been issued since 1980. However it is well known that servants come into the UK with their employers. This is completely outside the immigration rules, and is a concession to rich or expatriate families who want to continue to employ servants who have worked for them overseas. The Home Office formalised this concession from May 1991 and has produced an information leaflet for domestic workers, copies of which should be given to workers and employers when the worker is granted entry clearance.

Under the terms of the concession:

- the worker must be at least 17 years old
- if the employer is visiting the UK, the worker must have been employed by that employer for at least 12 months
- if the employer is coming to the UK for any other purpose, the worker must have been employed by that employer for at least 24 months
- the worker must have entry clearance before travelling to the UK. The British embassy or high commission should check the type and hours of work involved, and that the worker wants to come to the UK. The British post must interview the worker, at least on the first application for entry clearance, to ensure that she or he understands the position.
- both worker and employer must be given a brief leaflet explaining the position; the leaflet stresses that the permission granted is a concession and that the worker will not be permitted to change employment in the UK.

When these workers arrive in the UK, the immigration officers usually give them leave to enter in line with their employers. If the employers are visitors, the domestic worker's passport will also be stamped as a visitor, with employment prohibited, even though it is fully realised that she or he is coming to work. When the family is coming to live in the UK, the worker's passport is usually stamped with leave to remain on condition that the holder does not take any employment paid or unpaid except with the named employer. If the employer is a British citizen or settled in the UK, the worker will normally be given leave to enter for a year.

Because this concession is completely outside the immigration rules, these workers have no rights. They have no right to change their employment and applications to do so will be refused, so the workers are completely dependent on their employers' goodwill. If they lose their jobs, or have to leave because of unbearable treatment and exploitation, they have no claim to remain in the UK and are in a very vulnerable position.

The Home Office information leaflet states that if a domestic worker applies for settlement after four years' work for the named employer the application may be granted, but this is completely outside the immigration rules. Some campaigns for exploited workers have been successful.

Exemption from control

Diplomatic work

Diplomats and others working at embassies or high commissions in the UK do not need work permits, because under international law they are considered to be employed in the country of the embassy. Their admission to the UK is therefore mainly the responsibility of the Foreign and Commonwealth Office, which is given lists by the countries concerned of their diplomatic staff. They require entry clearance explaining their status, but this will be granted on proof of their employment. The entry clearance states that they are 'exempt' from immigration control and therefore their passports are not stamped, or may be stamped only with the date, when they travel into the UK. They are free to remain for as long as they are employed by the embassy or high commission. Time spent exempt from immigration control does not qualify a person for settlement.

When a person who is exempt from control leaves the job at the high commission or embassy, for whatever reason, the exemption continues until the Home Office specifically cancels it. When the Home Office is informed that the job has ended, it will remove the exemption, and write to the person concerned to state this and to grant leave to remain for a period of 28 days, in order that the person may either make arrangements to leave the UK or make a new application for permission to remain longer. There is a right of appeal against removal of exemption, but the appeal cannot succeed unless the person is still employed in an exempt category. If the person wishes to remain longer in the UK, it is important to make a fresh application to the Home Office within the 28 days' leave granted, so that there will be a right of appeal against any refusal.

It is not possible for people who are in the UK in another capacity to change status in order to work at an embassy or high commission. They need to leave the UK to apply for entry clearance. Occasionally if the person has been in the UK in breach of immigration control, he or she will be refused permission to return for this type of employment as the immigration authorities cannot then control how long the person remains.

Training and work experience

The Employment Department can approve schemes to give people, mainly from developing countries, the chance to have some training and work experience in the UK. The employers need to obtain permits from the Employment Department, showing that they are offering a genuine training programme to the applicant which would not be available in the country of origin which will be of use to the person when he or she returns. It may be possible for students who have qualified in the UK to be granted training permits to obtain six months' or a year's work experience in the subject they have been studying academically, before leaving the UK. It is important that both the employer and the trainee understand and sign a declaration on the application form that the employment is temporary and that the person will be leaving the UK at the end of the training period.

Some students can qualify in their subjects only with work experience. This is a common way of qualifying in the accountancy profession, where most students do articles with an accountancy firm while they are taking a series of examinations. This work is essential to their studies and will cease after they have become qualified, or have had a limited and definite amount of post-qualification experience. The Employment Department needs to be satisfied that the firm is providing adequate training and that the person is progressing.

Trainees have to keep the Employment Department informed of their progress towards qualification. People may be given training permits for the expected period their exams will take, or the permit may be extended on a yearly basis while they are qualifying. The permit will usually be extended if they are unsuccessful in an examination, to give them three chances to pass each examination in the stages towards qualification. If they have been unsuccessful three times at the same examination, the Employment Department will usually refuse a further extension of the permit.

It is the trainee's responsibility to ensure that the employers apply to the Employment Department for extensions of their permit and stay within the time given, so that they do not become overstayers. Home Office decisions about granting further leave to remain depend on Employment Department decisions about permits. The Home Office refuses the student permission to stay if an extension of the permit has been refused. There will be a formal right of appeal, as long as the application was made in time. During the appeal period, students can continue training, so it may be possible for them to make a fourth attempt during any appeal period and, if successful, to reinstate their trainee position.

Student nurses

Student nurses are treated as students, not trainees, throughout their training period. They deal only with the Home Office to extend their permitted stay, even though it is clear that they are working while they are training and are being paid. The hospitals do not have to apply for permits for their student nurses. Student nurses are the only people for whom the rules make provision to work in the UK after their studies are completed. When they are qualified nurses, if the hospital wishes to employ them as such, it must obtain work permits for them, and the other criteria of the work permit scheme must be met. The hospital may apply while the nurse remains in the UK and continues to work at the hospital. He or she does not have to leave the UK while the work permit application is pending.

Other ways of being able to work in the UK

British-born grandparents

Commonwealth citizens with a British-born grandparent can come to the UK to work or to seek work. They need to prove their legitimate descent from the person born in the UK, by having the grandparent's birth certificate, the grandparents' marriage certificate, the birth certificate of the father or mother descended from them, the parents' marriage certificate and the applicant's birth certificate. People coming to the UK for this purpose need entry clearance; people already in the country, for example as visitors, may be permitted to change their status. People will be allowed to enter or remain for four years, without any restrictions on employment. At the end of the four years, whether they have been working all the time or not, they may apply for settlement.

Working holidaymakers

Commonwealth citizens, aged between 17 and 27, may be allowed to come to the UK for up to two years on a working holiday. They have to show that any work they will take will be incidental to their holiday, and that they have the money to support themselves without recourse to public funds and to pay their return fare. In practice, this provision is mainly restricted to white Commonwealth citizens; in 1989, 9349 Australians and 1886 Canadians came but only three Indians applied; two were refused and one withdrew his application.

Au pairs

Young women (not men) between the ages of 17 and 27 who are unmarried, who have no dependants and who are citizens of any EC member state, Andorra, Austria, Cyprus, Czechoslovakia, the Faeroes, Finland, Greenland, Hungary, Iceland, Liechtenstein, Malta, Monaco, Norway, San Marino, Sweden, Switzerland, Turkey or Yugoslavia may come as au pairs for up to two years. An au pair is supposed to be living as a member of an English-speaking family, and doing light housework and childcare in return for pocket money and time off in order to attend English language classes. It is not possible to remain as an au pair for more than two years. There are no provisions for young men to be au pairs.

Unauthorised workers

People who are restricted or prohibited from working under the immigration conditions of their stay do sometimes work. If they do so while their leave to remain is still current, they are committing an offence under section 24(1)(b)(ii) of the Immigration Act 1971. They can be charged to appear in a magistrates' court or the Home Office can make a decision to deport them, on the grounds of a breach of their conditions of stay (▶see chapter 14 for more details of these processes). They are therefore in a dangerous position and are liable to pressure and blackmail from employers. Unauthorised workers may be working in very bad conditions or for very low pay, but dare not take action to force improvements because they are vulnerable to the employers informing the Home Office of their work or sacking them summarily. Although unauthorised workers have the same legal rights to contest unfair dismissal etc. they are unlikely to do so as this will draw attention to their presence in the UK.

People may also be working illegally without being aware of this. Students often believe, erroneously, that they are free to work during their holidays, or that the fact that they have been able to obtain national insurance numbers gives them permission to work. This is not the case. Some students are completely prohibited from working and need to apply to the Home Office for this prohibition to be removed before they can work. Other students' passports state that they can only work with the consent of the Employment Department. This means that the employer needs to obtain permission from the local Jobcentre to employ the student before the student is legally free to work (▶see chapter 9 for full details).

Overstayers who are working are not working illegally because any restrictions on working placed on their stay came to an end when the leave to remain finished. If they are caught, they can be prosecuted or deported because of their overstaying, but not because of working in breach of conditions.

Business people, the self-employed and persons of independent means

Business people

The immigration rules are designed to ensure that only wealthy business people will be permitted to come to set up or to join businesses. Entry clearance is necessary. People have to show:

- they have at least £200,000 capital of their own to put into the business. This has to be capital which is readily available, either in the UK already or easily transferable to the UK, which can be put into the business. The immigration authorities are entitled to ask about its provenance, so borrowing money from a rich friend will not be adequate. The business should need this amount of new financial investment.

- they will be involved full-time in running the business, will be able to meet their share of any liabilities and there is a genuine need for their time and investment. This means that they should not have other time-consuming activities outside the UK and they will not be allowed to do other work in this country or abroad. This is intended to ensure that people coming to do business are actually required for the business and that this part of the rules is not being used as a way for rich people who do not otherwise qualify to come to join their relatives.

- they have to show that new, full-time employment will be created for at least two people already living in the UK as a result of the admission of the business person from abroad

- if they are planning to set up a new business, they have to show that they have enough money left over after the investment of the £200,000 to support themselves and their family, without doing any other work, until the business can reasonably expect to make a profit

- if they are joining an existing business, they need to show its audited accounts for previous years and a written explanation of the terms on which the new partner will be joining. They need to show that the share of the profits they will receive is likely to be adequate to support them and any dependants.

Business people are normally granted leave to enter for a year initially and can apply to the Home Office to extend this near the end of the year. If there is evidence that the business is continuing, the money has been invested and the new employment has been created, an extension of three years should be granted. The spouse and children under 18 of the business person may be granted entry clearance to accompany or to come to join him or her and will be granted an extension of stay in line with the business person. After four years, they can all apply to settle, and this will be granted provided the business is still continuing and is making enough profit to support them.

Self-employed people

People intending to establish themselves as self-employed also need to make an investment of at least £200,000. They have to explain exactly what they are planning to do with the money and how these activities will support themselves and their family without doing any other work. They also have to create employment for at least two people and show they will be devoting a substantial amount of time to the business. This category includes people wanting to set up as professionals, for example, architects, accountants or doctors in private practice. There is however a special concession for overseas lawyers setting up as consultants in the law of another country, who do not need to have £200,000 capital.

The spouse and children under 18 of self-employed people may be granted entry clearance to accompany or to come to join them. They will be granted extensions of stay in line with the self-employed person and can apply to settle near the end of four years. This will be granted provided the self-employment is still continuing and is making enough money to support the family.

Writers and artists

There is a specific provision in the rules for self-employed writers and artists. They do not need to have £200,000 but have to show that they will be able to make enough money to support themselves and any dependants without recourse to public funds, from the proceeds of their art or writing. They are not able to take any other employment in the UK but if they also have savings or private means they may use them to support themselves as well as their art or writing. Writers may include freelance journalists; artists may include art photographers but not performing artists, who need to obtain work permits. Writers and artists will be allowed in for four years; the spouse and children under 18 will be granted extensions of stay in line with the writer or artist and they can all apply to settle near the end of the four year period.

Persons of independent means

£200,000 capital is required, or a guaranteed income of at least £20,000 a year. People must apply for entry clearance and show that they have the requisite amount of money and that they plan to live on it, without doing any work or business, and that this will produce enough money to support themselves and their dependants. They also have to show that they have a 'close connection' with the UK and that their presence is in the general interests of the UK. 'Close connection' has been interpreted as having close relatives either settled or living in the UK for some time, for example as students, or the applicant having spent a substantial period of time in the UK in the past. There is an unwritten practice that people who have £500,000 to bring with them will be allowed to come whether or not they have any previous connections with Britain.

The spouses and children under 18 of persons of independent means can be given entry clearance to accompany or to come to join them. They will all normally be given permission to stay for four years on arrival and can apply to settle near the end of that time. This will be granted as long as the money and capital is still available and they have not needed to have recourse to public funds.

8 Visitors

Visitors who are visa nationals (see glossary) have to obtain entry clearance from a British high commission or embassy before travelling. Visitors who are not visa nationals do not need to obtain entry clearance but may do so if they wish or may apply for permission at a British port or airport. They have to satisfy the same requirements of the immigration rules whether they are applying in the UK or abroad.

▶See chapter 11 on the advantages and disadvantages of applying for optional entry clearance and for the procedure of applying for entry clearance. All statistics show that there is a higher refusal rate for people applying at British posts abroad than there is for people applying to immigration officers at a port of entry, although the formal requirements of the immigration rules are the same. In Jamaica in 1989, for example, the refusal rate of entry clearance applications was 1 in 7, while the refusal rate at the airports was 1 in 40.

WHAT THE RULES SAY

The immigration rules on visitors state:

'A passenger seeking entry as a visitor, including one coming to stay with relatives or friends, is to be admitted:

- if he satisfies the immigration officer that he is genuinely seeking entry for the period of the visit as stated by him

- and that for that period he will maintain and accommodate himself and any dependants, or will, with any dependants, be maintained and accommodated adequately by relatives or friends, without working or recourse to public funds, and can meet the cost of the return or onward journey

- Leave to enter is to be refused if the immigration officer is not so satisfied, and in particular, leave to enter is to be refused where there is reason to believe that the passenger's real purpose is to take employment or that he may become a charge on public funds if admitted

- A passenger admitted to the UK as a visitor, and any dependants accompanying him, should be given leave to enter for a period of six months unless the immigration officer is satisfied that there are particular circumstances which justify the giving of a shorter period of leave. Visitors should normally be prohibited from taking employment.'

WHAT THE RULES MEAN

People may wish to come to visit the UK for many different reasons – to see relatives or friends, purely on holiday, to make or renew business contacts, to help in a family crisis or emergency. The immigration rules are the same for visitors, whatever the purpose of the visit, but the way they are interpreted for people from different countries and economic backgrounds is very different.

The intention test

• that they are 'genuinely' seeking entry for the length of time they ask for

This is the most difficult part of the rule to satisfy, because it is a subjective test of a person's intention which cannot be proved either way. Immigration officials will go into details about the person's life and background to see if they believe the person's story. They may ask a lot of questions: why will you need to go back after only two weeks? who will look after your children/farm/business while you are away? surely you can't afford to spend this amount of money on so short a time; aren't you planning to stay longer? if you found a place to study in the UK, would you do so? They will often search luggage and read any correspondence, including letters carried by the passenger to give to other people in the UK, making inferences from what is said, or not said.

If there are definite reasons why visitors have to return, they should try to have evidence of this. For example, a person in employment could have a letter from his or her employer, confirming the length of holiday and when the person is expected back at work. A student could have a letter from the college, confirming when the next term will begin. For someone without such a structured life, it can be more difficult and immigration officers openly admit to using something they call 'nose' – their alleged sixth sense telling them when someone is not genuine. They are also encouraged to think 'would I do that?' in connection with information they are told, but they may not appreciate the differences in cultures which place greater importance on particular events. Because it is up to the visitor to prove intentions, not up to the immigration officer to disprove them, it is very easy for officers to refuse without any objective proof.

Certain groups of people are more likely to be refused because officials are not satisfied about their intentions. They are: people from poorer countries; people who are relatively poor by the standards of the country from which they come; people with many relatives in the UK, particularly if the visitors are young and single, or elderly; people who are unemployed or who have just finished their studies. A list is circulated to immigration officials every month of the 'top five nationalities' refused entry in that month; once a country appears on that list, its nationals, especially those in the above categories, will be subject to close examination.

The support and accommodation test

- that during that time they will be able to maintain and accommodate themselves, or be maintained and accommodated by relatives or friends, without working and without using public funds

This means that officers are able to inquire into the money that visitors are bringing with them and the money that their friends and relatives may have to support them. When people apply for entry clearance abroad, entry clearance officers usually require evidence of financial support. If visitors are bringing their own money, evidence such as their bank statements or a letter from their employers confirming their salary will be required. If they are being supported by friends or relatives in the UK, a letter of invitation from the person confirming willingness to support the visitor is necessary, together with the sponsor's bank statement or other evidence of resources.

Immigration officers may decide that a person has either too little money, and therefore may want to work or to try to claim benefits here, or too much money and may therefore be planning to stay for a longer period than that stated. This is a very subjective calculation; what might be considered too much money for a Guyanese citizen, for example, could be thought perfectly adequate for a North American. Immigration officers may also make suggestions – would you work if you could find a job? – and use the answer, if affirmative, as a reason for refusal.

When visitors come without entry clearance, it may be useful for the sponsor to come to the airport to meet them, with evidence of the financial support available. If the sponsor does not go to the airport it is useful if the visitor has a telephone number for the sponsor, so that the immigration officers can make contact without delay.

Meeting the cost of the return journey

This usually means that the visitor should have a return or onward ticket, or the means to purchase one. However, officials will not automatically assume that the possession of a return ticket means that a person is a genuine visitor who plans to return: they may say that the return half of the ticket can be traded in if a person decides not to leave.

Length of time for visits

Since February 1988, the immigration rules have stated that in most cases visitors should be admitted for six months automatically, even when they intend to stay only for a few days. However, if a visitor *asks* for six months, this may well be interpreted as indicating a wish to stay longer than a 'normal' visit; the support and accommodation requirements will also be much more difficult to fulfil. Immigration officers can give less than six months, but only if they believe that there is a good reason for it, for example a particular short course of medical treatment.

Working holidaymakers

The immigration rules provide for 'young Commonwealth citizens between the ages of 17 and 27' to come to the UK for 'working holidays' of up to two years. They have to satisfy immigration officials that they are intending to be in the UK on holiday, that they are able to support themselves if they do not find work and that they can pay for their trip home. They have to show that any work they take is 'incidental to their holiday' and is not the main purpose of coming to the UK and that they do not intend to settle into long-term work. This provision is mainly intended for young people from Australia and New Zealand and Canada 'doing Europe'; it is unusual for people from other countries to be allowed in for this purpose.

Arrival in the UK

Leave to enter

People who are admitted as visitors will have their passports stamped with the immigration officer's square date stamp, showing the date and the port at which they entered, and 'leave to enter for six months, employment prohibited' (▶see chapter 13 for examples of passport stamps). *It is the passport stamp given at the airport that shows how long people can stay in the UK*, not the entry clearance from a British post overseas. The time begins to run from the date on which this stamp was given. Visitors should keep a note of this date separate from the passport so that even if the passport is lost they will know how long they can stay and when they need to apply for an extension of stay if that is necessary.

Work and business

Visitors are not permitted to work in the UK. This includes voluntary and unpaid work and other activities which would not normally be considered work. The Immigration Appeal Tribunal has decided that people coming intending to spend their visit looking after a relative's children cannot be treated as visitors but would be working as childminders (a job for which work permits are not available).

Visitors are able to 'transact business' in the UK. People who are in business abroad but who want to make or consolidate contacts in the UK, to investigate new markets or to learn new business techniques may do this while they are visitors. They may not set up in business in the UK, or set up a branch office and train staff for a business based abroad, as they would then have to obtain entry clearance as business people (▶see chapter 7). Business visits are only expected to last for a few days or weeks, though the people will be admitted for six months like other visitors.

Refusal of entry

Visitors who already have entry clearance will probably not be asked many questions by immigration officers as they have already been questioned in detail abroad. They can be refused at the airport if the immigration officer has reason to believe either that they lied, or deliberately concealed relevant information, in order to get entry clearance or that there has been a change in circumstances since entry clearance was granted, which means that the person no longer qualifies for it. If they are refused, they have the right to appeal against the refusal and to remain in the UK while the appeal is pending.

Visitors who do not have entry clearance may be refused entry if they do not satisfy immigration officers that they qualify under the immigration rules for entry. If they are refused entry, they can be sent straight back without any right of appeal until after they have left. Representations can be made to the immigration officers as to why they have made the wrong decision (▶see chapter 12 for further information).

Applying for extensions

WHAT THE RULES SAY

There is now *no* provision in the immigration rules for extending a visit beyond six months, except for medical visitors and working holidaymakers.

Visitors who have been admitted for less than six months initially may apply for visit extensions, up to the six month limit. If they do this, they must show a good reason for their change of plans. The application can be granted if the total time for the visit will not be more than six months and the other requirements of the rules – about maintenance and accommodation, and about the visitor's intention to leave at the end of the visit – are still satisfied.

Any applications to remain as a visitor beyond the six-month limit are outside the immigration rules, and therefore are dealt with at the discretion of the Minister. The Home Office has stated that such applications will only be granted in exceptional circumstances.

This does not prevent people from applying. Provided that an application is made before the existing leave runs out, the visitor will be legally in the UK until a decision is made and will also have a right of appeal if permission is refused. This means that the visitor will be able to remain legally in the UK for a considerable period of time, whatever decision the Home Office eventually makes.

However, these applications are almost certain to be refused and appeals are bound to fail. People's passports will be marked to show that they have been refused an extension. This may make it difficult to return to the UK, or to travel to other countries, in future. Even if the visitors leave the UK before the Home Office replies, they will be on record as having asked for something outside the rules. The Home Office assumes that everyone knows what the rules are and that applicants for extensions deliberately asked for something which is not allowed. Officials may not be satisfied that the visitors intend to leave the UK at the end of the next visit because they did not do so the previous time.

Visitors should therefore be advised about the possible long-term consequences of applying for extensions. It is important only to apply to extend a visit if it is really necessary, to set out the reasons for staying and the length of time required, and as far as possible to show that the visitors have done what they said they would do and left when they said they would.

A change in the immigration rules from 21 October 1991 states that visitors who have been admitted for six months 'will not be permitted' to extend their visit beyond that period. It is not clear at the time of writing whether this wording will mean that the Home Office will no longer consider applications made exceptionally, or whether it will mean that any appeals against almost-inevitable refusals of extensions beyond that time will not be considered fully.

How to apply for an extension

▶See chapter 11 about applying for extensions. It is important to be as clear as possible about the reasons for staying longer and the length of time required. There are no formal application forms; a simple letter will do, stating something like: 'I want to remain in the UK for another two months as a visitor before I have to return to college in my country' or 'I want to remain as a visitor for another three months in order to look after my sister whose baby is expected next week'. If there is any evidence to support either the reasons for the application or the necessity to leave the UK at the end of the further time, this should be sent to the Home Office. This might be confirmation of the reason why the person has to leave or a doctor's letter about any medical reasons for the visitor to remain longer. It is usual to send the passport to the Home Office with the application. People may request the return of their passports at any time; but ▶see page 161 about the possible dangers of doing so.

People who have come to the UK as visitors for medical treatment may be granted extensions to continue their treatment. They will need to have confirmation from the doctor treating them that the treatment is still necessary and continuing, and proof that they still have the means to pay for the treatment privately, as well as for their general maintenance and accommodation. They will not normally be granted extensions if the treatment is under the National Health Service.

If the application is refused, as long as it was made in time, before the previous permission to stay ran out, the person will have the right to appeal against the refusal, and to remain in the UK while the appeal is pending. ▶See chapter 16 for more information about appealing against refusals.

Visitors changing their status

The immigration rules provide for some changes of status for people who have come to visit the UK and prohibit others. The rules allow visitors:

- to apply to stay and settle with some close relatives; for example, parents coming to visit their children settled in the UK may apply to stay and settle with them (▶see chapter 4)
- to marry and to apply to stay with their spouses (▶see chapter 2)
- to apply to stay as working holidaymakers (▶see above)
- to apply for asylum (▶see chapter 5)
- **if they are not visa nationals**, to apply to stay as students (▶see chapter 9)

They should make applications to the Home Office before the time limit in their passport runs out, asking for a change of status and showing how they fit into the relevant parts of the immigration rules concerning their new status. It is important to explain why their plans have changed since they came in for the visit and what has made them decide to remain for a different purpose.

The rules do not allow visitors:

- to stay in order to work or to be self-employed
- to stay in order to set up a business
- if they are visa nationals to stay as students

This does not mean that they cannot apply for such changes, but that any application is likely to be refused. The Home Office would need to be satisfied that there were very exceptional reasons for considering them. People should be referred for specialist advice about the consequences of such applications.

Travel outside the UK

Frequent visits

There are no restrictions in the immigration rules on how frequently people can visit the UK. However, each time people return, they have to convince the immigration officers again that they fit into the immigration rules. Even if people just go on a day-trip to France, they need to prove all over again that they qualify to re-enter and they can be refused entry if the officer at Dover is not satisfied. It can be sensible to take proof similar to that which was used on the original entry.

Immigration officers can also consider information about past visits. This is particularly likely when people stay almost for the six-month visit limit and then return after a very short absence. For example, a person who has just spent five and a half months in the UK and has been away for three days may have difficulty in showing that he or she is a genuine visitor on return. The immigration officer may suspect that the person is attempting to get round the six-month visit period and may have other reasons for seeking to remain in the UK. This may be particularly difficult for people with close family members living in the UK.

Visa nationals

Most visa nationals need visas for every entry to the UK (▶see glossary for list of visa nationals). Visa national visitors may have obtained either single-entry or multiple-entry visas from the British post which gave permission initially. A single-entry visa can only be used once. A multiple-entry visa is valid for any number of visit entries within the time for which it is given, usually six months, two years or five years. People who are considering travelling and returning to the UK should apply for multiple-entry visas initially: for example, if they are planning to go to other European countries as well as the UK, or want to go on haj with relatives living in this country and visit them before and afterwards. Visitors who are visa nationals and who do not obtain multiple-entry visas have to apply to the British post in the country they visit for a new visa if they want to return to the UK. It is no longer possible for people to obtain re-entry visas in the UK. The previous practice of granting re-entry visas to visitors at the Home Office or Passport Office in the UK was discontinued in May 1991.

9 Students

Students who are visa nationals (see glossary) have to obtain entry clearance from a British high commission or embassy before travelling. Students who are not visa nationals do not need to obtain entry clearance but may do so if they wish or may apply for permission at a British port or airport. They have to satisfy the same requirements of the immigration rules whether they are applying in the UK or abroad.

▶See chapter 11 on the advantages and disadvantages of applying for optional entry clearance and for the procedure of applying for entry clearance.

WHAT THE RULES SAY

The immigration rules on people coming to the UK as students state that a student must show:

- 'that he has been accepted for a course of study at a university, a polytechnic or further education establishment, an independent school or any bona fide private education institution
- that the course will occupy the whole or a substantial part of his time
- that he can, without working and without recourse to public funds, meet the cost of the course and his own maintenance and accommodation and that of any dependants during the course

An applicant is to be refused if . . . the officer is not satisfied that the applicant is able, and intends, to follow a full-time course of study and to leave the country on completion of it.'

People who have genuine and realistic intentions of studying in the UK but who have not yet been accepted for a full-time course may be admitted as prospective students.

Visa nationals who did not enter the UK with a visa as a student or a prospective student will be refused permission to change their status in the UK to become students.

WHAT THE RULES MEAN

Educational institutions

All government-run institutions are assumed to be bona fide, as are private fee-paying schools for children. The Home Office does not have a formal procedure for the recognition of other private educational institutions, but is believed to have its own list of institutions which it suspects are not providing education or are carrying on fraudulent practices. In 1988 there were well-publicised raids aimed at two establishments, the London School of International Business and various institutions at Wickham House, London E2. Some students from the colleges were arrested and others were refused extensions of stay. Some students at the Academic College of Education have been refused on the grounds that the college they were attending was not adequate. However refusals of entry on the grounds that colleges are allegedly bogus are rare.

Full-time studies

Students will normally need a letter from the college at which they intend to study, confirming that they have been accepted on a particular full-time course. Depending on the college and the level of studies, the immigration authorities may also ask for details of the precise number of hours per week the student will be studying. They expect that the letter will also state whether the fees, or a deposit towards them, have been paid.

'Full-time' for immigration purposes normally means at least 15 hours organised daytime classes per week. This can occasionally be two or more part-time daytime courses which together make up 15 hours, if the student can show that this is the only or the most convenient way to do a course. If two part-time courses are taken, they should be related and should both contribute towards a common academic goal. If the course is of first degree level or higher, it is assumed that the 15-hours requirement is met, even though there may not be formal classes for this number of hours.

Financial support

Students must show that they have the money to pay their fees and to live in the UK without needing to work and without recourse to public funds (▶see box on page 124 for definition). Overseas students now have to pay full-cost fees for their courses, which are usually several thousand pounds. Although they may be allowed to work part-time (▶see page 115 for details), any earnings from any job they may obtain will not be taken into consideration by the Home Office in assessing their financial viability. If a student's wife has been permitted to stay in the UK with him and to work, her earnings may be taken into consideration.

Students may provide evidence of their financial support in several different ways. If they are supported by a government or other scholarship, a letter from the scholarship-giving agency will probably be sufficient, confirming the amount of the money and the arrangements made about fees. If students are being privately supported, a letter from the sponsor confirming willingness and ability to support them and evidence to prove this, such as recent bank statements or pay slips to show that money is available, will be necessary. When it is a friend supporting the student, or anyone else who has no immediately obvious interest in doing so, the immigration authorities may ask more questions about their and the student's motives.

Ability to follow the course

Immigration officials also have to be satisfied that the student is academically able to follow the course – though they have no qualifications with which to make this assessment and may go just on their views of the student's proficiency in English when answering their own questions. The Immigration Appeal Tribunal decided in the case of *Pattuwearachchi* (1991 Imm AR 341) that it is valid for a student coming to do a vocational course to decide at entry to follow an English language course first, and this change did not invalidate the entry clearance granted.

Intention to leave the UK

Students have to show that they intend to leave the UK at the end of their course of studies.

It is of course impossible to prove at the outset of a course what a person will do at the end of it and immigration officers therefore make subjective decisions. Because official scholarship or sponsoring agencies often stipulate that a student must return, this part of the rules is rarely a problem for officially-sponsored students. However, privately-sponsored students may encounter difficulties. The immigration authorities may ask what benefit the course will be to a person after returning home and about the student's future career plans. It may be helpful to have evidence of job advertisements from the country of origin which specify the qualification the student hopes to obtain, or even a job offer for return. It is certainly important to relate the qualifications to be obtained to employment prospects in the home country. Other evidence of commitments in the country of origin, for example having a spouse and children there, could also be helpful.

If students wish to continue to follow higher-level courses after the one for which they are seeking entry, they should explain this. The immigration authorities can decide whether these plans appear to them to be realistic either academically or financially. If a student has many other relatives who have become settled in the UK, particularly if they entered as students in the past, immigration officers may be particularly suspicious about their longer-term intentions.

Students who have not yet been accepted on a course

People hoping to study in the UK may not have made definite arrangements to do so before travelling. They may be travelling to the UK to look for a suitable course, or to come for interview at a particular institution. In these circumstances it is important that they explain their intentions to study to the immigration official and seek entry to the UK as a 'prospective student'. They then have to satisfy the immigration officials that they have the money to support themselves for the period while they are arranging their studies and that if they are not successful in obtaining a place they will leave the UK by the end of the period of stay granted.

Students or those seeking advice on their behalf may feel that, as they have no specific study plans, they should seek entry as visitors. This is not advisable. It is important that students make their intentions clear on arrival. The dangers of entering as visitors and seeking to change status once studies have been sorted out are twofold:

- people could be treated as illegal entrants (▶see chapter 14) because they did not reveal their true intentions, or the period for which they wished to remain, on arrival

- visa nationals cannot change their status while in the UK to become students

Since June 1989, the immigration rules have made it impossible for a *visa national* who enters the UK in some other capacity, for example as a visitor, to change to become a student while in the UK. It is necessary for such people who want to study in the UK to leave the country and then return after obtaining another visa abroad for the purpose of studies. People who hope to study but who have not yet obtained a place at a college to do so may obtain visas as 'prospective students' for this purpose and then apply to extend their stay in the UK if accepted. The provisions for gaining a prospective student entry clearance are similar to those for students except that they have to show they have 'genuine and realistic intentions' of studying rather than a definite place at a college. Students from countries which have strict foreign exchange control regulations, for example Nigeria, may have problems in showing their financial support to undertake a course before they have been accepted on it.

Arrival in the UK

Leave to enter

Students will normally be allowed in for a year at a time, or for the duration of their course, whichever is shorter. Higher-level degree students may be admitted for the full three years of their course. The length of time and conditions will be stamped on their passports (▶see chapter 13 for examples of passport stamps).

Students will either be given a *prohibition* on working or a *restriction* on working. A student admitted for a short time or who has a scholarship may be prohibited from working. Most students will be given a restriction on working, meaning that they can only work if they obtain permission from the Employment Department first (▶see pages 115–116 for details).

Students who are not Commonwealth or EC citizens and who are admitted for more than six months may also be required to register with the police. This means going to the local police station, or, in the London Metropolitan Police area, to the Aliens Registration Office, Lambs Conduit Street, London WC1, within seven days, to give the police details of name, address, marital status and occupation, and to pay a fee (▶see appendix) for obtaining a small green police registration certificate. Students do not need to continue to report on a regular basis but any changes in the information recorded on the certificate are supposed also to be reported to the police.

Refusal of entry

Students who obtained entry clearance in advance of travelling have the right to appeal against any refusal of leave to enter and to remain in the UK while the appeal is pending. Students who are not visa nationals do not need to obtain entry clearance before travelling. However, if they are unable to satisfy an immigration officer at a port of entry that they qualify to enter, they may be refused entry and can be sent straight back. Representations may be made to the immigration officers as to why they have made the wrong decision (▶see chapter 12 for more details).

Unless there is some very important new evidence or exceptional and compelling compassionate reasons, it is very unusual for immigration officers to change their minds once a decision to refuse has been made. If they are not satisfied that a student is able to follow the course that he or she intends to do, further evidence from the academic institution may be helpful to show that the student does meet its admission criteria. If the reason for the refusal is related to the intention to leave at the end of studies, it is very difficult to alter the decision.

Families of students

Male overseas students in the UK may be accompanied or joined by their wives and children under 18, provided that there is adequate support and accommodation available to them without recourse to public funds (▶see chapter 10 for definition). The status of the family is dependent on that of the student; they will be given the same time limit on their stay as the student himself. Wives of students will be prohibited from working if their husbands are, but will have no restrictions at all on working if their husband has a restriction rather than a prohibition. This means that they are free to work in any job, without the employers needing to obtain a work permit.

However, work in this way does not give the wife any independent claim to remain in the UK in her own right. She is still expected to leave with her husband.

The families of students are entitled to state education, child benefit, National Health Service medical treatment and any other benefit for which they meet the qualifying conditions.

Female overseas students have no claim under the immigration rules to have their husbands in the UK with them. Any application for a husband to come is discretionary and will only be granted in exceptional circumstances. Some scholarship agencies, for example the Association of Commonwealth Universities, make specific provisions in their grants for the spouse of a student; when this is the case the husband will normally be allowed to come with his wife. In other instances it will depend on the particular factors in the couple's situation, for example whether they can show that the husband can be supported financially, or that the husband needs to come to look after the children while the wife is studying. Husbands will not be allowed to work in the UK unless they can obtain work permits in their own right. If the husband is not in the UK, female students can only have their children with them if the children fit into the immigration rules for children joining lone parents (▶see page 37 for more details).

Applying for extensions

WHAT THE RULES SAY

The rules state:

'A student or prospective student . . . may be granted an extension for an appropriate period if:

- he produces evidence, which is verified on a check being made, that he is enrolled for a full-time course of daytime study which meets the requirements for admission as a student

- that he has given and is giving regular attendance during the course or has in the past given regular attendance during any other course for which he has been enrolled

- and that he is able to maintain and accommodate himself and any dependants without working and without recourse to public funds.

An extension should be refused if there is reason to believe that the student does not intend to leave at the end of his studies or if the Home Office is not satisfied that the applicant is able, and intends, to follow a full-time course of study.

Extensions of stay should not be granted to students who appear to be moving from one course to another without any intention of bringing their studies to a close.

An extension of stay will be refused if it would lead to more than four years being spent on short courses...a short course is one of less than two years but includes a longer course where this is broken off before being completed'.

WHAT THE RULES MEAN

Full time studies; maintenance and accommodation

The Home Office requires evidence that students are still enrolled for a full-time course of study, that the money for maintenance and accommodation is still available and that they intend to leave the UK at the end of their studies. These can be shown in the same way as when the students first applied to enter, ▶see above.

Regular attendance

Students have to prove that they have been in regular attendance on the course they have been following. The Home Office can check their attendance records with their colleges. This may be done by a formal written questionnaire but the Home Office may also telephone colleges and make decisions based on information given over the telephone, the source of which cannot later be traced. JCWI and UKCOSA advise institutions not to respond to telephone inquiries but to ask the Home Office to put the request in writing, so that the information can be checked by a person qualified to do so and so that the college will also have records of what the Home Office has been told. If students have not attended regularly for good reasons, for example illness, it is important that this should be explained to the Home Office and evidence should be sent in, for example medical certificates for the relevant period that the students were unfit to attend classes.

Moving from one course to another

The Home Office will refuse extensions of stay if students 'appear to be moving from one course to another without any intention of bringing their studies to a close'. This provision can be used against students who change their career or study plans while in the UK. The Home Office prefers students who follow obvious study paths to an academic goal and is suspicious of those it believes may be 'perpetual students'. If students have a radical change of plans, it is important to explain the reasons for it, if possible backed by letters from course tutors or lecturers supporting the change. This rule may also be used against students who start a new course after they have already been studying for many years as the Home Office may suspect that they are hoping to bring themselves within the ambit of the 'ten-year concession' (▶see page 160) to be able to stay permanently.

Short courses

The rules state that extensions of stay should also not be granted to students who would be spending more than four years on short courses. Short courses are defined as courses of less than two years' duration, but include longer courses which were abandoned before completion. This is unnecessarily restrictive for some students whose planned courses are short or who may change their minds during courses; the Home Office has stated that it may be flexible about this in some individual cases. It is important to explain in the application the reasons for abandoning a particular course, or why the student is continuing on short courses, if possible with supporting letters from the institution(s) concerned, to show that this is part of a regular and coordinated plan of studies.

How to apply for an extension

Students who wish to remain longer in the UK than the initial time they have been given need to apply to the Home Office for permission to remain longer. It is very important to do this before the time given runs out – as long as the application is made in time, people are still legally in the country while the Home Office is considering it. If the application is refused, there is a formal right of appeal against the refusal. If the application is made late, the students are illegally in the UK even while it is under considera-tion and if it is refused, they have no right of appeal. It is therefore vital to apply in time even if not all the documents required for the application are available, as they can be sent later. All that is necessary is that a letter is sent to the Home Office, before the permission to stay expires, asking for an extension (▶see chapter 11 for more information on making applications).

Applications can be made either in writing or in person at the Home Office, or in person at one of the regional Public Enquiry Offices of the Home Office (▶see chapter 19 for addresses). There are also arrangements whereby immigration officials visit certain universities and colleges near the beginning of the autumn term, in order to deal with routine extensions. This may be most convenient for students if it is arranged at their college, but it is very important they should not allow the time to run out just because an immigration officer is going to visit a few days later.

Permission to work

When a course involves a period of employment or practical training, including work, it is the responsibility of the college either to negotiate with the local Employment Department Jobcentre a general permission for all the overseas students on the course to do this, or to make sure that the individual organisations in which the students will be working obtain per-mits. It is important that this should be done, or a student on a sandwich course may find that he or she is working illegally. Before taking up employment, students should check with the course tutor, or other person in the college responsible for permits, that this has been done.

If students want to obtain employment unrelated to their course, this may be possible. If the students' passports are stamped with a prohibition on working, they need first to apply to the Home Office for this to be varied to a restriction on working. This may be done if the Home Office is satisfied that the students do not need to work in order to be able to continue to pay for their studies.

If a student's passport is stamped with a restriction on working (▶see chapter 13 for an example of this stamp) it is possible to get permission to do a particular job, as long as a complicated procedure is followed. Students wishing to undertake either part-time or vacation work must first get permission from their local Jobcentre. They must take their passport (and police registration certificate, if they have one) to their local Jobcentre, where the staff will check to ensure that they are not prohibited from working. The Jobcentre will give the student form OSS1, which is divided into three sections. Part 1 must be completed by the student, Part 2 by the prospective employer and Part 3 by the academic institution. When the form is completed it should be returned to the Jobcentre, to consider the application for permission to work. It is unlikely that permission will be granted for more than 20 hours per week. The Jobcentre is more likely to grant the application if the job is related in some way to the student's course and if it has been advertised previously.

It is very important that students who want to work during their studies, even when it is just a short-term holiday job, are advised to follow the correct procedure. Working without obtaining permission is a breach of conditions of stay and a criminal offence. Students who are found working illegally may either be prosecuted under section 24(1)(b)(i) of the Immigration Act 1971, or the Home Office may make its own administrative decision to deport them.

The consequences of working without permission have become more severe since the passing of the Immigration Act 1988, because there is now no full right of appeal against deportation for people who last entered the UK less than seven years before the decision to deport them. In most cases, therefore, students caught working without permission can only appeal on the facts of the case (which would mean arguing that the student had not been working, or had obtained permission to do the work). In the past, students caught working in breach of conditions were rarely deported but faced problems when it came to extending their stay. Now, such students are regularly forced to leave the UK. ▶See chapter 12 for more details of what to do when people are threatened with deportation.

Fees and grants

Overseas students normally have to pay full-cost **fees** for their courses and are not normally entitled to local authority awards. Under the Education (Fees and Awards) Act and Regulations, differential fees can be charged to overseas students. In general, in order to qualify as home students, and therefore to be charged the lower level of home student fees, students must satisfy the educational institution that:

- they have been ordinarily resident (▶see glossary) in the UK for the three-year period before the course began, from 1 January, 1 April or 1 September, depending on the month the course started and

- at no time during this period were they ordinarily resident wholly or mainly for the purpose of receiving full-time education.

Thus in most cases people who have been granted leave to remain as students, even if they have been in the UK for more than three years, will not qualify for home student fees. People who have been allowed to remain in the UK for another purpose, for example as the children of a work permit holder, or who are settled, but who happen to have been studying during that time, will qualify as home students.

Some people do not have to live in the UK for three years to be treated as home students for fees purposes. They include:

- people granted refugee status and people granted exceptional leave to remain after making a claim for asylum. Once either of these statuses has been granted, the person may be treated as a home student immediately. This does not apply to asylum-seekers waiting for a decision to be made on their case, who may be required to pay full-cost fees. However, as soon as they are granted leave to remain, their status changes and they may be treated as home students, even in the middle of a course of studies.

- people who do not have the right of abode (see glossary) but who have been granted settlement in the UK. This provision was intended mainly for families of those granted special quota vouchers for settlement (▶see page 227) but also applies to people granted settlement on other grounds, for example marriage to a settled or British person. Once settlement has been granted, the student will be eligible to pay home fees for any *new* course undertaken.

- people who cannot meet the three year ordinary residence requirement only because they were temporarily absent abroad during all or part of the relevant period may also be excepted from the regulations and qualify as home students

- the spouse or child of a person who would be an excepted student

- EC nationals who have been ordinarily resident in the EC for the relevant three-year period prior to the course of studies will be eligible to pay the home fees rate.

The student **grants** regulations have similar requirements of three years' ordinary residence, not for the purpose of studies, so most students from abroad are not entitled to grants. There are similar exceptions to the three years requirement although a student granted exceptional leave to remain will not be entitled to a mandatory award on that ground alone. Similarly, a student who has recently become settled will not automatically qualify for an award, and will still need to satisfy the three years' residence requirement. EC nationals will only be eligible if they have been ordinarily resident in the UK for the relevant period. Applications should be made to the local authority in which the student is resident.

Student grants and fee reimbursements are not counted as 'public funds' for immigration purposes. If a student is receiving a grant, this will be acceptable to the Home Office as evidence of financial support.

Studies including training

Some studies normally include a large amount of practical work, for example nursing or accountancy. Such students are not treated consistently under the immigration rules. Nursing students are counted as students for immigration purposes, even though they are being paid. They do not have to show other means of financial support than their pay from the hospital. People coming for interviews at hospitals may be granted visas, or leave to enter at a port, as prospective students and may apply for extensions as students if they are offered a place. After qualification, they may be permitted to remain to work; ▶see pages 95 and 122 for further information.

The immigration rules treat most other students who are being paid as **trainees** and their employers need to obtain training work permits for them.

The immigration rules on entry state only:

- 'the holder of a current work permit, including a permit for training and work experience, should normally be admitted for the period specified in the permit, subject to a condition permitting him to take or change employment only with the permission of the Department of Employment'.

The immigration rules for applications within the UK state:

- 'a person holding a [trainee] permit . . . will have been admitted for the period specified in the permit up to a maximum of two years and subject to a condition restricting him to approved employment. When a trainee who is subject to such a condition applies for an extension of stay in order to continue or complete the training for which he was admitted, the application may be granted

- if the Department of Employment confirm that his training is continuing and that he is making satisfactory progress

- and if there is no reason to believe that the applicant does not intend to leave the UK on completion of his training.

• visitors and students may be granted extensions of stay as trainees if the Department of Employment consider the offer of training satisfactory . . . provided there is no reason to believe that the applicant does not intend to leave the UK on completion of his training; otherwise an extension should be refused'.

Being granted leave to enter or remain as a trainee therefore depends on the Employment Department approving a trainee permit. The person has to find an employer willing to employ him or her and willing to go through the procedure of applying to the Employment Department for a trainee permit. Thus, for example, accountancy students who want to study by training with a firm, rather than by studying at a college, need trainee permits. Their firms need to apply to the Employment Department, on form WP2 or OW22, to obtain trainee work permits for them, showing that they will be following a recognised training programme. The Employment Department may query the training and experience proposed, and the salary offered, before deciding to approve the training.

People coming to the UK as trainees must have obtained their permits, through their employers, before travelling. When they arrive, they may be given leave to enter for up to two years to follow the training, with a restriction on employment.

Applying for extensions

From 1 October 1991, applications for leave to remain in the UK *as a trainee* must be made direct to the Employment Department, not to the Home Office. Since the employers normally make this application, it is important for the trainee to check that it has been done in time, in order to remain legally in the UK. The Employment Department states that any passports sent in with the application will be sent on to the Home Office while it considers the trainee application. If the Employment Department approves the continued training, it will inform the Home Office, which will grant leave to remain.

Most people given trainee permits progress through a series of examinations before qualifying. The Employment Department normally gives them three chances at every examination stage, but if they fail one paper three times, it will probably not renew their trainee permission. As long as the application for extension was made in time, there will be a right of appeal against any refusal, and the trainee may remain in the UK, and continue training, during the appeal period. If there is time to take the paper again successfully, the training permit may be renewed.

People who wish to do practical training in the UK in fields with less-established paths to qualifications will have to negotiate individual programmes with their prospective employers, who will then need to apply to the Employment Department to obtain trainee permission. These are considered on a case-by-case basis.

EC students

EC citizens are not subject to British immigration law and rules but to EC law (▶see chapter 6 for more details). This means that they do not require leave to enter the UK and are free to travel between EC countries to work, to seek work, to do business or be self-employed or to provide or receive services. If they are engaged in any economic activity, they are able to obtain 'residence permits', documents which confirm their right to live in a particular EC country. At present EC citizens are not entitled to residence permits simply because they are studying in another EC country.

However, EC law provides that no obstacles should be put in the way of EC citizens travelling for the purpose of studies. They have to show that they are studying full-time, but as they are able to work freely, their earnings or potential earnings can be considered in deciding whether they can support themselves. They should be entitled to home fees in the same way as home students, provided they satisfy the ordinary residence requirements in the Education (Fees and Awards) Regulations (see above). Three years' ordinary residence in the UK may also entitle EC students to mandatory awards. However, the majority of EC students are not entitled to British mandatory awards. If the studies are being paid for by the student, it is possible to argue that the student has moved to another EC country to 'receive a service' and therefore is in the UK for an EC purpose and should be granted a residence permit, but the law on this is still not clear.

EC citizens are entitled to work in other EC countries, so an EC student also doing a part-time job in the UK is entitled to a residence permit.

An EC directive on students was agreed on 28 June 1990 (90/366/EEC), to come into force on 30 June 1992. It provides that EC students and their spouses and children will qualify for residence permits for the period of the student's studies in the UK, provided that the student and his or her family:

- 'has sufficient resources to avoid becoming a burden on the social assistance system of the host Member State during their period of residence
- the student is enrolled in a recognised educational establishment for the principal purpose of following a vocational training course there and
- that they are covered by sickness insurance in respect of all risks in the host Member State.'

This means that EC students will be able to have their husbands or wives with them while they are studying and the spouse will be free to work.

Becoming a student when already in the UK

People who are not visa nationals and who have entered the UK for any purpose, for example as visitors, can apply to the Home Office to change their status to become students. If people apply to become students shortly after gaining entry in some other way, the Home Office may wish to ascertain that there has been a genuine change of mind to become a student, and that this decision took place after they entered. If at the time of their entry people had already considered studying, or had definite plans to do so, the Home Office could treat them as illegal entrants, on the grounds that they had deceived the immigration officers when they arrived in the UK. ▶See chapter 14 for more details about illegal entry and its dangers.

Visa nationals (▶see glossary for list) who entered for any purpose other than studies will normally be refused permission to change their status to become students. They may have to leave the UK and apply at a British embassy or high commission abroad for a student visa.

Students changing their status

The immigration rules provide for some people who have been students in the UK to change their status and prohibit others from doing so. The rules allow students:

- to apply to stay and settle with some close relatives; for example, children studying in the UK whose parents later gain settlement may apply to stay and settle with them (▶see page 41 for details)
- to marry and apply to stay with their spouse (▶see chapter 2 on spouses and fiancé(e)s for more information)
- to apply to stay as working holidaymakers (▶see page 103 for details)
- to apply for asylum (▶see chapter 5)

They should make applications to the Home Office before the time limit on their passport runs out, asking for a change of status and showing how they fit into the relevant parts of the immigration rules for their new status. ▶See chapter 11 for more details of making applications.

The rules do not allow students to stay:

- in order to work or to be self-employed
- in order to set up a business

This does not mean that they cannot apply for such changes, but that any application is likely to be refused. The Home Office would need to be satisfied that there were very exceptional reasons for considering them. People should be referred for specialist advice about the consequences of such applications.

Temporary stay

Students may wish to remain in the UK after their formal studies are over, perhaps in order to attend a degree-giving ceremony, or to continue to write up a PhD thesis after the formal period of study is over. This may be possible, provided an application is made in time and with the support of the academic institution, and provided the student has the money to live in the UK for this additional period without needing to work or to have recourse to public funds. There may be difficulties if the student has been in the UK for nearly ten years, because the Home Office may believe that he or she does not intend to leave at the end of the studies; see page 160 for further details about the 'ten-year concession'.

Working after studies

It is not usually possible for students to stay in the UK after completing their studies in order to work. If students have lived legally in the UK for more than ten years, the Home Office has stated that it will consider making an exception to the immigration rules to grant them indefinite leave to remain because of the length of time they have spent in the UK; ▶see page 160 for more details of this 'ten-year concession'.

Normally, however, students wanting to work in the UK after their studies are over need work permits. Work permits are normally only issued to people who are outside the UK and whose prospective employer applies to the Employment Department for a permit. One of the criteria for the grant of a work permit is that the person should have had several years' experience of work in a similar job outside the UK, so it is rare for students to qualify. There are three exceptions to this:

Work experience

When students want to gain practical experience of working in their subject for a year or so, they may qualify under the Employment Department's work experience scheme. This is a scheme permitting employers to offer work and training, for a limited period, in particular to students from developing countries. The employers need to obtain work experience permits from the Employment Department, showing that a programme has been worked out for the student, who will be gaining useful experience, and that it is understood that the student will leave the UK at the end of the training. Students with training or work experience permits will not normally be allowed to change to ordinary employment later.

Nurses

Students who have trained as nurses in the UK may be permitted to remain to work as nurses after they have qualified. They may remain in the UK while the hospital which wishes to employ them applies for a work permit and their experience of working while training will be taken into account. Permits may be granted, depending on the general employment situation for nurses in the area. This concession does not apply to nurses who are in the UK for some other reason; a visitor who is a qualified nurse will not usually be permitted to remain to work. ▶See also pages 95 and 118 for information about nurses.

Academics

Students who wish to continue with an academic career may be able to do so in the UK, if the academic institution is willing to apply for a work permit on their behalf. The research that they have been doing and the job the institution wants them to fill are likely to be highly specialised and it may be possible to show that there was no other suitable candidate.

Travel outside the UK

Students can travel outside the UK and return within the time limit stamped on their passports. They may expect to be readmitted until the same date, as long as they still satisfy the requirements of the immigration rules on students. Usually their passports will be stamped 'given leave to enter section 3(3)(b) until [date]' which is what this section of the Immigration Act 1971 means. Visa national students who have been given permission to stay for more than six months do not need a visa to re-enter the UK within the time they have been given. Visa national students coming for less than six months may have obtained multiple entry visas; if they did not, they will need to apply at the British post in the country which they are visiting for a new visa before they can return.

Students cannot obtain any formal assurance while in the UK that they are likely to be readmitted after any absence. They have to satisfy an immigration officer when they re-enter that they still qualify to enter. It is therefore sensible for them to take letters from their college confirming their studies, and proof of their financial support, with them to show to the immigration officers on their return.

If a person has a visa and is then refused re-entry to the UK, usually on the grounds that there have been changes in circumstances since the visa was issued, or full facts were not given in order to obtain it, there is a right of appeal against the refusal and the person is able to remain in the UK while that appeal takes place.

If students travel out of the UK when an application for an extension of stay is pending, the application for leave to remain automatically lapses. They may expect immigration officers to question them in detail on return before deciding whether to grant entry. For further consequences of requesting passports back from the Home Office in order to travel, ▶see pages 161–2.

10 Immigration, benefits and other state provisions

The purpose of this chapter is briefly to explain the connection between immigration status and entitlement to some means-tested benefits. It is not intended to give detailed advice on benefit entitlements or on which benefits people may be able to claim.

Under immigration law people may be admitted to the UK subject to the requirement that they do not have recourse to public funds. The box below shows which benefits count as public funds. There is never any endorsement on people's passports to show that they are subject to the public funds requirement. Moreover, there is often no way that the people themselves could be aware of this, unless they have a detailed knowledge of the immigration rules; immigration officers will not tell a husband coming in to the UK to join his wife, for example, whether he may claim any benefits.

PUBLIC FUNDS

The first paragraph of the immigration rules defines public funds as: '**housing** under Part III of the Housing Act 1985, Part II of the Housing (Scotland) Act 1987 and Part II of the Housing (Northern Ireland) Order 1988 and **income support**, **family credit** and **housing benefit** under Part II of the Social Security Act 1986 and Part III of the Social Security (Northern Ireland) Order 1986'.

When the immigration rules mention that a person must satisfy an immigration official that he or she can be supported and accommodated without recourse to public funds, these are the only benefits and services that are meant. This list is complete and exhaustive; nothing else counts as public funds for immigration purposes.

Any other benefit not listed – for example, child benefit, community charge benefit, invalidity benefit – is not public funds and claiming it cannot affect anyone's immigration status. Any other parts of the welfare state – medical treatment under the National Health Service, gaining council accommodation in any way other than as a homeless person, children receiving free state education – are not public funds. Claiming anything other than the four benefits listed can have no direct immigration consequences for a person legally in the UK.

124

Who is not affected by the public funds requirement?

- British citizens
- Commonwealth citizens with the right of abode (see glossary)
- people who are settled (allowed to stay permanently) in the UK. It does not matter why settlement was granted; once a person has been allowed to stay permanently, he or she has full entitlement to claim any benefits, subject only to any qualifying condition attached to that benefit.
- people who have refugee status
- people granted exceptional leave to remain (see chapter 5)
- work permit holders (but their families are subject to the requirement)
- EC citizens. The position of EC citizens is confusing in law. Under EC law, EC citizens are free to move between EC countries to take or to seek work, to set up in business or self-employment, and to provide or receive services. They do not require leave to enter or remain and do not have to show that they can support themselves without recourse to public funds. British immigration law has not yet caught up with this; section 7(1) of the Immigration Act 1988 passed in order to bring British law into conformity with EC law is not yet in force at the time of writing. ▶See chapter 6 for further details.
- citizens of other countries with which there is a reciprocal agreement. There are reciprocal arrangements about eligibility for some limited benefits between the UK and Australia, Austria, Bermuda, Canada, Cyprus, Finland, Iceland, Israel, Jamaica, Malta, Mauritius, New Zealand, Norway, the Philippines, Sweden, Switzerland, Turkey, the USA and Yugoslavia. The benefits authorities may ask for evidence of the nationality of a claimant, but this should be only in connection with establishing whether the person is eligible under any bilateral reciprocal arrangements. The DSS Overseas Branch of the Benefits Agency, Newcastle-upon-Tyne NE98 1YX or the relevant embassy or high commission could give details of individual agreements.

Who is affected by the public funds requirement?

The immigration rules state in many places that people must satisfy an entry clearance or immigration officer that there will be 'adequate maintenance and accommodation without recourse to public funds for the applicants and their dependants' and they may be refused permission to enter or remain in the UK if the officer is not satisfied. These groups of people are:

- people given leave to enter as spouses, to join a British or settled partner, during the first year of leave
- children given leave to enter to join a British or settled parent, during the first year of leave

- fiancés and fiancées
- students and members of their families
- visitors
- working holidaymakers
- au pairs
- people given permission to enter or remain as business people, self-employed people, workers who do not need work permits (permit-free employment) and people of independent means, and people admitted as members of their families
- the spouses and children of work permit holders.

These people will be refused entry clearance overseas, or entry to the UK, if they cannot convince an official that they will not need to claim public funds.

Sponsorship

People coming to visit or study in the UK, or to join a relative in order to settle permanently, will have had to show that support and accommodation without recourse to public funds is available. The person providing this support is known as a 'sponsor'. Sponsorship is proved by the person concerned confirming in writing his or her willingness to provide the support required, and evidence that this can be done. For example, a person sponsoring a student should have a recent bank statement or recent pay slips to show the money that is available to pay the college fees and to support the person while he or she is studying.

It is possible for people to fill in a 'sponsorship form' which will provide the necessary information and send this together with the evidence to the British embassy or high commission. Sponsorship forms are optional; they are merely a convenient way of recording information which may be required by the British authorities. Some advice agencies prepare their own, to help the sponsor in the UK compile information but the information required is also clear from the entry clearance application forms at the British posts abroad. Sponsorship forms do not need to be in any particular format and they do not need to be witnessed or attested by a solicitor.

Undertakings

The immigration authorities can also ask people to sign 'undertakings' to confirm that they will support the person (see appendix for copy of undertaking). These undertakings can be required under the Social Security Act 1986 and the Immigration Act 1971, but should not be signed unless they are specifically requested. Where an undertaking has been signed, the DSS has the authority to claim back any income support (but not any other benefit) that the sponsored person has been paid. Action would be taken through its Benefits Agency, the official name for the benefits side of the DSS since April 1991, at local office level.

A sponsored person who is in the UK as a visitor or student is not entitled to receive any income support, because under the income support regulations he or she does not qualify. A sponsored person who has indefinite leave to remain can claim, even when an undertaking has been signed. The effect of the undertaking is that the sponsor can be asked to repay any income support which the sponsored person has claimed. It is government policy that if sponsors' financial circumstances change and they are no longer able to sponsor the person from abroad, they will not be required to repay benefit. The Benefits Agency may want to interview the sponsor, in the same way that other 'liable relatives' may be pursued, to see whether the changes in financial circumstances are good enough reasons for the failure to maintain.

At the date of writing JCWI knows of only one case where the DSS has taken a person to court to attempt to recover income support claimed by a sponsored person from the sponsor. The case was taken against a man who had sponsored his widowed mother to come to join him for settlement and had signed an undertaking to support her. He believed that as a resident in the UK she should exercise her entitlement to claim. The court ordered him to pay towards her support. The DSS Benefits Agency local offices have however written many threatening letters to sponsors, implying that prosecution will follow. In all the other cases JCWI knows about an accommodation has been reached, often by the sponsor agreeing to pay a small weekly sum, and the matter has not been taken any further.

Possible effects of claiming

If people are admitted with limited leave subject to the requirement that they can support and accommodate themselves without recourse to public funds, and then receive one of the public funds benefits, if the Home Office finds out this may affect their immigration status.

A claim for a public funds benefit may result in:

- leave being curtailed
- an extension of leave being refused
- temporary rather than permanent leave being given
- the possibility of being refused entry to the UK when attempting to return after previously having claimed public funds.

Advisers are often therefore reluctant or unsure whether to advise a person whose immigration status is subject to the public funds requirement to claim benefit because of the possible immigration consequences. There are close links between the Home Office and the DSS and established procedures for reporting claims for income support to the Home Office.

However there are no known established channels of communication between the benefits and immigration authorities in respect of family credit, housing benefit and housing for homeless people. It is very difficult to give clear cut advice because law and practice differ and two public funds benefits (housing benefit and rehousing of homeless people) are administered by local authorities whose practices vary.

It is important to be clear that there are two different authorities and sets of regulations involved in assessing whether someone can or should claim a public funds benefit:

i) **the Home Office immigration rules** which may lead to a refusal of entry or a refusal to extend someone's leave to remain if public funds have been claimed and are thought likely to be needed again

ii) **the DSS benefit regulations** which bar some people in the UK temporarily from some benefits on the ground that they are 'persons from abroad'; this includes, for example, spouses during their first year of residence in the UK.

Advisers will therefore need to assess whether people *can* claim a particular benefit and also whether they *should* do so, if this might jeopardise their immigration status.

Home Office practice

The Home Office does not always enforce the full extent of the legal requirement not to have recourse to public funds. It is normal practice to ignore short periods of reliance on public funds. The Home Office has stated, in a letter from the then Minister, David Waddington, to Max Madden MP in December 1985: 'We would not use this power [to refuse] if a person had become dependent on public funds for a short time through no fault of his own. Moreover, if a sponsor here is dependent on public funds the relevant question will be whether *extra* funds were necessary to support the applicant.' (our emphasis)

For example, a British woman and her children who have been rehoused under the homelessness provisions of housing law require the same sized accommodation as a woman and man with children. Thus if the husband applies from abroad to join the family, he will be able to show that there is adequate accommodation for him because it was not provided for *his* needs but for the rest of the family. Once the husband has been allowed in, under the social security regulations, he is not eligible to receive any income support (see below for further explanation). The wife is eligible to claim for herself but will not receive anything for her husband. Under the immigration regulations, if the wife claims income support for herself and receives money, this could be used by the Home Office to refuse her husband permission to remain on the grounds that the couple cannot support themselves without recourse to public funds. Thus if they need to claim during that year, or if either or both of them is claiming at the time the husband's application for settlement is made to the Home Office, this could be used as a reason to refuse the application. If at all possible, it is advisable not to be claiming a benefit classed as public funds for immigration purposes at the time of an application for settlement.

If the extension or settlement application is refused on public funds grounds, and the spouse is able to appeal against the refusal, he or she may remain in the UK while the appeal is pending, and is permitted to work. If the person later finds work and is able to stop claiming, the Home Office should be informed, with proof of the other source of money, and it is likely that leave to remain would then be granted and the person be asked to withdraw any appeal. It is unusual to be refused leave to remain on public funds grounds; only 46 husbands and wives were refused on these grounds in 1990. However, the numbers of spouses being refused entry clearance on these grounds is rising.

In general, the safest advice that can be given is that where a person is subject to the public funds requirement, claiming a public funds benefit should be a last resort and the claimant should be aware of the possible immigration consequences.

'Public funds' benefits

Income support

Benefit regulations

There are more detailed regulations about eligibility for income support than any other benefit. Although income support is intended as a safety net, not all people in the UK are entitled to receive it.

The income support regulations give a list of people who are not eligible for normal income support, who are called 'persons from abroad'. They are:

- people who have limited leave subject to a requirement not to have recourse to public funds (▶see list on pages 125–126 for categories of people who come under this heading)
- people on temporary admission (▶see glossary)
- people waiting for a Home Office decision on their application
- people who have remained in the UK beyond the time allowed them (overstayers)
- people subject to a deportation order
- people who the Home Office alleges are illegal entrants.

The DSS tells the Home Office about claims from people who it believes may be 'persons from abroad' and the Home Office may follow up this information. It is therefore dangerous for people in the UK without permission to apply for benefits if they have not already applied to the Home Office to regularise their immigration status. After applications have been made to the Home Office, they are eligible to claim income support but will receive it at a reduced rate (see below).

People in the country legally, but with a requirement not to have recourse to public funds, who apply for benefits may receive warning letters from the Home Office and their leave to remain may be curtailed, or any extension refused.

Urgent cases benefit

'Persons from abroad' can qualify for this, lower, rate of income support if they meet one of the conditions listed in income support regulation 70. These are:

a) they have entered in a category which refers to there being no recourse to public funds and their funds which come from abroad are temporarily disrupted. Provided they have been self-supporting during their stay and there is a reasonable chance that their funds will be resumed, they can get income support for up to 42 days (six weeks) in any one period of leave granted. When this applies to students, they can also claim housing benefit, for the whole of their 'eligible rent' under housing benefit regulations, for this six-week period.

b) they are awaiting a decision on their application for leave to remain in the UK to be varied and are applying for a type of leave which does not have a public funds condition attached to it, for example, settlement or refugee status. In such cases they can get income support while the application is pending, until they are sent a decision. If the application was made to the Home Office while they still had leave to remain and it is refused, they are given 28 days' leave in order to make arrangements to travel. They may continue to claim benefit for those 28 days.

c) they are awaiting the determination of an appeal under the Immigration Act

d) they have overstayed their leave and have applied to the Home Office for leave to remain, and they are applying for a type of leave which does not have a public funds test attached to it

e) they are the subject of a deportation order but their removal from the UK has been deferred in writing

f) they are not subject to a deportation order, but have been given permission to stay pending the removal of another person who is subject to a deportation order (as in (e) above)

g) they are being treated as illegal entrants by the Home Office but have been allowed, in writing, to stay

h) a direction for their removal from the UK has been made but the removal has been deferred in writing

ENTITLEMENT TO INCOME SUPPORT

Immigration status	Immigration rules	Benefits regulations
settled person (for whatever reason)	full entitlement	normal qualifications
spouse (1 year's stay)	public funds requirement	not eligible to receive benefit
British citizen or settled person with spouse with 1 year's stay	able to claim	claim for self only – partner not eligible to receive benefit
work permit holder	able to claim	able to claim *but* availability for work?
student	public funds requirement	not eligible to receive benefit *except* for six weeks with temporary disruption of funds from abroad
visitor	public funds requirement	not eligible to receive benefit *except* for six weeks with temporary disruption of funds from abroad
refugee/exceptional leave to remain	able to claim	normal qualifications
application pending to Home Office for leave with public funds requirement (e.g. fiancé(e) to spouse)	public funds requirement	not eligible to receive benefit
application pending to Home Office for leave without public funds requirement (e.g. asylum-seeker)	able to claim	urgent cases rate only
appeal against Home Office refusal	able to claim	urgent cases rate only; may affect appeal outcome

i) they have exhausted all rights of appeal but have been allowed to stay whilst representations are being considered by the Home Office

j) they have been granted temporary admission or are waiting for the Secretary of State to make a decision on their immigration status.

In cases (b) to (j) above, the claimants will be entitled to income support, at the urgent cases rate, until leave to remain is granted or until the date of removal from the UK or until a decision is reached on their immigration status.

When the DSS Benefits Agency considers a claim under income support regulation 70, *all* capital will be taken into account. People will be paid only 90% of the basic income support personal allowance (though children's personal allowances will be met in full); any extra premiums to which they are entitled will be met. Housing costs under income support regulation 17(e) will be met. The Benefits Agency has no power to recover benefit from the claimant or anyone else, but it is always paid at this reduced rate.

If a British or settled person has a partner and/or children who are 'persons from abroad' benefit is modified for the family. The settled partner can claim but will only receive the income support applicable amount paid to support a single person, plus any additions for children who are not persons from abroad. Thus the 'person from abroad' effectively has no 'applicable amount' and will receive no money. However the family's joint resources will be assessed, including those of the 'person from abroad', in deciding the amount payable. Premiums will be paid only for those family members eligible to claim. Housing costs will be met as normal.

In some circumstances, for example when an application for settlement is pending at the Home Office, both partners may be eligible to claim – the 'person from abroad' could claim urgent cases benefit for the whole family or the settled partner could claim a reduced amount of income support. In this case a 'better off' calculation should be done. But if people subject to the public funds requirement receive public funds this could jeopardise their immigration status.

Immigration consequences

Because the DSS routinely informs the Home Office about claims from 'persons from abroad', claiming income support is most likely to have an immigration effect. People who need to apply to the Home Office for extensions or for settlement after making income support claims may need to explain in the application why the claim was necessary and what steps they have taken to avoid the need to claim in the future. Students or visitors who have claimed income support can expect applications for extensions to be refused. People applying for settlement with British or settled relatives should explain why they have had to claim and how, if the application is granted, they will not need to claim in the future.

People applying for asylum, or for leave to remain on exceptional grounds because of their particular personal or compassionate circumstances, are entitled to claim urgent cases rate of income support while the application is pending and this should not affect the Home Office decision.

Family credit

Benefit regulations

Eligibility for family credit depends, in addition to the financial requirements, on the claimant having responsibility for a child, being in paid work for at least 24 hours a week, the claimant and heterosexual partner (if any) being ordinarily resident in the UK and obtaining at least some of their income from work in the UK. There is no specific residence period required and immigration status is not mentioned in the regulations. If benefit is paid, the amount of money received is the same for a single adult claimant as for a couple.

Immigration consequences

When one partner is subject to the public funds requirement and the other is not it may be possible for the settled partner to make a claim without affecting the immigration status of the other. There is no automatic contact between the DSS and the Home Office in connection with family credit.

Housing benefit

Benefit regulations

Under housing benefit regulations, people may claim regardless of their immigration status. There is no duty on a local authority to inform the immigration authorities of the status of recipients of housing benefit.

The housing benefit regulations on eligibility specifically exclude a group of people – most students, including overseas students. There are reciprocal agreements on eligibility between the UK and the other countries of the EC, Iceland, Malta, Norway, Sweden and Turkey. Students from these countries may claim housing benefit, and are entitled to receive the money, but this could have an effect on their immigration status. The regulations therefore give the local authority administering housing benefit a reason to check applicants' immigration status. If it is found that the people are overseas students, this means that they are ineligible for this benefit unless they are claiming urgent cases income support. Some local authorities have taken policy decisions not to ask about status because they disagree with passport checks; others inform people about possible immigration risks or suggest they should seek advice on their immigration status before continuing the claim; others may inform the Home Office about claims.

Advisers therefore need to know whether their local authority is aware of the above issues and whether their policies are likely to ensure confidentiality of information. Some local authorities do not keep records of immigration status for precisely this reason. Housing benefit records are computerised and their contents cannot be divulged under the Data Protection Act. More problematic is the fact that once the information about a person's immigration status is known, a member of staff could pass the information on to the Home Office.

Immigration consequences

If the Home Office is aware that housing benefit has been obtained by people subject to a public funds requirement, this could lead to an extension of stay being refused. For example, a student from Norway, with which there is a reciprocal agreement, might be entitled under the benefit regulations to obtain housing benefit but might have his or her application for an extension of stay as a student refused by the Home Office, on the grounds of inability to support him or herself without recourse to public funds.

Homeless persons' accommodation

Housing regulations

Homeless persons' accommodation is administered by local authorities. There are no uniform practices; different councils have different procedures and policies. Immigration status is irrelevant in deciding whether an individual or a family is in priority housing need and therefore immigration questions should not be asked. The only relevant questions are about housing need.

However, the Asylum Bill, published on 1 November 1991, proposes that asylum-seekers should be treated differently from other homeless people. They would not be eligible for rehousing if they have any accommodation, however temporary, available to them and should only be provided with temporary accommodation while they are asylum-seekers. This is not yet in force at the time of writing.

Immigration consequences

If people subject to the public funds requirement are rehoused as homeless they could be refused permission to remain longer if they make an application for an extension of stay to the Home Office. It is comparatively rare for the Home Office to inquire how they have obtained council property. The Home Office has also stated that when a couple are in homeless accommodation it is only concerned with whether that accommodation had to be provided in order to meet the needs of a person from abroad. For example, if a British mother and her children are in homeless accommodation, this would not preclude her foreign husband coming to join them, as the same size accommodation would be necessary whether or not the husband were living there.

Deciding whether to claim

It is important to weigh up the financial and the immigration consequences of claiming or not claiming a 'public funds' benefit. Often when people seek advice on benefits they will be in dire financial straits. Whilst it is important that they understand the immigration implications of claiming, financially they may have no choice but to do so, at least in the short term. The following checklist may be helpful in deciding how a claim can most safely be made:

• **Can the partner claim instead?** This will serve to mask the fact that people subject to the public funds requirement have claimed, and may also mean that no public funds are paid for these claimants themselves.

- **Is there a financial alternative?** Clearly this needs to be immediate; a short-term claim might be necessary until other funds are investigated, for example, charities, sponsors' friends, student welfare organisations, any embassy welfare provisions.
- **Will the claim be for a short or long period?** Short-term recourse to public funds can possibly be explained by 'mitigating circumstances'. The Home Office has indicated that when considering applications for family settlement a short-term claim may not prejudice the application.
- **Will the Home Office find out?** If the benefit claimed is income support, the DSS will report the claim to the Home Office. If it is a benefit administered by the local authority, policies on confidentiality and on contacting or informing the Home Office vary. Local advice centres may have information.
- **Will a sponsor be pursued?** If the claim is for income support, sponsors who have signed undertakings may well be contacted about the claim and should be advised. If the relationship between the sponsor and the sponsored person has broken down, or if the sponsor no longer has the money, it is unlikely that the Benefits Agency will take action against a sponsor. If the claim is for any other benefit, there is no liability for the sponsor.
- **How imminent is a Home Office decision?** A claim made when the Home Office is about to decide whether a person should be allowed either to remain indefinitely or for a further limited period may prejudice the decision. A claim made soon after leave has been granted may not cause similar problems.
- **What is the claimant's immigration status?** The Home Office is less likely to be sympathetic in dealing with applications for extensions from students and visitors and others in the UK for short-term purposes who have claimed 'public funds' benefits than from people who may qualify for settlement, such as spouses.

If all else fails and a claim has to be made, it may be worth considering 'mitigating circumstances' *in advance* so that these can be explained when the person needs to make an application to the Home Office. If it looks as though the Home Office is likely to refuse leave to remain, a detailed application should be made through an advice agency, with full reasons why the person does now qualify to remain or why an exception should be made.

Benefits which are not 'public funds'

All other welfare benefits are not classed as 'public funds' for immigration purposes and therefore have no direct effect on immigration status and on applications to remain.

Residence requirements

Most benefits are subject to a residence test, either directly or indirectly. National insurance benefits (for example, unemployment benefit, invalidity pension) require contributors to pay into the scheme for approximately two years before they qualify for benefits.

Non-contributory non-means-tested benefits are often paid only where the claimant has been in the UK for a specified period. The rules vary with the benefit – for example, child benefit is paid after either the child or the parent has been present in the UK for six months, or earlier if the parent is working. Severe disablement allowance (the non-contributory version of invalidity pension) is payable after ten years residence and disability benefit if the person is ordinarily resident and has been in the country for a specified period.

Other means-tested benefits have their own entitlement regulations. The public funds rule is not incorporated into other benefit law as it is for income support. Entitlement to income support, housing benefit and community charge benefit (which is not public funds) may be immediate, depending on immigration status and other circumstances, but the amount of benefit may be affected by the length of residence. This is because entitlement to more than the basic level of benefit can depend on receiving a non-contributory benefit (for example, getting a disability benefit means the claimant gets a higher rate of income support).

Council accommodation

Living in council accommodation as such is not recourse to public funds; it is quite safe for an overseas student, for example, to be living in council property and for the Home Office to know this, provided that it was not obtained through the homeless persons provisions. People's immigration status is irrelevant for joining a council waiting list.

National Health Service

Immigration status and eligibility to use the National Health Service are not directly related. From 1 October 1982 people defined by the NHS as 'overseas visitors' can be charged for their NHS hospital medical treatment. This does not mean that all people from overseas are liable to pay for their NHS treatment; there are many exemptions from this. In particular, anyone who is ordinarily resident (▶see glossary) in the UK, or is allowed to stay permanently or intends to stay permanently, is exempt from charges.

Hospitals interpret the regulations in their own ways, most commonly that people who intend to remain for less than six months are liable to be charged. Deciding on whether a person is ordinarily resident may also be complicated and hospitals may tell people they are liable, or send out bills, when this is not correct. When bills are challenged, hospitals will often correct them.

Exemptions from charges

Certain sorts of medical treatment are exempt from charges:

- out-patient or day patient treatment
- treatment in casualty and accident and emergency departments, including dental and ophthalmic emergency departments (but as soon as an emergency patient is transferred to an ordinary ward, liability to pay may begin)
- the diagnosis and treatment of certain communicable diseases (including TB and sexually transmitted diseases). This includes having a test for the HIV antibody, and counselling connected with the test, but not any further treatment if the test is positive.
- compulsory psychiatric treatment (ie detention under the Mental Health Act or treatment conditional on a probation order)

Some people are exempt from charges:

- anyone who has been in the UK for at least 12 months
- anyone who has come to the UK with the intention of remaining permanently. If an application for settlement is pending with the Home Office, the person is exempt.
- anyone who has come to the UK for the purpose of working
- members of HM Forces, other Crown servants and British Council staff recruited in the UK but serving overseas who have come back for treatment
- students who are on courses which last at least six months
- people working overseas who have had at least 10 years' residence in the UK and have either been working abroad for less than five years, or have been taking leave in the UK at least once every two years, or have a contractual right to do so or a contractual right to a passage to the UK at the end of their employment
- seafarers on UK-registered ships
- war disablement pensioners and war widows
- certain UK pensioners living overseas if they had lived in the UK for at least 10 years or been 10 years in Crown service
- refugees, people with exceptional leave to remain and asylum-seekers
- people in prison or detained by the immigration authorities
- the spouses or children, up to the age of 16, or 19 if still in full-time education, of any of these people
- citizens of the other countries of the EC and other countries with which the UK has reciprocal medical treatment agreements. These are Anguilla,

Australia, Austria, British Virgin Islands, Bulgaria, Channel Islands, Czechoslovakia, Falkland Islands, Finland, Gibraltar, Hong Kong, Hungary, Iceland, Isle of Man, Malta, Montserrat, New Zealand, Norway, Poland, Romania, St Helena, Sweden, Turks and Caicos Islands, USSR, Yugoslavia. These agreements vary; some only cover treatment for conditions which have arisen during the visit. People from these countries who do not fit in to any of the other exemptions may be charged for medical treatment for a pre-existing condition as this is not covered in agreements. The full details of individual agreements should be checked with the consulate of the country concerned.

Liability for charges

People who do not fit into any of these exemptions and who cannot argue that they are 'ordinarily resident' in the UK are liable to be charged for hospital treatment. This applies mainly to visitors, to students who are attending courses of less than six months' duration and to people who already had the medical condition for which they require treatment before they came to the UK and who are not otherwise exempt.

Ordinary residence in this context means that people are legally in the UK, for a settled purpose, as part of the regular order of their lives for the time being. This was defined by the House of Lords in the case of *Akbarali v. Brent London Borough Council* (1982 QB 688), which decided that overseas students were ordinarily resident in the UK for the period of their studies. It is not directly connected to immigration status; a person who has entered as a visitor, for example, but who has applied to the Home Office for permission to settle, has shown his or her intention to remain permanently in the UK and is therefore ordinarily resident in the country and not liable to charges.

Many hospital administrators have a rule of thumb that people intending to stay in the UK for less than six months are liable to pay for treatment. However, people in the UK for less than six months may be ordinarily resident, if they are in the country for a settled purpose. A student enrolled on a three-month course of studies, for example, may argue that, because of this purpose of the stay, he or she has become ordinarily resident and therefore not liable to be charged.

Procedures

People who come to a hospital for treatment for the first time should be asked up to three brief questions to determine whether they are eligible for free treatment or not. If they answer yes to any one of the questions, they have shown that they are entitled to free treatment. The questions are:

- Have you (or your husband or wife, or parent for a person under 16) been living in the UK for the past 12 months?

- Are you/spouse/parent going to live in the UK permanently?
- On what date did you/spouse/parent arrive in the UK?

Hospital administrators are not supposed to ask to see passports at this stage, unless they have any reason to believe that they have not been told the truth. There are however many reports that requests for passports are routine.

Only if the patient has answered no to the first two questions should any further questioning be carried out. Hospitals call this Stage 2 questioning and the *NHS Manual of guidance on health service charges* gives complicated flowcharts for administrators for use in establishing whether people are exempt from charges. Instructions say that it is only at this stage that people's passports may be requested and then only to check whether they are citizens of a country with which the UK has a reciprocal agreement on treatment.

The charges levied on people are the normal private rates for treatment, without any extra consultants' fees. The Department of Health publishes a list of the fees for particular treatments, drugs and operations as well as boarding fees. These vary according to the type of hospital, with prestigious teaching hospitals being more expensive.

Hospitals have no authority to charge anyone other than the patient from overseas for medical treatment. They have no authority to ask the relatives or friends of a visitor to pay or to underwrite payment for medical treatment and any requests for such guarantees should be resisted. Some health authorities have stated that it is not worth their while pursuing debts abroad.

Private medical treatment

There are provisions in the immigration rules for visitors to come to the UK for medical treatment, but this treatment has to be private, and people have to show that they have the means to pay for it and to support themselves without working or having recourse to public funds. Having come to the UK for medical treatment does not stop people from becoming exempt from charges after being in the country for a year. They will then be eligible for free NHS treatment, but any application to the Home Office for permission to remain in the UK for NHS treatment would be outside the immigration rules, at the discretion of the Home Office. The chances of success would depend on the seriousness of the illness and the necessity of the treatment.

General practitioners

The NHS regulations do not apply to treatment from GPs. GPs are technically self-employed and have their own discretion about accepting or refusing any patient on to their lists. Department of Health guidelines suggest that they should accept people who are in the UK for less than six months only as private patients. Some GPs ask to see passports when registering new patients and this has inhibited many people from abroad from registering with a GP and obtaining a NHS number. However, visitors and other people in the UK for short periods are entitled to register with GPs and to receive a GP service through the NHS, if they can find a doctor who will register them.

State education

Educating children of compulsory school age (5 to 16) at state schools is not counted as recourse to public funds. Overseas students, work permit holders, business people and any others who are subject to the public funds requirement are entitled to send their children to state schools. There is nothing to stop visitors' children from attending state schools, but the schools are entitled to refuse admission to a child who is only going to be in the UK for a short time, on the grounds that the disruption caused to the child and to the rest of the class is disproportionate to the benefit gained by a few weeks' schooling. However, if the parents are planning to remain longer the school should accept the child; immigration status in itself is not an adequate reason for refusing admission to school.

A child will not be granted leave to enter or remain in the UK as a student in his or her own right in order to attend a state school. Children may come to the UK as students, but they have to be attending private fee-paying schools and have the money available for this, and arrangements have to be made for their care, either living with foster-parents or at a boarding-school with adequate arrangements being made for school holidays. If a child who has been granted leave to remain as a student is transferred from a private to a state school, any application for leave to remain for that purpose is likely to be refused.

Status checking

Department of Social Security

There is evidence of collusion between different government departments which pass on information. This is most clearly seen in the DSS Benefits Agency which has official instructions to inform the Home Office about claims made by people subject to immigration control. For example it has to inform the Home Office about income support claims made by:

- citizens of countries which have signed the European Convention on Social and Medical Assistance (Austria, Cyprus, Finland, Iceland, Malta, Norway, Sweden, Switzerland and all EC countries)

- people applying for a change of status or to extend the length of their stay, where they are not entitled to normal income support but to the urgent cases rate (see above).

The Benefits Agency may also ask questions about people's immigration status and then contact the Home Office to confirm what the claimants have said. If the Home Office cannot trace the person's file or confirm status, this may delay the claim. The income support application forms ask if the claimant or a person for whom he or she is claiming has come to live in the UK within the last five years. If the answer is yes the claimant will be interviewed by the Benefits Agency and this is a licence to ask immigration questions. It may also discourage people with an entitlement to benefit from claiming, if they are not secure in their knowledge of their position.

People are also often asked to show their passports when they are applying for a national insurance number. The Benefits Agency can issue NI numbers when these are requested for benefits purposes without regard to immigration status. As people born in the UK are allocated a NI number automatically, it is assumed that anyone who needs to apply will be subject to immigration control and must be checked. Benefits Agency officials are not always aware of the meaning of immigration stamps and they have no authority to demand passports, though in practice there may be complications and delays for the claimant if this is refused.

Register offices

When people want to get married and signify their intentions to the marriage registrar, he or she is required to be satisfied as to their identity, their age and that they are free to marry. Instructions from the Registrar General's department state that the most convenient way to prove the identity of a person from abroad is by seeing the person's passport. This has understandably caused worries for people who are in the UK without permission.

In general, the registrar is looking at the passport for evidence of identity and age and nationality (as the marriage laws of some countries require extra procedures if the marriage is to be recognised there as well as in the UK). Alternative evidence such as a birth certificate may be acceptable but this is at the discretion of the registrar. A minority of registrars also act as immigration officials and attempt to check immigration status. JCWI knows of arrests in connection with weddings at Westminster and Hackney (where an investigation into alleged marriages of convenience was run by the *News of the World*) and of inquiries relating to immigration status being made in Southwark and Haringey (the latter denied that this was policy).

Opposition to status checking

Community groups have often taken up the issue of internal immigration checks and controls in particular areas. Examples include the No Pass Laws Here! group which was active from 1979 to 1987, the Hackney Anti-Deportation Campaign which produced a useful booklet on internal checking in Hackney and the Committee for Non-Racist Benefits, which has produced useful leaflets for claimants.

The effect of checks is often to discourage people who have every right to claim but who are worried about their status, rather than to find or arrest people who may not be entitled. JCWI opposes immigration status checks by non-immigration authorities and believes it is important that such checks should be challenged and stopped.

11 Coming, going and staying: the practicalities of travel

This chapter discusses the practicalities of travel to the UK, both when entering the UK for the first time and travelling in and out of the country after having been given permission to remain. It also covers the practical details of making applications to the Home Office for variation and extension of leave.

Entry clearance

Entry clearance is permission from a British embassy, high commission or consulate to travel to the UK. It may be called either a visa, an entry certificate or a letter of consent. People applying for entry clearance have to satisfy officials at a British post that they qualify under the immigration rules to enter the UK in the category in which they are applying.

People who need entry clearance

There are three groups of people who need to obtain entry clearance before travelling to the UK. They are:

- **people who are visa nationals** (▶see glossary for list) who must have entry clearance before travelling to the UK for any reason
- **people who are coming intending to stay permanently:** this usually means people coming to join relatives in the UK, for example spouses, children or parents.
- **people who are coming in order to work or to do business**, including all the categories of permit-free employment in the immigration rules (▶see chapter 7), self-employment and diplomatic work.

How to apply for entry clearance

People apply for entry clearance to the British embassy, high commission or consulate in the country in which they are living before travelling to the UK. The procedure is that they have to fill in the official application form IM2A (▶see appendix for example) and any other form relevant for their application. Form IM2B is for people applying for settlement, Form IM2C for people applying to work, Form IM2D for people claiming the right of

143

abode and Form IM2E for anyone who has previously applied for entry clearance and been refused. The forms are obtained from the British post. They can also be obtained from the Migration and Visa Department of the Foreign and Commonwealth Office in the UK, and the relative in the UK may fill them in on behalf of the person abroad. However, the person abroad should sign the forms and take or send them, with the fee, to the British post. The fee (▶see appendix) is payable in local currency and is not refundable.

The application is made on the day the British post receives the form and the fee; if the fee has not been paid, the application is not considered to be valid. The date of application is particularly important in children's settlement applications, as they must be under 18 at the date of application. In some countries, the application will be dealt with straight away. In others, for example the countries of the Indian subcontinent, the Philippines and Jamaica, there are long delays for people applying for settlement and may be delays for visitors.

Applications for settlement

The entry clearance officers at the British post interview all people applying to come to the UK for settlement with family members, except children under 10. Children between 10 and 14 should be interviewed only in the presence of an adult who is associated with their family, and should only be asked simple questions about their immediate family. All applicants have to satisfy the entry clearance officer that they are related as claimed to the person they are applying to join, and that there is adequate support and accommodation for them.

Documents required

The British post requires some standard information both about the applicant and the person he or she is coming to join (the sponsor). This includes:

- **photocopies of the sponsor's passport**. If she or he is a British citizen, the first five pages; if not, all the pages with personal details and all the pages with any immigration officers' stamps on them. Because passports should not be sent through the post between countries, British posts will accept photocopies, but they must all be certified by a solicitor as genuine copies; the solicitor should write on each photocopied page 'I certify this is a genuine copy of . . . ', sign the statement and add an official stamp. In general, the immigration authorities will not accept photocopies of documents, on the grounds that a photocopy might not reveal a forged or altered document, unless the copies have been certified by a solicitor in this way.

- **the sponsor's birth certificate** if he or she was born in the UK

- **evidence of adequate financial support in the UK**. If the sponsor in the UK is working, this could be recent pay slips, or a letter from the employer confirming the job and salary, or recent bank statements covering at least the past three months showing money coming in and out. If other friends or relatives will be supporting the applicant, a letter from them will be necessary, confirming that they are able and willing to do so and similar evidence to the above that they are able to do so. If the sponsor in the UK is running a business, the business accounts or bank statements could be sent.

A spouse from abroad applying to come to join a British or settled spouse in the UK may also provide evidence of his or her own means or plans, for example a letter from an employer offering a job when the spouse arrives. Other relatives must show that the sponsor is able to support them.

There is no separate immigration law definition of what 'adequate' support is; as long as the money coming in is above the level of income support that would be payable to the household, this should be considered adequate. However, the Immigration Appeal Tribunal has held in a recent case (*Azem*, 7863) that the level of support should be above the basic income support level, because a person on income support receives other things free, like prescriptions and eye tests and free school meals for children, therefore income support cannot be considered adequate total support.

- **evidence of accommodation**. Accommodation does not have to be owned; council or privately-rented accommodation is quite satisfactory. If it is being bought on mortgage, a letter from the building society or other organisation giving the mortgage, confirming the ownership of the accommodation and the number of rooms available should be adequate. If it is council accommodation, a letter from the council confirming the tenancy, the size of the accommodation, and that there is room for the extra person to live there will be necessary. This can be difficult to obtain from overworked council housing departments which may take a long time to provide letters that they do not see as immediate emergencies. If it is privately rented, a letter from the landlord confirming the size and tenancy of the accommodation and that he or she has no objection to the extra person coming should be sent. When landlords are unwilling to write, or when the accommodation is owned outright, some council environmental health departments are prepared to write to confirm that accommodation is adequate.

There are no special immigration law standards for the adequacy or size of accommodation; the standard laid down under the Housing Act 1985 applies – that is, that two people, of the opposite sex and at least one of them over the age of 10, and who are not married or living in a relationship similar to marriage, should not have to share the same room to sleep in. The number of rooms includes bedrooms, living-rooms and kitchens, but not bathrooms and toilets.

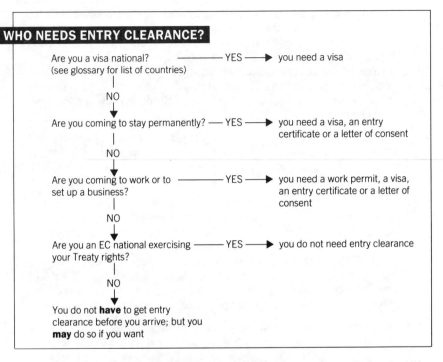

WHO NEEDS ENTRY CLEARANCE?

Are you a visa national? ——————— YES ——▶ you need a visa
(see glossary for list of countries)
                          |
                         NO
                          ↓
Are you coming to stay permanently? —— YES ——▶ you need a visa, an entry
                          | certificate or a letter of consent
                         NO
                          ↓
Are you coming to work or to ——————— YES ——▶ you need a work permit, a visa,
set up a business?   an entry certificate or a letter of
                          | consent
                         NO
                          ↓
Are you an EC national exercising ——— YES ——▶ you do not need entry clearance
your Treaty rights?
                          |
                         NO
                          ↓
You do not **have** to get entry
clearance before you arrive; but you
may do so if you want

- **the applicant's current passport**. If the person has travelled to the UK before, he or she may also be asked for old passports, to show that he or she did leave the UK as required.

In addition to the general requirements, there are further requirements for people applying to come for particular reasons. They are listed in the relevant chapters.

Applications to work

The British post will need evidence of the work offered. For most employment, the employer in the UK has to obtain a work permit for the person from the Employment Department in the UK and the British post will need to see this. As the Employment Department only issues permits when it is satisfied about the pay and conditions offered for the job, and that the employers could not find a suitable worker already resident in the UK, the British post will not normally make further checks. If the employment does not require a permit (▶see chapter 7) the British post will need a letter of confirmation from the employers about the job and the pay and conditions offered in order to consider whether it meets the requirements of permit-free employment.

If the application is for business or independent means, full details of the money and business proposals are necessary. The British posts frequently refer business applications to the Home Office for decision, so that it can check on the feasibility of the enterprise.

Applications for temporary stay

People who are not visa nationals and who are not coming to settle, work or do business in the UK do not need to get entry clearance before travelling. They have the choice of applying for entry clearance abroad, or of travelling to the UK without it and seeking entry from the immigration officer they see at the port of entry. There are advantages and disadvantages in applying for entry clearance when it is optional, but the final decision on whether it would be wise to do so depends on the person and the facts of the case.

Advantages and disadvantages of applying for optional entry clearance

The advantages are:

- people know in advance whether they satisfy the requirements of the immigration rules and therefore they are unlikely to have problems or delays when they arrive in the UK
- if they are refused entry clearance, they will have spent money only on the entry clearance fee, not also on the ticket to the UK
- if they get entry clearance but are nevertheless refused entry when they arrive in the UK, they can appeal against the refusal and remain in the UK while the appeal is pending, and give evidence at the appeal hearing

The disadvantages are:

- in some countries there are delays in considering applications and there may also be further delays where the applications are referred to the Home Office
- there is a fee for entry clearance, which is not returned if the application is refused, and an application may involve more than one long journey to the nearest British post
- the refusal rates for entry clearance overseas are much higher than those at ports of entry in the UK
- if entry clearance is refused, the person's passport will be marked to show this and information about the refusal may be passed on to the authorities in the UK, so that travel to the UK (and to some other countries) will be more difficult in future.

If the application is successful

If the entry clearance officer is satisfied, the person will be given entry clearance. There are different names for this depending on the nationality of the person applying – ▶see chapter 13 for examples. If they are visa nationals, they will be given a visa, which looks different for Commonwealth and non-Commonwealth citizens. If they are non-visa Commonwealth citizens, they will get an entry certificate, which is similar to a Commonwealth visa. If they are non-visa, non-Commonwealth citizens, they will not have a stamp in their passports but will be given a separate letter of consent, which is literally a letter they need to carry with them and their passport when they travel to the UK. Most of these stamps or documents also state 'valid for presentation at a UK port within 6 months'. This does not mean that people will be admitted to the UK for a six-month period. It means that they must travel to use the clearance within six months. If they do not travel within this time, they will need to get a new clearance, as the old one will no longer be valid.

If the application is refused

If the entry clearance officer is not satisfied, the application will be refused. This must be done in writing and the person must be informed of his or her right to appeal against the refusal and be given forms to fill in to appeal. The appeal must be received by the British post which refused within three months of the date of refusal; see chapter 16 for more information about appeals.

Arrival in the UK

On arrival at a UK air- or sea port, people who are subject to immigration control must be examined by an immigration officer to see whether they satisfy the requirements of the immigration rules for leave to enter. If they are granted leave, immigration officers stamp their passports with a square stamp showing the date and port of entry, and the time limit and any conditions on their stay (▶see chapter 13 for examples). The time limit is from the date on this stamp, the date on which the person was granted permission to enter, not from the date on which any entry clearance was granted. For example, a person granted visit entry clearance on 3 January who was admitted to the UK on 30 March for six months is permitted to stay until 30 September. Before 30 September, the person should either leave the UK or apply to the Home Office for permission to remain longer. It is worth keeping a record of the date separate from the passport, so that if the passport is lost, the person knows the date to which he or she is allowed to remain and can make any application to remain longer in time, before the permission runs out.

If immigration officers put a time limit on a person's stay in the UK, they may also impose other conditions, either a restriction or a prohibition on employment, and/or a requirement to register with the police.

If people are refused entry to the UK, they may be able to contest this refusal. See chapter 12 for more information.

Illegible passport stamps

When people are admitted as visitors for six months, the stamp put on their passports is usually a standard rubber stamp stating 'leave to enter for six months employment prohibited'; ▶see chapter 13 for examples. If the immigration officer does not press hard enough, or does not have enough ink on the inkpad, the stamp may not be legible. The Immigration Act 1988, in force since 1 August 1988, provided that where an entry stamp is illegible, the person is deemed to have been granted leave to enter for six months, with a prohibition on employment.

Before 1 August 1988, an illegible stamp was deemed to have granted the person indefinite leave to enter. This was because the Immigration Act 1971 provides that people must be given notice in writing of the time limit and conditions on which they have been granted entry. When these could not be read, it was decided that no valid time limit or conditions had been imposed on the person's stay. Thus people who last entered the UK before 1 August 1988 and had no legible time limit placed on their stay may apply to the Home Office to confirm that they are settled in the UK. They should obtain specialist advice before approaching the Home Office.

Entry through Ireland

The UK and Ireland, together with the Isle of Man and the Channel Islands, form a Common Travel Area. This means that there are no immigration controls between the two countries and most people do not require leave to enter when travelling from one to the other. People's passports are not usually stamped as they are not examined by immigration officers. Irish citizens entering the UK automatically become settled on arrival, as do British citizens entering Ireland. The Prevention of Terrorism Act, used to control the movement of British citizens between Britain and Northern Ireland, is beyond the scope of this book.

The Immigration (Control of Entry through Republic of Ireland) Order 1972 applies to most people who are not Irish citizens. It provides that, although not requiring leave to enter, people subject to immigration control who enter the UK through Ireland for the first time are deemed to have been granted leave to enter for three months, with a prohibition on employment and business. Nothing will be stamped on their passports and there will usually be no evidence of their date of entry other than the travel ticket, if they have kept it. If they wish to remain in the UK for more than three months they should apply to the Home Office for an extension of this stay, with any evidence they have of the date of arrival (so they will not be treated as overstayers) and showing how they fit into the immigration rules to remain longer.

Both the UK and Ireland have their own lists of countries whose citizens require visas to enter and there is not a common visa for both countries.

Visa nationals intending to travel to both countries should obtain visas from both the embassies concerned before setting out. This is necessary even though it is unlikely that passports will be checked while travelling. A visa national who has been given a visa endorsed 'short visit' to enter the UK from a British embassy or high commission and who enters through Ireland is deemed to have been given a month's leave to enter, with a prohibition on employment and business and a requirement to register with the police. People with visas for any other purpose are deemed to have been given three months.

People who have limited leave to remain in the UK and who travel between the UK and Ireland and return to the UK within the currency of their leave still have the same length of time left. People who are granted leave to enter the UK for a limited period, who travel to Ireland and return after that leave has expired are deemed to have been granted seven days' leave to enter the UK again.

The Immigration (Control of Entry through Republic of Ireland) Order does not apply to visa nationals who do not have visas, or to people who have previously entered or remained in either the UK or Ireland without permission, or against whom there are current deportation orders. They still require leave to enter. If they enter without seeing an immigration officer to grant this leave, they are deemed to have entered in breach of the immigration laws and can be treated as illegal entrants who entered by deception (▶see chapter 14). Even though they have not been examined by an immigration officer, and did not know that they should have been, the Court of Appeal decided in the case of *Bouzagou* (1983 Imm AR 69) that people in this situation are illegal entrants. They are liable to removal with no right of appeal until after they have left the UK.

Travelling in and out of the UK

The immigration rules provide for people who have been granted leave to enter or remain in the UK to return after being abroad during this time. The provisions are different for three groups of people – those with leave to enter or remain for six months or less, those with leave to enter or remain for more than six months but who still have a time limit on their stay, and those with indefinite leave to enter or remain. There are also provisions for people who are applying to the Home Office for leave to remain at the time they want to travel. People with the right of abode always qualify to re-enter but those not travelling on British citizen passports should obtain a certificate of entitlement to the right of abode before travelling.

People who always qualify to re-enter

People with the right of abode

These people are not subject to immigration control and therefore can enter the UK at any time. People who are British citizens and are travelling on British passports are able to enter just by showing this document. Immigration officers only have to be satisfied that the person travelling is the rightful holder of the passport. Occasionally they make more detailed checks when they suspect that a person is travelling on a forged passport or on a passport issued to someone else, and people can be refused entry for this reason. It is up to the immigration officers to prove their case that a person travelling on a full British passport is not entitled to do so, and the person travelling has the right to appeal against refusal and to remain in the UK while the appeal is pending.

British Visitor's passports

All kinds of British nationals (see chapter 17) who are resident in the UK are able to obtain travel documents through the Post Office. These are called British Visitor's passports and are normally valid for one year and for western European countries only. The Post Office does not usually demand evidence from people to show that they are British, but issues these documents on request. Because evidence of the person's British nationality may not have been shown, immigration officers may not accept a British Visitor's passport as proof that a person is British or is entitled to re-enter the UK.

The case of *Minta* (QBD 3.6.91) decided that Mr Minta's British Visitor's passport did not prove that he was a British citizen. He was born in the UK of Ghanaian parents, had returned to live in the UK in 1978 and had travelled abroad for a month's holiday. The court held that the document was not a full British passport, and that Mr Minta had not satisfied an immigration officer he was born in the UK, so he should be removed and only had the right of appeal after removal. The Home Office barrister in the case admitted that this decision meant that 'British citizens – particularly those from ethnic minorities – would not be well advised to travel on British Visitor's passports, for obvious reasons'. People who attempt to return to the UK on British Visitor's passports and who do not hold full British passports may therefore be refused entry and returned to the country from which they have come in order to prove their status there.

Certificates of entitlement to the right of abode

People born in the UK before 1983 are automatically British citizens, as are people born in the UK from 1983 onwards if either parent was a British citizen or was settled in the UK at the time of their birth. They may also be entitled to another nationality by descent from a parent and therefore may be travelling on the passport of the other country. This may be when the other country, for example Malaysia or Nigeria, does not allow dual nationality or places restrictions on the stay of people using non-national passports. These people with the right of abode need to have their passports stamped with a 'certificate of entitlement to the right of abode' (▶see chapter 13 for example) as proof of their status in order to qualify to enter the UK. These certificates of entitlement can be obtained either from the Home Office, if the person is in the UK, or from a British embassy or high commission if the person is abroad. There is a fee payable (▶see appendix for amount). Difficulties sometimes arise in countries where the British authorities are suspicious of documents shown.

Other Commonwealth citizens with the right of abode also need certificates of entitlement before travelling to the UK. They may have the right of abode through the birth of a parent in the UK or through a marriage, before 1 January 1983, to a man with the right of abode (▶see glossary for further explanation). They also need to show original documents to prove their claim to the right of abode. In some countries where there may not be contemporaneous birth or marriage certificates to prove the relationship people may have difficulties in convincing the British authorities that they qualify.

Certificates of entitlement are valid for the same length of time as the passport on which they are stamped. When people renew their passports they can then apply to the British authorities for a new certificate of entitlement.

People with leave to enter/remain for six months or less

Most people with leave to remain for six months or less are visitors, but some students on short courses may be admitted only for the period of the course and others coming for short-term work, like summer agricultural work, may also be given less than six months stay. When they are given leave to enter at a British air- or sea port, they have permission to stay for the time stamped on their passports. If they travel out of the UK, the leave they have been given lapses, that is, has finished. If they return, immigration officers will treat them as new arrivals and question them again to decide if they qualify to enter.

Thus people given leave to enter for six months as visitors, for example, who travel to mainland Europe after two months and then seek to re-enter Britain cannot assume that they will be given the further three months leave left to run. They must again satisfy the immigration officers of their claim to enter as a visitor. They may be refused permission to enter if the immigration officer is not satisfied, and can then face removal to the country from which they have travelled, rather than to their country of origin.

Visa nationals need a visa for every entry to the UK. Visa national visitors who are planning to travel out of and into the UK during their visit need a valid visa for each entry. They should therefore apply initially for multiple-entry visas, not single-entry visas, so that they will be able to return. Once people with single-entry visas have travelled to the UK and been admitted, the visa is no longer valid. If they want to return, they need a new visa.

Until May 1991 it was possible for such people to apply to the Passport Office in London for multiple-entry or single-entry re-entry visas, while they were in the UK on holiday, and then travel out of the UK and return. Since 16 May 1991 re-entry visas have been abolished and visas can only be obtained outside the UK. Thus visa national visitors with single-entry visas who want to travel out of the UK and return must apply to the British post in the country to which they have travelled for another visa before returning to the UK. If they return without a new visa, they are liable to be refused entry just for this reason. Immigration officers do have the discretion to readmit people who they believe genuinely did not know about the visa requirement (and may then mark their passports with a large 'W' to show they have been warned about this) but it is not safe to count on it.

People with leave to enter/remain for more than six months but with a time limit

From 16 May 1991, people who have been granted leave to enter or remain for more than six months can travel and return to the UK and expect to be allowed in again for the rest of that time without detailed questioning by immigration officers on their return. This is because paragraph 1 of the Schedule to the Immigration Act 1988 came into force on that date. It provides for leave to enter to continue after an absence. As long as people coming back are still doing the same thing for which they were originally granted entry, they should not have difficulties on return. Thus, for example, a student who is still following the same full-time course of studies and who still has the financial support available to do this should be readmitted for the same time as he or she had before leaving. If the student has stopped studying, or has married a settled or British person and seeks entry as a spouse, he or she could be refused entry because the entry sought would be in a different category and a new entry clearance would be necessary.

Visa nationals returning within the time given do not need visas. They are exempt from requiring visas if they return during a period of leave of more than six months. This is universal; until 16 May 1991 only nationals of eleven countries (Algeria, Bangladesh, Ghana, India, Morocco, Nigeria, Pakistan, Sri Lanka, Tunisia, Turkey, Uganda) were exempt from requiring visas in these circumstances. The Home Office and immigration officers used to endorse their passports to confirm that they were exempt from requiring visas. Now all visa nationals are exempt in the same circumstances, but visa exemption stamps are no longer used. This means that people have nothing in writing to show that they do not require visas. They may therefore have problems in convincing other authorities, for example airline staff, that it is safe to allow them to travel and that they do not need visas (as airlines can be fined £2000 if they bring in someone who needs a visa and does not have one).

People who have indefinite leave to enter/remain: the returning residents rule

People who are settled (have indefinite leave to remain) in the UK are free to travel out of and into the UK, provided they do not stay out of the UK for more than two years. This is called the returning residents rule. Visa nationals are exempt from requiring visas if they return within this time. But see above for possible problems following the discontinuing of visa exemption stamps.

WHAT THE RULES SAY

The immigration rules state that people must satisfy an immigration officer that:

- they are returning for the purpose of settlement
- they had indefinite leave to enter or remain in the UK when they last left the country
- they have not been away for longer than two years.

WHAT THE RULES MEAN

Returning for the purpose of settlement

This means that immigration officers have the power to question people returning to their homes in the UK about the purpose of their travel. Although this may not happen each time they travel, there is always the possibility that they may be asked personal and intrusive questions about their intentions. In order to retain their settlement rights, people who have lived in the UK must satisfy the immigration officers that they are intending to remain indefinitely on this particular occasion.

In the years before 1 May 1990, settled people returning within two years of departure were automatically admitted again for settlement. It did not matter how long or short a period they had remained in the UK on their last entry and immigration officers did not have the power to inquire into their intentions. Returning to the UK for short periods in order to retain settlement rights is now more difficult, because immigration officers are more likely to question people who have spent long periods outside the UK about their current intentions.

Indefinite leave when they last left the country

People who once had indefinite leave to remain but lost it because they returned and were granted only limited leave now have no way under the immigration rules to qualify again for settlement. Even if they have spent most of their lives in the UK, by being admitted for a limited period they are applying at the discretion of the Home Office for settlement.

Young people who have spent most of their lives in the UK but who have gone abroad for postgraduate study, for example, may wish to return to their homes during summer holidays. Strictly speaking, they would not be returning 'for settlement' as they plan to leave the UK at the end of the holiday to continue studies, before returning to stay permanently at the end of the course. Women of Asian origin whose husbands have been refused permission under the primary purpose rule to live in the UK with them may spend long periods abroad with them and may intend to go abroad again but also return to the UK to see their parents and other relatives living in the country. If questioned by immigration officers, they would explain this – and could then be admitted as visitors, rather than for settlement. The next time they returned it would be for settlement – but they would not then fit into the rules as returning residents as they would not have been admitted with indefinite leave on their last entry. It is therefore important that returning residents should always make it clear that they intend to continue to live in the UK, and this country is their home.

Not been away for more than two years

This is a clear requirement and is strictly interpreted. Settled people who have been out of the UK for nearly two years and who are unable to return within this time should apply to the British embassy or high commission in the country they are in for entry clearance as returning residents. There is a fee for this; ▶see appendix for the amount. If the application for entry clearance is made before the two-year period is finished, and the people explain the reasons for the delay in travel, it is likely to be granted.

People who have been away for more than two years before returning or applying for entry clearance to return are in a more difficult position. The immigration rules state that an application may still be granted in certain circumstances, for example if people have 'lived here for most of their lives'. Thus people who came as young children to join their parents and were educated in the UK but who have then spent three or four years abroad without returning home may be able to qualify because of the length of time they have spent in the UK.

The rules do not give any other examples of exceptional circumstances which would allow people to return to their homes. The courts have decided in the case of *Khokhar* (1981 Imm AR 56n) that being too ill to travel at the relevant time (when detailed medical evidence has been provided) and in the case of *Armat Ali* (1981 Imm AR 51) that having the passport detained by the authorities in connection with legal proceedings have been strong enough reasons. It is important for people to explain in full, with evidence, the reasons why they have not been able to return to the UK within two years and why they are doing so at the time of application.

If the application is successful

If people are applying abroad they will be granted entry clearance as returning residents and this will be endorsed on their passports. They must travel to the UK while the entry clearance is still valid, usually within six months. On arrival at the port of entry, they will be given leave to enter for an indefinite period. If people are applying at a port in the UK, they will be admitted for an indefinite period.

If the application is refused

People who have applied for entry clearance have the right to appeal against any refusal. The entry clearance officers have to give them a letter giving brief reasons why the application was refused and forms to fill in to appeal against the refusal. The forms must be returned to the entry clearance officers within three months of the date of refusal. People who apply for entry at a sea- or airport have a right of appeal but if they did not have entry clearance they can only appeal after they have been sent back. People who are given limited leave when they enter can challenge this by applying as returning residents after entry. If they are refused, they have a right of appeal as long as the application was made before their leave to remain ran out. However, there is no provision in the immigration rules for people to be granted returning resident status after entry to the UK, so these appeals are unlikely to succeed. See chapter 16 on appeals for more details.

Applying to the Home Office

People who have been allowed to enter or remain in the UK for a certain period or under certain conditions may apply to the Home Office to extend the time or to change the conditions.

Applying in time

If at all possible, **people should apply to the Home Office in time**, before their present permission to stay runs out, even if all the necessary documents, including the passport, are not available. This means that a letter should be posted or faxed to the Home Office, or people should go there to apply, before the time stamped on their passports has expired. If an application for an extension is made before the time runs out, the person is still legally in the UK while the Home Office considers the application, however long this takes. During this time, any restriction or prohibition on working still applies. If the application is refused, there is a formal right of appeal against the refusal.

If people want an answer quickly, they may decide to go to the Home Office to apply in person. The application may be decided on the day, but this is not always possible. Otherwise, it is normally best to write to the Home Office, particularly if there are any unusual circumstances in the case. In an emergency, a simple letter such as:

[address of person applying]

Under Secretary of State
Immigration and Nationality Department, Home Office
Lunar House, Wellesley Road, Croydon CR9 2BY

Dear Sir/Madam [date]

My leave to remain in the UK will expire on [date]. I am now writing to request that it be extended. I will send further details and evidence in support of this application later.

Yours faithfully

[name of person applying]

---

is enough to keep the person legally in the UK. The letter should be sent by recorded delivery post and the person should keep a copy. If the application is faxed to the Home Office, it should be sent by post as well.

Applying after leave to enter has expired

If the person's permission to remain has already expired it is often still worth applying to the Home Office, particularly if the person fits into the rules apart from the overstaying, or has a strong compassionate case. If an application is made late, it is important that the person has advice and makes as full a case as possible for the Home Office to consider. It is usually best to make the application through an advice agency, both so the Home Office knows that the person is receiving competent advice, and so that the Home Office may not immediately know the person's address.

If the application is made late, after the time stamped on the passport has run out, the person is in the UK without permission while the application is under consideration and there is no right of appeal against any refusal. While the application is under consideration, the person is still an over-stayer and thus liable to deportation. However if the police or immigration service come across the person, the fact that an application has been made gives some protection. It is unlikely that further action against him or her will be taken while the Home Office is dealing with the application. If the application is refused, although there is no formal right of appeal against the refusal, further representations may be made to the Home Office.

Dealing with the Home Office

It is important to remember that the Home Office Immigration and Nationality Department exists to carry out the immigration law, *not* to give advice, either to advisers or individuals. If advisers want further information before being able to advise someone, they should not ask the Home Office first, but should get in touch with an independent specialist source – JCWI, UKIAS, the local law centre, NACAB – where information will not be recorded for use against the person later, and which will give independent advice.

There is no compulsion to provide all the information or evidence the Home Office may request when this is not pertinent to the application. There is no need to give the private address of a person who is represented; c/o the advice centre is quite sufficient. If the Home Office asks for detailed information on the telephone, there is no need for advisers to give it; they may ask for the request to be put in writing.

Do not assume that everything the Home Office says is correct. Staff turnover at Lunar House, the Immigration and Nationality Department of the Home Office, is high. Advisers are likely to know just as much about the law as many Home Office staff do. Home Office threats are not always carried out. For example, a standard Home Office reminder letter states that if information is not received within two weeks, the application may be refused. This is most unlikely to happen, particularly if the person or the adviser is in touch with the Home Office explaining the reason for any delay in providing evidence.

Do not give up just because the Home Office has refused, or has sent out threatening letters. Even when people have been told to leave the country without delay, under threat of deportation, decisions can still be altered.

Home Office discretion

The Home Office and the immigration authorities have the power to make decisions outside the immigration rules, if they are satisfied that there is sufficient reason to do so. When a person has strong compassionate or other reasons for needing to remain in the UK, but does not fit into the immigration rules, an application for treatment outside the rules may be made. Full details should be given of the reasons why the person needs to remain, together with any available evidence to support this.

If the person has already been through the formal processes of dealing with the Home Office – making an application, appealing against a refusal, losing the appeal – it may be worth making any further application through the local Member of Parliament. It is important to write to the MP with full details of the case and ask him or her to send that letter on to the Home Office Minister, with any further covering letter. If an MP takes up a case, this means that the correspondence and the file will be dealt with by the

CHANGES OF STATUS ALLOWED UNDER THE IMMIGRATION RULES

This table lists changes which are specifically allowed under the rules. **This does not mean that an application will automatically be granted; people have to satisfy the Home Office that they qualify.** See relevant chapter for details. Other applications may be made, but they are *outside* the immigration rules, at the discretion of the Home Office. For example, there is no provision in the rules for a person in the UK to become a fiancé(e), but such applications may be granted when there are strong reasons for delaying the marriage. BUT applying to change status may cast doubts on the person's original intentions; ▶see chapter 14.

1 visitor
can change to 8, 9, 10
can change to 2 if *not* a visa national
can change to 6, 4 if specified nationality
cannot usually change to 3, 5, 7, 11
cannot extend 6 months stay as 1

2 student
can change to 8, 9, 10
can change to 4 if specified nationality
cannot usually change to 3, 5, 6, 7, 11
can apply to extend stay as 2 until end of
studies
can change to 1 for short period after end
of studies

3 work permit holder, permit-free employment
can change to 8, 9, 10
can change to 11 after four years in
approved employment
can change to 2 if *not* visa national
can change to 4, 6 if specified nationality
cannot change to 5, 7
can change to 1 for short period after end
of work

4 working holiday-maker
can change to 8, 9, 10
can change to 6 if specified nationality
can change to 2 if *not* visa national
cannot change to 3, 5, 7, 11
can change to 1 for short period at end of
stay

5 business, self-employed, independent means
can change to 8, 9, 10
can change to 11 after four years
residence
can change to 2 if *not* visa national
can change to 6 if specified nationality
cannot change to 3, 4, 7
can change to 1 for short period at end of
stay

6 au pair
can change to 8, 9, 10
can change to 2 if *not* a visa national
can change to 4 if specified nationality
cannot change to 3, 5, 7, 11
can change to 1 for short period at end of
stay

7 fiancé(e)
can change to 8 after marriage
if marriage plans fail, can change to 1, 9,
10
can change to 2 if *not* visa national
can change to 4, 6 if specified nationality
cannot change to 3, 5, 11

8 spouse with one year's leave
can change to 11
if marriage fails, can change to 1, 9, 10
can change to 2 if *not* visa national
can change to 4 if specified nationality
cannot change to 3, 5, 6, 7

9 refugee
can change to 11 after four years
can change to 8

10 asylum-seeker granted exceptional leave to remain
can change to 11 after seven years
can apply for 9
can change to 8

11 settled – indefinite leave to remain
no immigration applications necessary
may be able to apply for British citizenship

office of the Minister responsible for immigration rather than at Lunar House. MPs' intervention is most useful as a last resort; if they intervene while an appeal is pending, for example, they will usually be told that their representations will not be considered until after the appeal has been decided.

The Home Office has stated some circumstances in which it will exercise discretion, outside the immigration rules, in a particular way. The 'under-12 concession' (▶see page 39) has been in existence since 1976 but has never been put into the rules. The granting of exceptional leave to remain instead of refugee status to asylum-seekers (▶see chapter 5) is outside the immigration rules. There are also policies about granting indefinite leave to remain to people who have lived in the UK for a long period.

The 'ten-year concession'

The Home Office has stated that if people remain in the UK legally (that is, with Home Office permission) for more than ten years they will normally be allowed to stay permanently. They will be granted indefinite leave to remain in the UK and thus become settled. Both the period and the legality of residence are interpreted strictly. Being in the UK with permission means precisely that; if a person was late in applying for permission, even if that permission was subsequently granted, the person was an overstayer for a period and therefore cannot fit into the ten-year concession. Time spent while waiting for an appeal against a Home Office refusal will only count towards the ten year period if the appeal was subsequently successful. If a person is waiting for an appeal at the end of the ten-year period, she or he will not be granted settlement then, but will have to wait for the outcome of the appeal and only if it is successful will settlement then be granted. Time spent exempt from immigration control, for example as a diplomat or other work for an embassy, does not count towards the ten-year period.

The people most commonly able to benefit from this policy are overseas students. However, as the immigration rules provide that students must intend to leave the UK at the end of their studies and as this 'concession' becomes more widely known, it is becoming more difficult for people who have been students for eight or nine years to obtain extensions of their stay. The Home Office is likely to ask ever more detailed questions about their plans and intentions after their studies and if they give any indication that they might want to apply to settle under this provision, they will be refused further student extensions.

The 'fourteen-year concession'

The Home Office has also stated that if people remain in the UK for over fourteen years, whether legally or illegally, this will also normally qualify them for settlement. Thus a student or any other person who has been in the UK for over ten years, but who has spent some time without permission, will have to wait until fourteen years have passed before it is likely that settlement will be granted.

Requesting return of passports

While the Home Office is considering an application for an extension of stay or variation of conditions, it is normal for it to keep the applicant's passport. The return of the passport can be requested at any time, if the holder needs it, for example as proof of identity for a bank or to show to a marriage registrar. However there may be dangers in requesting a passport *in order to travel*.

The Home Office has stated in correspondence with JCWI that it will grant three months leave to remain in some circumstances when a passport is requested in order to travel. This is when the application to the Home Office is for an extension in the same capacity as that previously granted, it appears that the person qualifies for the leave requested but the Home Office has not yet had time to look at the application. When the person returns, he or she is likely to be readmitted for a period of two months in order to make a further application to the Home Office.

Variation of Leave Order

However it is more common for a different procedure to be followed. Under the Immigration (Variation of Leave) Order 1976, amended in 1989, when people have made applications for extensions to the Home Office before their leave to remain expires, this leave is automatically extended for the period the Home Office is considering the application. This leave to remain expires either 28 days after the date the Home Office decides the application or the date the application is withdrawn. The Home Office has stated that if people request their passports in order to travel this *automatically* withdraws the application for leave to remain longer.

In these circumstances, the Home Office will return the passport as requested but without any further endorsement. If the previous leave has not yet expired, it is still valid. If the previous leave to remain has already expired, the Home Office will send a letter stating that the person must leave the UK within 28 days as the application for leave to remain has been withdrawn. This is a grace period within which the Home Office will not take any further steps to force the person to leave. If the person's plans change and he or she does not travel but instead returns the passport to the Home Office to continue to apply to remain, the Home Office treats this as a new application, made on this date. Thus if the person's previous leave to remain had expired, this will be treated as a late application and there will be no right of appeal if it is refused. The person will also become an overstayer after the 28-day period is up, and therefore liable to arrest and deportation.

It is therefore very important that people who want their passports for any purpose other than travel should make this clear in their request to the Home Office. *An application is only withdrawn if the request for the passport is for the purpose of travel; it remains pending if the passport is taken away from the Home Office for any other purpose.*

Travelling before an application is decided

It is risky for people to travel and to expect to be able to return when the Home Office has not yet decided an application. They will be able to leave the UK without difficulty but when they return they will have to satisfy the immigration officers that they fit into the immigration rules. Their passports will show the previous leave to enter or remain, and the triangular stamp showing the date of departure from the UK. If there is a period of time between these two dates, immigration officers will ask why and will then contact the Home Office to check the position.

If the application to the Home Office was straightforward, and if people can satisfy the immigration officers that they qualify to enter, they may be granted leave to enter for the period they request. If the application appears more complicated but it seems likely that it would be granted, people may be admitted for two months and told to apply again to the Home Office within this time. If the application was for a change of status, especially if this was one for which entry clearance is necessary, people may be refused entry. For example, an overseas student who marries a British citizen in the UK, applies to remain as her husband but travels before the application has been decided, will not qualify to re-enter. He does not qualify as a student, because he no longer intends to leave the UK when his studies are completed; he does not qualify as a husband because he does not have entry clearance for that purpose.

People who need to travel while the Home Office is considering an application sometimes believe it would be easier to obtain emergency travel documents from their own embassies or high commissions and travel on these while the Home Office continues to consider the application. This is not a safe procedure. It is unusual for a travel document to be issued in these circumstances, but if one is, it does not alter the holders' immigration status – that an application for further leave to remain had been made, but not decided, when they left. When they return, immigration officers will see a departure stamp on the travel document but no other evidence of the person's status in the UK. They will certainly need to know what that was; when they know that an application was pending they will contact the Home Office about the reasons for the application and what is happening about it. It is not safe to expect leave to enter to be granted.

12 Problems and emergencies

Many people find giving immigration advice very frightening, because of the possible consequences of making a mistake, especially in situations which require urgent action. However, it is not as complicated or difficult as it sometimes seems. It is largely a question of keeping within deadlines, knowing who to contact and being prepared to be persistent. This chapter discusses the main immigration problems in which urgent, or time-limited, action may need to be taken.

Refusal of entry clearance overseas

A relative or friend may seek advice on behalf of someone who has been refused a visa or entry clearance overseas. ▶See chapter 11 for more details about applying for entry clearance.

1 Find out what the person was applying for (e.g. visit, family settlement).

2 After being refused, the person abroad should have been given a written notice of refusal and an appeal form.

3 Ask whether the person in the UK has copies of these documents. If not, ask him or her to get copies and return with them.

4 If the person abroad has *not* been given a notice of refusal and appeal forms, then he or she has not legally been refused. Unless the person wants to withdraw the application, he or she should go back to the British embassy or high commission and insist that the application be either granted or formally refused.

5 The notice of refusal will state (very briefly) why the person has been refused (but this may be too vague or subjective to be very helpful).

6 The appeal forms must be filled in and returned within three months of the date of refusal. ▶See chapter 16 for how to fill in appeal forms. The 'representative in the UK' can be a friend or relative in the UK, or an adviser, and arrangements for someone to act as representative at the appeal itself can be made later.

7 Full details of the reasons for refusal (and possibly a record of the interview at the British embassy or high commission) will be sent to the appellant's representative after a few months. At this stage, if the person has not already arranged for someone to represent at appeal, this should be done.

Problems on arrival in the UK

One of the most common emergencies is to be contacted on behalf of someone who has been refused entry on arrival. This situation most commonly arises when people coming for a temporary purpose, such as visitors or students, are unable to satisfy immigration officers that they intend to leave at the end of their stay. Advising them will almost certainly mean negotiating with immigration officers at the port or airport where the person arrived.

It is important not to be intimidated by immigration officers. They are ordinary people who are not omnipotent; a chief immigration officer may sound important but he or she is only the second tier of official with a barrage of inspectors and chief inspectors above. Be firm with immigration officers and assume that negotiation is possible. If they do not alter their decision, ask to speak to a chief immigration officer and then an inspector to continue the negotiations.

1 **As soon as possible try to find out the following details about the passenger:**

- name (preferably as on his or her passport)
- nationality
- date of birth
- port of entry (including which terminal at Heathrow or Gatwick) and approximate time of arrival
- purpose of travel
- port reference number (if possible; this will be on any papers that he or she has been given by immigration officers)
- from which country and port or airport the passenger travelled (with flight details)
- does the passenger have entry clearance?
- what did the passenger say to the immigration officers?
- what evidence to support his or her statements was shown to them?
- what information have the immigration officers given about why they are not satisfied and what they are doing next?
- has the passenger been in the UK, or attempted to come to the UK, before? (with full details)
- what is the passenger's marital status?
- if married, what is the nationality, whereabouts and intentions of spouse and children?
- what does the passenger want to do now?

2 **Find out whether the person has been refused entry,** or whether he or she is still being questioned before a decision has been made.

If the person is still at the airport or port, this can be found out by contacting the immigration service there. The immigration officer will need to know from where and when the passenger arrived, his or her name and nationality, and if possible date of birth.

If the person has been released from the port or airport, look at the documentation he or she has been given. If the reference number includes /RLE/ the person has been refused entry; if not, there has still been no final decision.

3 **If the person has not yet been refused entry,** it is much easier to try to convince the immigration officers to allow him or her in. Get as much information as possible from immigration officers about why they are suspicious and check this with the person him or herself or with the friends or relatives in the UK. If there are any obvious misunderstandings or errors which can be corrected, the immigration officers may be satisfied and may grant the passenger entry.

4 **If the person is refused entry,** and if he or she had obtained a visa or an entry clearance before travelling, there is a right of appeal against refusal and the passenger can remain in the UK until the appeal has been decided. This means that, whatever the final decision, he or she will be able to stay for some time. Forms for appeal will be handed to the passenger at the same time as the refusal notice. They must be filled in and returned to the port or airport where the refusal took place within 28 days of the date of refusal. ▶See chapter 16 for more details about filling in appeal forms.

5 **If the person did not have a visa or entry clearance before travelling,** he or she has a right of appeal against refusal, but only after being removed from the UK. The passenger will be issued with a refusal notice and either given temporary admission until a fixed date (which can often be very soon) or detained at an airport detention centre until removal.

6 **If there is no right of appeal before removal,** the remedies available to refused passengers are very limited, but should nevertheless be tried.

i) Contact the immigration officers at the port or airport. Try to convince them that they have made a mistake. They are unlikely to change the decision, but it may be possible to negotiate an extension of temporary admission, if this has been granted, so that the person is able to stay for at least a week. If the person is detained, try to negotiate temporary admission. The person will need an address and sponsor. Immigration officers will need to be convinced that he or she will return when required to leave the country. Detention has to be authorised by a chief immigration officer, so insist on speaking to him or her and if necessary go higher (to the inspector in charge of the port or airport terminal).

ii) See whether there are any grounds for involving an MP. MPs used to be able to intervene very effectively in port refusal cases and removal was always deferred while their representations were being considered. Since

January 1989 this is no longer done. The Home Office will only defer removal if the MP is able to bring forward exceptional compassionate circumstances which the immigration officer knew about but did not properly take into account. If such circumstances have been put to an immigration officer and have not been properly considered, it may be worth involving an MP. Use the constituency MP of one of the friends or relatives the person is coming to be with. However, some MPs refuse to take on such cases at all now, or need a great deal of persuading to do so. MPs can be contacted at the House of Commons (071 219 3000) which may also be able to give the number of the MP's secretary or constituency office.

iii) See whether there are any grounds for asking the courts for leave to apply for judicial review of the refusal. However, judicial review is rarely granted in port refusal cases, as the courts have held that there is an appeal right (though only after removal) and therefore that judicial review is inappropriate. If it is a really strong or compassionate case, the passenger may wish to take legal advice about judicial review, but it is of little use in most refused visitors' cases.

7 **If the person is eventually removed,** make sure that he or she fills in and returns the appeal forms provided. The appeal must be received within 28 days of the date of removal. This is important, even if the person's visit has been ruined and he or she does not plan to try again immediately. If the refusal is not challenged, it will form part of the person's immigration record. Refusals are marked on the passport (in the form of a cross through the square entry stamp, ▶see chapter 13 for example). This will mean that the passenger will have problems whenever he or she tries to enter the UK again, and may also have problems entering other countries.

Late applications to the Home Office

Often people come for advice about extending their stay either just before their existing leave to remain runs out, or after it has done so.

1 **If the person's leave is about to expire,** it is vital that he or she should apply for an extension **before** the existing leave runs out. An application should be posted (recorded delivery), faxed or taken to the Home Office immediately. It does not matter if all the information and evidence needed are not available, or even if the person does not have his or her passport; any other evidence to support the application can be sent on later.

2 **If the person's leave expired recently,** the Home Office will probably consider the application as though the relevant immigration rules applied (check the relevant chapter for a description of the rules and how they are interpreted). If the application is straightforward (for example, a student who is in the middle of a recognised course, has paid the fees and has adequate support), the person can make the application him or herself, explaining and apologising for the lateness. The person becomes an overstayer the day after leave runs out. Any application to extend stay is

completely discretionary, outside the immigration rules, and there is no right of appeal against a refusal. But if there may be problems fulfilling the other requirements of the rules, the person should seek further advice.

3 **If the person's leave expired some time ago,** there may be difficulties with the application. The Home Office may begin deportation action as soon as it is contacted; or indeed may already have done so without the person knowing about it. Before advising the person to contact the Home Office, check:

i) whether he or she has been in the UK continuously for seven years or more. If so, there is a full right of appeal before deportation and the Home Office is likely to give the case more serious consideration.

ii) whether there are strong reasons for the person to stay (for example, marriage to a British or settled person, strong compassionate reasons).

iii) whether the person has received any threats of deportation from the Home Office.

If people decide to make an application to the Home Office it should be through an adviser, partly so that the Home Office does not need to know the address and partly so that it knows that they will be properly represented if deportation action is threatened. ▶See chapter 14 for more information about the process of deportation and the ways to challenge it.

Arrest and threatened deportation or removal

Advisers are often contacted on behalf of people who are being held by police or immigration officers, on the grounds that they are illegally in the UK, and threatened with deportation or removal.

As soon as possible, find out the following information:

- the detainee's name, date of birth and nationality
- the Home Office or immigration service reference number
- where the person is detained
- under what authority the person is detained – for example, as an alleged illegal entrant or because a deportation decision has been made
- are there any plans to send the person away, and if so, when
- has the person been given any papers and if so, what
- what the detainee wants – for example, to contest the situation in every possible way, to return to the country of origin as quickly as possible, to be released for a short period to make arrangements to leave

Speak to the officer dealing with the case, at the Home Office or the immigration service office, to register interest in the case and ensure that you will be informed of any decision or action that is taken.

1 **Find out whether the person has been charged** with any criminal, or

immigration, offence. If no charge has been brought, try to ensure that the person does not say anything, and certainly does not sign anything, until a solicitor or adviser can be present. The police may call on a duty solicitor, but some do not know very much about immigration law.

2 If the person has not been charged, find out whether he or she is being treated as an illegal entrant, or is threatened with deportation:

- alleged illegal entrants will have been given a form called IS 151A. They may have signed a 'confession' while in custody, possibly without understanding what this meant, and the decision on their status may be based on this. Alleged illegal entrants will need legal advice if they wish to challenge this decision; ▶see chapter 14 for more details about illegal entry.

- people threatened with deportation will have been given a form called APP 104. This is a 'notice of intention to deport'; ▶see chapter 14 on the deportation process and possible action.

3 **Try to negotiate temporary release,** or bail if the person is appealing against a decision to deport. The factors which the immigration service will consider include:

- does the person have a stable home? For example, how long has he or she lived at that address, is this with family or close friends with whom he or she would want to keep in touch?

- is the person in employment, and for how long?

- has the person abided by any immigration or bail conditions in the past?

- what incentive does the person have to keep in contact with the immigration service?

- how strong is the person's case?

It is less likely that a woman or child will be detained, but probable that a young man without close family ties, who has not lived at the same address for long and who does not have a strong immigration case, will be.

If the person is not released, *visit* as soon as possible, to find out exactly what he or she wants to do and to advise on whether this is feasible.

If there are plans to remove the person very quickly, and he or she wants to contest removal, speak to the chief immigration officer or the Home Office official dealing with the case. If there is new information or arguments which have not been considered before, it is possible that the person's removal will be delayed while representations are considered.

If the person does not have a right of appeal against the immigration decision, representations from the MP for the area where he or she lives or works may delay removal. Under Home Office guidelines to MPs in force since January 1989, if the MP agrees to take up the case, he or she should contact the officer dealing with it to say so, and to give an outline of the 'new and compelling evidence' which will be put forward. The MP then has eight working days in which to submit written representations. If nothing is received by that time, arrangements for the person's removal will proceed.

If the MP makes initial telephone representations and thereby secures a delay in the person's removal, the adviser should write to the MP with full details as soon as possible. The MP will probably pass the adviser's letter on to the Home Office, with a covering letter, so the adviser should state all the relevant facts and arguments in the letter to the MP. If the person is detained, arguments for his or her release should be repeated, as the intervention of the MP may add further delays to the consideration of the case.

Judicial review

When all attempts to make the Home Office reconsider a case have failed, it may be possible for the person to apply to the courts for a judicial review of the Home Office decision. Courts will only grant leave to appeal if they believe that the Home Office was wrong in law, or that there were serious procedural defects in its practice. If the person wants to attempt judicial review, it is important that he or she is referred quickly to a solicitor who is experienced and knowledgeable in immigration law and who will advise honestly about the chances of success. Legal aid is available for court cases on immigration on the same basis as for any other legal matter – when the person meets the financial criteria and the Legal Aid Board is satisfied that there is an arguable case.

13 Passport stamps and codes

This chapter gives examples of common passport stamps and codes used by the immigration authorities. It is intended for reference, to help advisers identify endorsements and make deductions from them and to familiarise people with Home Office practices.

Interpreting passports

The stamps which the Home Office and the immigration service put on people's passports or travel documents have specific meanings. The Home Office and the immigration service also have private codes which they use as well as the official stamps, so that an immigration official, whether from the UK or another country, often has more information than is known to the holder of the passport. It can be important for people to know what these codes mean as the endorsements on their passport may seriously affect their chances of being allowed into the UK again or of being granted an extension of stay, even when there is no apparent reason why they should face difficulties.

Entry clearance

British embassies and high commissions endorse passports when they deal with entry clearance applications from people wanting to come to the UK. When an entry clearance application is made, the entry clearance officer will want to see the passport and at that time it is likely that 'entry clearance applied for' and the date will be written on the first blank page of the passport.

An entry clearance passport endorsement is called either a visa or an entry certificate. It may be a certificate stuck into a passport and then embossed with the post's official stamp, or an inked stamp placed directly in a passport, or it may be a separate official 'letter of consent' from the post.

The entry clearance will include written information to show why it was granted, for example 'settlement to join mother' or 'visit'. It will also state 'valid for presentation at a UK port within six months of issue'. This means that the entry clearance is valid for six months from its date of issue and people should use it to travel within that time. If they are unable to travel during that time, they must apply to the British embassy or high commission to extend the validity of the entry clearance.

Entry clearances state whether they are valid for a single entry or multiple entries. A single-entry entry clearance may be used for only one journey to the UK; it is not valid for any subsequent re-entry. If the person is a visa national and wishes to travel out of the UK and to re-enter, a new visa is necessary.

A Entry clearance sticker

B Certificate of entitlement to the right of abode

Certificates of entitlement to the right of abode

People who have the right of abode (▶see glossary for definition) but who are not travelling on British passports need to get this right confirmed by the British embassy or high commission before travelling. They will be given a certificate of entitlement to the right of abode, which is a sticker like the entry certificate sticker. Before 1983, this was called a certificate of patriality, which means precisely the same thing. If people apply to the Home Office for confirmation of their right of abode, the Home Office can also give the certificate of entitlement.

Passport stamps at ports of entry

When a person subject to immigration control arrives at the borders of the UK and is admitted, the passport will be stamped with a square date stamp. This will have the date on which the person arrived, the name of the port, and the number (in brackets) of the individual immigration officer who dealt with the application. Any time limit stamped on the passport runs from the date of this square stamp, *not* from any date from which entry clearance was granted abroad.

C arrival
stamp

Immigration officers may also impose conditions either prohibiting or restricting work or business. They may also require the person to register with the police. If there is only a time limit on the person's stay, that means that there are *no* restrictions on what that person may do while in the UK for that time. If there is no time limit on a person's stay the person has indefinite leave to remain (settlement) and there can be no other conditions either.

Visitors

It is usual for visitors to be admitted for six months, even if they only intend to stay for a shorter period. Most people admitted as visitors will have stamp **D** and the date stamp.

If the immigration officer was not totally satisfied but did not have enough evidence on which to base a refusal, there will be a more detailed stamp **E**

| LEAVE TO ENTER FOR SIX MONTHS | **D** |
| EMPLOYMENT PROHIBITED | |

E

Leave to enter the United Kingdom on condition that the holder does not enter employment paid or unpaid and does not engage in any business or profession is hereby given for/until

SIX MONTHS

AB 1 2 3 456

and a computer reference number. If the suspicions are particularly strong the time may be written as 'SIX (6) MONTHS', which will alert any immigration official dealing with that person in the future to ask more questions than she or he otherwise might to try to elicit evidence for a refusal. It does not appear to the person concerned that there is anything unusual.

When a visitor is merely transiting through the UK, he or she will usually be given a shorter period. When a person has requested a very short period as a visitor, occasionally the precise period may be given. Immigration officers may also give a shorter period than six months if they feel there is a particular reason for doing so, for example a person coming for a particular short course of medical treatment. Any shorter period will also alert another immigration official to something unusual about the applicant.

Students

The most common stamp on a student's passport is **F**. This stamp is known as a 'restriction on working'. Although this long rubber stamp is often fairly illegible, its conditions are still valid even if not known by the person. It

F
Leave to enter the United Kingdom on condition that the holder does not enter or change employment paid or unpaid without the consent of the Secretary of State for Employment and does not engage in any business or profession without the consent of the Secretary of State for the Home Department is hereby given for/until

TWELVE MONTHS

means that if the student wants to work in the weekends or evenings, the prospective employer must apply for a work permit to the Employment Department (▶see chapter 9) for the work to be legal. If the student wants to be self-employed, for example giving private coaching, she or he must approach the Home Office to request permission to do this.

Some students will have the same stamp as a

visitor (▶see stamp **E**) with the time in handwriting, for example 'TWELVE MONTHS'. This stamp is known as a 'prohibition on working'. If more than six months has been given initially, the person must have come in as a student, because a visitor will never be given more than six months. Some scholarship agencies discourage their students from working. If a student has been admitted for less than six months for a very short course, or as a prospective student, he or she may be prohibited from working.

It is possible for the student to try to alter this by applying to the Home Office to request that the stamp be changed to a restriction on working. It is important not to give the Home Office the impression that the student needs to work for financial reasons; ▶see details of the support and accommodation requirements in chapter 9.

Students' wives may be allowed to live in the UK with them while they are studying. If the student is prohibited from working, his wife will be also and will have the same time limit as her husband.

If the student has a restriction on working, his wife's passport will be stamped as **G**, for the same length of time as the husband.

G Leave to enter the United Kingdom is hereby given for/until

T̲W̲E̲L̲V̲E̲ ̲M̲O̲N̲T̲H̲S̲

This means that the wife is free to work; there are no restrictions on what she can do in the UK during the time she has been admitted. She does not need to get permission from the Home Office or any separate work permit and she will be given a national insurance number on request.

Students' husbands have no claim to be with them in the UK under the immigration rules. If the Home Office decides to make an exception and to allow a husband to be here while his wife studies he will be allowed to stay for the same length of time as his wife but will be prohibited from working.

Workers and business people

People admitted with work permits or for permit-free employment or as business people or self-employed will have a stamp restricting employment (▶see stamp **F**), with 'TWELVE MONTHS' or 'FOUR YEARS' in handwriting.

The spouses of work permit holders and business people will have no restrictions on working, merely the same time limit as their spouse. This means that spouses are free to work; there are no restrictions on what they can do in the UK during the time they have been admitted. They do not need to get permission from the Home Office or any separate work permit and they will be given national insurance numbers on request.

People admitted as persons of independent means, and their spouses and children, will have a prohibition on working (▶see stamp **E**) with the time, usually 'FOUR YEARS', in handwriting.

Refugees and those granted exceptional leave to remain

Refugees' passports are not stamped, because they cannot use them without forfeiting their refugee status. They will be given a letter from the Home Office which explains their position as refugees and some of their rights in the UK and which states that they have been given leave to remain until a certain date. They may be given refugee travel documents, issued by the Home Office under the United Nations Convention relating to the Status of Refugees and their leave to remain will be stamped on them. The travel documents are valid for all countries except the refugee's country of origin.

People granted exceptional leave to remain may use their national passports and will have leave to enter or remain stamped on them. If they cannot obtain passports, they may be given Home Office brown travel documents, but this is always discretionary. These will be endorsed with leave to remain without restrictions on employment or occupation (▶see stamp **G**). Leave is usually given for one year initially, then for two periods of three years and then settlement may be granted.

Registration with the police

After the time limit and conditions, some people will have an extra passport stamp **H**.

H The holder is also required to register at once with the police. This is a requirement which may be imposed on people who are not Commonwealth or EC citizens, who are over 16 and who have been allowed to enter the UK for more than six months or who have come in to work for more than three months. It is normally imposed on students and workers of the relevant nationalities, and on refugees and people granted exceptional leave to remain, but not normally on people given leave to enter or remain as spouses. If the requirement to register with the police has not been stamped on people's passports, even in situations where it could have been, they do not have to do so. When the requirement is imposed, it should be taken seriously.

'At once' means within seven days. The person should go to the Aliens Registration Office, 10 Lambs Conduit Street, London WC1 3MX if he or she lives in the London Metropolitan Police area, or to the central police station of the town if living outside London. The police need the person's passport, two photographs of the person and the fee (▶see appendix). The police record the person's full name, date of birth, address, marital status, occupation in the UK and immigration conditions in the UK and note all this in a green police registration certificate. A person required to register with the police must inform them of any change in any of these particulars within two months of the change occurring. When people are allowed to settle, they no longer have to register with the police and this is endorsed on their passports.

Family members

Most family members coming for settlement will be admitted for a year initially. Their passports will be stamped with leave to enter the UK for this period and with no other conditions (▶see stamp **G**). They are free to work or to study or to do anything else they wish during that time.

Re-entering the UK

Section 3(3)(b)

People who have been granted more than six months' permission to enter or remain in the UK and who travel out of and into the UK within the period of time that they have been given may expect to be allowed in again for what is left of that time, on the same conditions. This will happen provided the immigration officers are satisfied that their circumstances have not changed to make them no longer qualify for leave to enter in that capacity. When they return, their passports are usually stamped as **I** and the same date as when their previous leave would have expired is in handwriting.

I Given leave to enter
to **[date]**
Section 3(3)(b)

3(3)(b) is the section of the Immigration Act 1971 which provides for readmission in these circumstances. It has applied automatically to people granted leave for more than six months since 16 May 1991.

Re-entry visas and visa exemption

Also from 16 May 1991, all visa nationals allowed to remain for more than six months are exempt from requiring visas if returning to the UK within the time of their previous leave. The issuing of re-entry visas has been discontinued. Visas can only be obtained from British posts outside the UK.

Visa national visitors still need a visa each time they enter (as they have leave only for six months). They should therefore apply for multiple-entry visas before coming to the UK if they are considering visiting other countries and then returning to the UK. If they do not do so, and travel and intend to return to the UK within the period of their visit they will have to obtain new visas from the British post in the country which they have visited.

Before 16 May 1991, most visa nationals needed visas for any entry to the UK. There was an exception for citizens of India, Bangladesh, Pakistan, Sri Lanka, Ghana, Nigeria, Uganda, Turkey, Algeria, Morocco and Tunisia given long-term leave to remain if they were planning to travel and return within the previous period of stay. If they wished to be sure that they would not be questioned about visas on their return, they could ask either the Home Office or the immigration officer they saw as they left the UK to endorse their passports as **J** overleaf.

| J | The holder is exempt from requiring a visa when returning to the United Kingdom within the period limited as above |

This was then evidence for airline staff, or any other officials who needed to know, that the person did not need a visa to travel back to the UK. All other visa nationals needed either to obtain re-entry visas in the UK before they travelled or to apply to the British post in the country to which they had gone for a visa to return.

Leave to remain

When the Home Office has any dealings with a person, the person is given a Home Office reference. This is a unique personal reference; it is normally the first letter of the person's surname followed by five or six numbers. If a woman marries, the Home Office changes her reference to that of her husband, if he already has a Home Office file, or gives her a new reference, from the first letter of his surname. For Arabic names, the Home Office uses the first letter of the first name. The reference should always be used in any correspondence and will help the Home Office to find any file. If the Home Office has ever held the person's passport, it writes the reference number on the inside of the back cover of the passport.

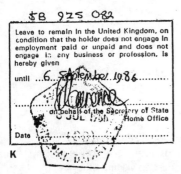

When the Home Office grants permission to stay, this is known as 'leave to remain', as the person has already entered the country. The Home Office uses larger stamps, with oblong borders, using broadly the same wording as immigration officers' stamps apart from the wording 'leave to remain' rather than 'leave to enter', as **K**

It is signed by the official who has granted the leave, then stamped 'on behalf of the Secretary of State, Home Office'. The Home Office date stamp is pentagonal, stating 'Home Office Immig & Nat Department', the date, and the number of the official in brackets.

Home Office-granted leave to remain may also have a requirement to register with the police.

Settled status

There are several different stamps a person who is *settled* in the UK may have on his or her passport. When a person has been granted entry clearance for settlement and arrives at a UK air- or sea port, the stamp put on the passport will state

| L | Given leave to enter the United Kingdom for an indefinite period |

If people have already been granted settlement but have travelled and returned after a holiday, it is not necessary to repeat the stamp to enter indefinitely again. They will usually just be given the square date stamp, (▶see stamp **C**) showing when and where they returned. This means exactly the same thing; the person has been admitted with no time limit and no conditions on his or her stay.

When a person is travelling for the first time on a new passport, it is sensible to carry the old passport as well, so that the immigration officer can immediately see what the person's status is. When a person enters the country for the first time on a new passport, it is usual for the 'Given leave to enter the United Kingdom for an indefinite period' stamp to be given again, so that the person's status will be clear to other immigration officers in the future. When this has been done, there is no need to continue to carry the old passport as well as the new one when travelling, though it should still be kept, if possible, in case the evidence is ever required.

M

imd	27B

Given leave to remain in the UK
for an indefinite period

[signature]

On behalf of the Secretary of State
Home Office

Dated 17 JUN 1991

(421)

When the Home Office grants settlement, it uses a stamp as **M** showing that there are no time limit and conditions on the person's stay.

When settlement has been granted, but the passport on which it was endorsed has run out, and the person obtains a new passport, this may be endorsed by the Home Office. Because the leave has already been granted, this will not be stamped again. The endorsement the Home Office then gives is either

N

There is at present no time limit on the holder's permitted stay in the United Kingdom	or	Holder's stay in the UK is no longer subject to a time limit

These mean exactly the same as indefinite leave. Many people are worried by the 'at present' phrase. It does not mean anything more temporary, or that the Home Office could impose a time limit in the future. The Home Office uses this form of wording because retaining settlement is conditional on the person not being out of the UK for a period of more than two years and qualifying to enter under the returning resident rules (▶see page 154).

Visa nationals who are settled do not require visas to return for settlement within two years. If they have been away longer, it might be wise to apply for returning resident visas; ▶see page 155 for further details.

Leaving the UK

When people leave the UK, their passports are stamped with a triangular stamp, showing the date and port of exit and the number of the immigration officer as **O** overleaf.

If there is a period of time between the expiry of the last leave to enter or remain granted and the date of departure, it will be clear that something unusual has happened. If the person tries to return in the future, the immigration officers may ask questions to find out the reason for this. It may be because an application for an extension had been made to the Home Office, but not decided when the person left, or an application had been refused and the person had appealed, or that the person has overstayed leave to remain. This will not affect the person when he or she leaves, as the passport is just stamped with the date of departure. However, the immigration officers will normally send a report to the Home Office of the person's departure, so that there will be a record should he or she attempt to enter again.

If the person is being deported or has been forced to leave under the supervised departure provisions (▶see chapter 14) the date will be underlined to show that the person left with some immigration problems.

If the immigration officers believe that the passport may be forged or there is some doubt about the person's immigration status, they will underline the immigration officer's number on the stamp. This will alert immigration officers in future should the person attempt to re-enter the UK.

Refusals and problems

When people apply for entry clearance abroad, the entry clearance officers write 'entry clearance applied for', followed by the place and date, on the first blank page of the passport. If the application is refused, they underline these words.

P

When people are refused entry to the UK, their passports are still stamped with the square date stamp but an ink cross is put through this to show the refusal of leave to enter.

When the Home Office refuses further leave to remain, it underlines the date to which the previous leave had been granted. This may not be noticed by the person but shows any other immigration official that there has been a refusal.

Leave to remain in the United Kingdom, on condition that the holder does not enter or change employment paid or unpaid without the consent of the Secretary of State for Employment and does not engage in any business or profession without the consent of the Secretary of State for the Home Department is hereby given

until 31St DECEMBER 1989 EMB

Q

If the passport is a new one, with no leave to enter or remain stamped in it, the Home Office underlines the person's Home Office reference number, written on the inside back cover of the passport.

The Home Office may also write 'EMB' by the side of the last leave to enter or remain granted, or on the inside back cover of the passport if there are no other British stamps on the passport. This means that when the person leaves, immigration officers are required to write a report to the Home Office to confirm the person's embarkation.

British passports

Since 1983, British passports have had the nationality status of their holders printed at the bottom of the first page. This may state: British citizen, British Dependent Territories citizen, British Overseas citizen, British subject, British Protected Person or British National (Overseas). British citizens automatically have the right of abode and are not subject to British immigration control. All other British nationals are subject to immigration control and therefore their passports have immigration stamps on them showing any time limit and conditions on their stay.

People who are settled in the UK will be given an indefinite leave stamp. They may also have a stamp on page 5 of their passports

R Holder has the right of readmission to the UK

which means that they are settled and can return after *any* length of absence. The normal two-year restriction on returning residents does not apply to British passport holders.

British passports issued before 1983 will state that their holders are: British subjects, citizens of the UK and Colonies; or British Protected Persons; or British subjects without citizenship. Page 5 of the passport may be printed

S Holder has the right of abode in the UK

which means that the person is a British citizen under the British Nationality Act 1981.

This printed phrase may have been crossed out, and page 5 of the passport may be stamped with stamp **R**, confirming that the person is settled in the UK and can return after any length of absence.

Alternatively, page 5 may be stamped

T Holder is subject to control under the Immigration Act 1971

which means that the person is not settled in the UK. The passport will have other immigration stamps giving limited leave to remain.

Special quota vouchers for settlement are stickers, like entry certificates, but have QV and a reference number written on them. The person should have been granted settlement on arrival (▶see stamp **L**).

14 Deportation, illegal entry and removal

Immigration control is enforced by both criminal and administrative sanctions. People who fall foul of immigration law may be dealt with:

- either through Home Office administrative powers, which are extensive, and which culminate in deportation or removal
- or through the criminal law and the courts.

Deportation means sending people away from the UK under an order signed by the Home Secretary and prohibiting their re-entry. The person will normally have entered the UK legally and been granted leave to remain; but then broken a condition of stay, for example by overstaying leave to remain or working without permission. If a person is convicted of a serious non-immigration criminal offence, deportation may be recommended by the courts, or may be carried out entirely through the Home Office's administrative powers. The person cannot return to the UK unless the deportation order has first been revoked.

Illegal entry means entering the UK without gaining permission from an immigration officer (and therefore in breach of the immigration laws, which require all people who do not have the right of abode in the UK to have such permission). People may be treated as illegal entrants if they bypass immigration control altogether, or enter in breach of a deportation order or deceive an immigration officer about their identity or their reasons for coming to the UK. Entry by deception is an area of illegal entry which has been expanded greatly by immigration officers extending the definition of 'deception'. The word used for the process of making an illegal entrant leave the UK is **removal**, not deportation.

Deportation – through the courts

Criminal offences under immigration law

When a time limit is placed on a person's stay in the UK it is an offence under section 24(1)(b)(i) of the Immigration Act 1971 for the person to remain beyond the time limit given. It is an offence under section 24(1)(b)(ii) to fail to observe a condition attached to leave to remain, for example working when forbidden to do so. These offences are popularly known as overstaying and as being in breach of conditions. They are the most common immigration offences; prosecutions for other offences, such as assisting illegal entry, or harbouring, are rare.

Overstaying

People are overstayers if they remain in the UK without permission after their immigration leave has run out. This includes people who applied to the Home Office after their permission to remain had run out, even if the application was only one day late and even though the Home Office is considering their application.

People who applied for extensions before any previous leave ran out and who are still waiting for a reply from the Home Office are *not* overstayers while the application is pending. Neither are people who are appealing against a Home Office refusal, even if their leave has expired.

Breach of conditions

The most common condition, as well as a time limit, to be put on a person's stay is a prohibition or a restriction on working. It is then illegal for the person to do any kind of work, paid or unpaid, even helping out at a friend's shop or business for a couple of hours, without the employer obtaining permission in advance from the Employment Department. Overseas students in particular often believe, erroneously, that they are permitted to work during their holidays, or for a specific number of hours a week, without seeking permission but this is not the case (▶see chapter 9 for details of how students may obtain permission to work). As the Home Office can take deportation action against a person found to be working without permission, it is important that students should not work without permission and without realising the seriousness of the possible consequences.

Criminal convictions for non-immigration matters

Some people may be recommended for deportation, as part of the sentence, if they are convicted of a non-immigration criminal offence. Anybody who is not:

- a British citizen

- a Commonwealth citizen with the right of abode (▶see glossary)

- a Commonwealth citizen who was settled in the UK on 1 January 1973 and who has lived in the UK for at least five years since then

can be recommended for deportation if convicted of a criminal offence for which he or she could be sentenced to imprisonment. This includes people who are settled in the UK and are convicted of a non-immigration offence. In order to be recommended for deportation it is not necessary for people to receive a custodial sentence. It is enough that they are convicted of an offence for which imprisonment is a possible sentence.

The court process

A police officer may arrest without warrant anyone he or she suspects to have committed an immigration offence and the person may be charged to appear before a magistrates' court. It is important that the person should have legal representation and that the solicitor should understand immigration law and the possible immigration consequences of conviction.

Overstaying is a continuing offence; people can be arrested for overstaying at any time after their leave has run out. People can only be convicted of the offence once during any one period of overstaying; if, after a conviction, the person still remains in the UK without permission, any further action would be under the Home Office's administrative powers.

If people who are liable to deportation are charged with an offence for which they could be imprisoned, they must be informed of their liability to deportation and be given a standard information sheet by the court explaining this. This sheet is written in legal language and may be frightening. It does not mean that people are to be deported, but that if they are convicted a recommendation for deportation is possible as part of any sentence. The case must be remanded for at least a week to enable them to seek advice and, if they allege they are not liable to deportation, to obtain evidence of this fact. The threat of deportation is particularly worrying to people settled or with close family in the UK. It is important that the solicitor representing in the criminal matter also knows about immigration law and the importance of arguing against a recommendation for deportation and appealing against any recommendation that is made.

People convicted of immigration offences may be fined up to £2000, imprisoned for up to six months, and recommended for deportation.

Recommendations for deportation

The official handbook for magistrates, *The sentence of the court*, gives them guidance on making recommendations for deportation. The person or representative should be asked to address the court specifically on the question of a recommendation, and the court should also consider the effects of a recommendation on others, such as the person's family. The handbook states, 'Those who have committed serious offences or who have long records are suitable for recommendations, as are those who are convicted of immigration offences.' The court is reminded that people recommended will be detained unless the court directs release, and that 'detention in custody (as opposed to bail) pending criminal proceedings is not normally appropriate unless there is reason to suppose that the defendant would abscond or commit further offences.'

If people are recommended for deportation, the recommendation is part of the sentence and the only formal appeal against it is through the criminal appeals system against conviction or sentence. If no appeal is made, or if the appeal is unsuccessful, the Home Office then considers whether to carry out the recommendation.

It is important to remember that the courts cannot deport people; they only recommend to the Home Office that the person should be deported. The final decision rests with the Home Office, which has to consider any representations made as to why it should not carry out the court's recommendation. If representations are made to the Home Office, it is important to explain any special or compassionate circumstances, or why deportation should be delayed, for example to enable a person to complete a course of studies. However, in 1990 the Home Office decided not to deport only 19 court-recommended people and signed 564 such deportation orders. It is therefore probable that a recommendation will be carried out.

Deportation – Home Office administrative powers

The most common reason for deportation is that people have remained in the UK without permission. It is becoming more frequent for the Home Office to use its administrative powers to force people out of the UK, rather than using the court system. The Home Office can make an administrative decision to deport a person who it believes has breached the immigration laws or whose presence it believes is not conducive to the public good.

The deportation process

The Home Office may come to know of people in breach of the immigration laws in many ways. They may have been in contact with the Home Office themselves. For example, they may have applied for an extension which was refused, or lost an appeal, and remained in the UK after this. The Home Office will normally send a standard letter to the person after an appeal has been dismissed, stating that he or she has no further right to remain in the UK and should make arrangements to leave without delay (▶see appendix). This is *not* a formal deportation notice or order, though many people think it is. If the person does not leave, or make any new application for leave to remain, the next letter from the Home Office will probably be another standard letter, reminding the person of his or her liability to deportation, and asking for a reply within 28 days stating any compassionate or other reasons why deportation should not be carried out. The immigration rules state that 'full account is to be taken of all the relevant circumstances known to the Secretary of State' before a decision to deport is made. It is therefore very important, if the person does intend to contest deportation, that all possible information on his or her behalf is given to the Home Office at this stage.

If the person has not been in contact with the Home Office, but has simply stayed beyond the leave granted or worked without permission, he or she may be traced either by the police or the immigration service or by both acting together. The police increasingly ask for evidence of identification and immigration status from black or 'foreign-looking' people they stop for other reasons – on suspicion of a traffic offence, at a demonstration, as a witness to an accident or crime. People may call the police because of a burglary or an assault and then be asked to prove their status. The police may raid a house looking for someone else and then ask any other people at that address to prove their identity. If it is then established or suspected that the person may be in breach of the immigration laws, the police can check with the immigration service or with the police national computer (which contains the names of people against whom deportation orders have been signed) to confirm their suspicions. They may then hold the person pending immigration officers coming to interview him or her and to take further action. The police or immigration service may receive information, often through anonymous letters, which they follow up with a raid.

Decisions to deport

When people are traced, it is more usual for the Home Office to initiate its own **administrative action** to deport them, rather than the police charging them with an immigration offence. If the Home Office decides to go ahead with administrative deportation, this is a two-stage process. First a decision to deport is made, and secondly, after any appeals have been exhausted, the Home Secretary signs a deportation order.

When a formal decision to deport is made it must be given in writing to the person. The Home Office standard letter (▶see appendix) stating the decision and the reasons for it also gives an explanation of the person's right to appeal against the decision within 14 days of the date of the notice. The Home Office also sends appeal forms to fill in.

Until August 1988, it was accepted that decisions to deport had to be authorised by a senior official at the Home Office, acting on behalf of the Secretary of State. From 1 August 1988, the Home Office changed its practice and authorised immigration officers, of the rank of inspector, to make deportation decisions. This resulted in decisions to deport being made by an immigration officer interviewing a suspect and making a quick telephone call to an inspector, with a resumé of the case and a recommendation for deportation action. This was usually confirmed. This devolution of power to a quite different class of official was contested in the courts, but in October 1990 the House of Lords decided, in the case of *Oladehinde* and *Alexander* (Imm AR 1991 111), that it was lawful for immigration officers to take these decisions. However, the House of Lords suggested that the procedures were of great concern. The Home Office has agreed to ensure that there are written records of the decision-making process and that instances where there are any compassionate aspects or where the person has been in the UK for a long time must be referred to the Home Office for decision.

The immigration rules state that when the Home Office considers whether to deport people it must take into account 'every relevant factor known', including the person's

- age
- length of residence in the UK
- strength of connections with the UK
- personal history, including character, conduct and employment record
- domestic circumstances
- the nature of any offence of which the person was convicted
- previous criminal record
- compassionate circumstances
- any representations received on the person's behalf.

After the Home Office makes a decision to deport people, it can also decide to detain them pending deportation or any appeal. ▶See chapter 16 for more details of the appeal process. If no appeal is lodged within the 14 days, or if the appeal is dismissed, the Home Secretary can then proceed to the second stage and sign a deportation order against the person. It is also possible to make written representations to the Home Office again at this stage, if there is relevant information which has not yet been considered.

Before 1986, the Home Office had a practice of making decisions to deport or deportation orders, and 'serving them on the file' at the Home Office without the person concerned being aware of it. This may have happened because records of the person's arrival at the airport and admission had been sent to the Home Office but they had not been followed by records of the person's departure or by any application for further leave to remain. The Home Office then assumed that the person had remained without authority. It also happened when a person moved and the Home Office was unable to find the new address and assumed that the person was still in the UK. As there is only a right of appeal against a deportation decision within 14 days of the decision, people may lose their right to appeal. If a decision is served some time later, when the person is traced, he or she may apply for leave to appeal out of time but it will be a matter for the appellate authorities whether the appeal can still be heard. If a deportation order has been signed, there is no appeal against the decision to make it. The Home Office now normally waits until a person has been traced and dates decisions to deport when they are sent to the person.

Rights of appeal against decisions to deport

People who have been in the UK less than seven years

The Immigration Act 1988 removed full rights of appeal against deportation for people who have been in the UK for less than seven years at the time of the decision. Although they can still appeal, the appeal can only be won if the facts on which the Home Office based its decision to deport were not correct. The Home Office can make the decision on the grounds of a person's overstaying, or on breach of a condition against working. The only arguments that can be considered at the appeal are whether the person was an overstayer or not, or whether the person had been working or did not have any restrictions on doing so. No other arguments against deportation, such as information about ties with the UK, family, marriage or other compassionate circumstances can be put at the appeal.

The *only* exception to this is if a person claims to be a refugee; this claim can be argued at the appeal. However the Asylum Bill, published on 1 November 1991 but not in force at the time of writing, provides for a new process of appeal against refusals of asylum; ▶see chapter 5 on refugees for more details. In any other case, the appeal will automatically be dismissed if the Home Office had its facts right. It may still be worth lodging an appeal, for example to give the person more time to make preparations for leaving, or, if the person is detained, to make it possible to apply for bail (▶see chapter 15). It is important, however, that the person realises the reasons for lodging an appeal and that the appeal itself cannot succeed.

People who have been in the UK for more than seven years

When people have been in the UK continuously for more than seven years at the time the Home Office makes a decision to deport them, the appeal can consider all the factors of the person's situation. Arguments can be put forward to show why the Home Office should have exercised its discretion differently and should not have made the decision. Any family, compassionate or other reasons can be argued. Witnesses can be called to testify to the suffering that would be caused or the loss to the community that would be sustained by the person's deportation as well as details about the individual's life. There is thus a possibility of the appeal succeeding and the adjudicator reaching a different decision from the Home Office about whether a person should be deported. There are other details about the appeals process in chapter 16.

When a deportation order has been signed

If an appeal against a decision to deport has been lost, or if no appeal has been lodged within the 14-day period, the Home Office may proceed to sign a deportation order. After an order is signed, there is no further appeal against deportation; the person only has the right to appeal against destination. This is also the case if an order has been signed after a court recommendation.

The Home Office normally deports people to their country of nationality, or to the country which has given them a travel document, because they will be readmitted there. If people want to appeal against destination, this should be stated at the time of lodging the appeal. In order to succeed in this part of the appeal, the person has to have proof that another country will allow him or her to be deported there. It is rare for this to be granted unless a person has very strong ties with another country.

It is possible to urge the Home Office to revoke a deportation order while the person is in the UK, but the application is only likely to be considered if the deportation order was signed a long time ago, there have been changes in circumstances since the order was signed and the person has only recently been traced. All the changes in the person's circumstances or any compassionate or family reasons, unknown to the Home Office at the time the order was signed, should be put forward.

Alternatives to deportation

Leaving the country quickly

Where there is no legal case to argue and no strong compassionate circumstances to put forward, and particularly where the person is detained or threatened with detention, he or she may not wish to contest refusal but instead to leave the country as soon as possible. This may be arranged without going through the whole deportation process, if the person formally renounces rights to appeal against the deportation decision and confirms his or her willingness to leave the country. There are then two processes – 'voluntary' departure and supervised departure – for leaving more quickly.

'Voluntary' departure

'Voluntary' departure is when the person is able and willing to pay the fare to the country of origin, and does so, while the immigration service makes the travel arrangements. There will still be evidence that the person was in fact forced to leave, as immigration officers will endorse the person's passport 'served with form APP 104' (the notice of the Home Office's decision to deport him or her) but no formal prohibition can be placed on the person's return.

Supervised departure

Supervised departure is when the immigration service pays for the ticket of a person against whom a decision to deport has been made, but the person has shown that he or she is willing to leave and has signed a formal disclaimer of any appeal rights. Again, the person's passport will be endorsed 'served with form APP 104' to show that a deportation decision has been made. It may be just as quick as 'voluntary' departure, but there is the power for the Home Office to prohibit the person's re-entry. It is not clear how often this power is used. Until 1988, supervised departure could only be used for people recommended for deportation after a court conviction, and was supposed to be restricted to 'young and first offenders'; it was rare. Since 1988, it can be used for anyone threatened with deportation and has become more common. In 1987, 779 people were deported and 147 left under the supervised departure procedure; in 1990, 577 people were deported and 1202 left under supervised departure.

The process of deportation

If any appeals against deportation and destination are lost, or if no appeal is lodged, the Home Office can proceed to make a deportation order. This has to be signed by the Home Secretary, or by another Secretary of State from a different department on his behalf. The immigration service then has to make the practical travel arrangements, for which the Home Office will pay; there is no advantage to the deportee in paying his or her own fare. The immigration service will also make sure that the deportee has a valid passport or travel document.

People can be detained pending travel arrangements being made; the immigration service will usually hold their passports or travel documents and will give them to the captain of the plane to hold and to pass to the national authorities. The passport will be marked, by the date of the triangular departure stamp being underlined (▶see chapter 13, stamp **O**), so that it will be difficult for the person to use that passport in future travel to the UK. The Home Office has stated that passports may be returned to deportees on the plane if this is requested through their advisers in advance of travelling. This is important for citizens of countries which may impose further penalties on their nationals if deported, or when people have applied for asylum in the UK, so that their deportation will not immediately be clear to the authorities of the country to which they are returning. It is difficult to check whether this is in fact done.

When people have left the UK with deportation orders signed against them, they cannot return while the order is still current. If they do gain entry while there is still a valid deportation order against them, they have entered illegally and can be arrested and removed as illegal entrants (see below). The order must be revoked before they can apply to return.

Returning to the UK

Revocation of deportation orders

It is possible to apply at any time for a deportation order to be revoked. If the person is abroad, he or she may apply either by letter or in person to the British embassy or high commission in that country, or by letter to the Home Office. Anybody else may write on the person's behalf to the Home Office. The immigration rules state that an order will not normally be revoked until the person has been out of the UK for at least three years. If an application is made sooner, it should contain full details of the exceptional circumstances justifying revocation earlier than normal. Having a spouse and children settled in the UK, who have reasons for being unable to join the deportee abroad, for example, may be strong enough compassionate circumstances. When people were deported after criminal convictions, the order is unlikely to be revoked before the conviction has become spent under the Rehabilitation of Offenders Act. If revocation is refused, there is a right of appeal against this refusal.

If a deportation order is revoked, this does not give the person the right to come back to the UK. It merely means that there is no legal obstacle to him or her applying for permission to return. The person will still have to fit in to all the requirements of the immigration rules in the category in which he or she is seeking to return. The Home Office is likely to consider the application in great detail, so even if the person is not a visa national it is advisable to apply for entry clearance rather than simply travelling to the UK, in order to minimise the risk of refusal at the airport.

After supervised or voluntary departure

Although there may be no formal bar, returning is difficult. If people apply for entry clearance it is likely that the application will be referred from the British post abroad to the Home Office and therefore that the details of their past immigration history will be known. This can be considered in deciding whether it is likely that they will abide by any conditions put on their stay in the future. The Home Office has not stated how often the power formally to prohibit re-entry after a supervised departure has been used; this is an area which requires further monitoring. There is no time limit set down for how long such a prohibition would last, or how the person would know about it.

Illegal entry: Home Office administrative powers

The Home Office can force alleged illegal entrants to leave the UK under its administrative powers. Illegal entry means entering the UK in breach of the immigration laws. There are three ways in which people can enter illegally:

- without seeing an immigration officer at all or by failing to obtain leave to enter when this was required
- entering the UK while there is still a valid deportation order signed against them
- by deceiving an immigration officer as to their identity or their claim to enter the UK

The concept of illegal entry was originally designed to cover people in the first two categories but the definition has been greatly expanded by the Home Office and the courts. If the Home Office alleges that people are illegal entrants, it can immediately make arrangements for their return to their country of origin, with no formal right of appeal until after they have been sent back. Representations can be made to the Home Office but the only formal process for contesting removal before departure is to apply for a judicial review of the decision to treat the person as an illegal entrant. It is rare for the courts to look into the reasons for the Home Office's decision.

Entering without leave

Without seeing an immigration officer

This is what was originally understood by illegal entry – for example, a small boatload of people arriving at midnight on a deserted beach, or a person hidden in a car boot, coming into the country. It is rare. If a person confesses to having entered by avoiding examination by an immigration officer there is no way of arguing that he or she is not an illegal entrant, but it is still possible to make representations to the Home Office to urge that the person should not be removed. If there are exceptional compassionate circumstances, for example a person who has been living in the UK for many years or who is married with children, he or she may still be allowed to remain.

Without obtaining leave from an immigration officer

Immigration officers are required to examine people subject to immigration control when they enter the UK, in order to decide whether to grant them leave to enter or not. If they fail to examine people subject to control and pass them through into the UK without stamping their passports with leave to enter, the people can be treated as illegal entrants because they have not obtained this leave. This was confirmed in the case of *Rehal* (1989 Imm AR 576). Mr Rehal was a British Overseas citizen whose passport was not stamped on entry because the immigration officer mistakenly assumed he was a British citizen and therefore not subject to immigration control. The court accepted that Mr Rehal had not deceived an immigration officer, but decided nevertheless that he was an illegal entrant.

Entry through Ireland

It is also possible for people who enter through Ireland to be treated as illegal entrants. There is no immigration control between the two countries, and normally people do not require leave to travel within the Common Travel Area (the UK, Republic of Ireland, Channel Islands and Isle of Man) so they do not have to see an immigration officer; ▶see page 149. However, some people do require leave, and if they enter without it, they have entered illegally. They are:

- visa nationals who do not have visas to enter the UK (even if they did have visas to enter Ireland)
- people who have previously been refused entry to the UK or have overstayed in the UK or in Ireland

• people against whom there are current deportation orders.

No records are kept of people entering through Ireland, so such people are only likely to be treated as illegal entrants if they apply to the Home Office for an extension or a change of status and the Home Office then makes checks on their entry.

In breach of a deportation order

If a person enters the UK while there is a deportation order signed against him or her that has not been revoked, the entry is illegal. It would be rare for a person travelling in his or her true identity to be readmitted, so there may also be another problem connected with this entry, such as obtaining a false passport. The only right of appeal is concerning the person's identity – arguing that he or she is not the person named on the deportation order.

'Deception' of an immigration officer

Most people treated as illegal entrants are so treated because the Home Office alleges they have entered by deception. A person who has ostensibly been legally allowed into the country and who has stamps on his or her passport granting leave to enter may be treated as an illegal entrant by deception. The Home Office may allege that he or she told lies when applying for permission to enter.

Alternatively, it may claim that the person did not give information which, if the immigration officer had known it, would have meant that the person did not qualify to enter and would have been refused. There is often no evidence to support the Home Office's view and the only way that the allegation can be substantiated is through the 'confession' or admission of the person concerned.

Entry by deception has been the subject of many court cases. The most important is *Khawaja and Khera* (1982 Imm AR 137). The House of Lords decided that the Home Office has to prove, on the balance of probabilities, that people accused of illegal entry have made false representations to the immigration authorities and that they were granted leave to enter on the basis of that false information. Mr Khera was found not to be an illegal entrant. He had applied as a child to come with his mother to join his father but had married in India while the application was still under consideration. He did not know that this made any difference and was not asked whether he was married, so it was accepted that he had not deceived the immigration authorities. Mr Khawaja was held to be an illegal entrant; he had entered as a visitor saying that he would spend a week with his cousin but applied to the Home Office shortly afterwards to remain as a husband, having married his wife in Belgium before travelling to the UK and married her again in the UK during his visit. He was held to have deceived the immigration officers on arrival and therefore to be an illegal entrant.

More recently, court decisions appear to be backtracking on this definition. It has been held in the case of *Durojaiye* (CA 13.6.91) that merely showing a passport with a previous immigration stamp of leave to remain to an immigration officer can count as deception if the reason for which the previous stamp was given is no longer current. For example, a student who is no longer studying but has several months' extension of stay and who travels out of and returns to the UK within this time might be considered to have deceived the immigration officers on return, because he was no longer a student. It is important to monitor these developments and to consider referring people for legal advice on possible judicial reviews of illegal entry decisions.

Establishing illegal entry

It is quite common for the Home Office to treat people as illegal entrants when they might instead be treated as overstayers, or are legally in the UK as visitors or students. For example, if a man who was given entry as a visitor is subsequently found working, it is likely that he will be questioned by immigration officers about his intentions when he first came to the UK – had he really intended just a visit? had he always wanted to work here? did he know before he came that he would work? had he always intended to stay longer than he said? If the answer to any of these questions is 'yes', immigration officers may allege that he had concealed his true intention, of coming to the UK to work, from the immigration officers. If this had been revealed, it would have resulted in refusal of permission to enter, therefore entry was gained by deception as he was never really a genuine visitor.

Most people are questioned by immigration officers shortly after arrest, or after being detained in a police station for some hours, and have not received advice. They do not know the reasoning behind the questions or what the officer is trying to make them say and are quite unaware of the crucial difference between remaining in the UK 'illegally' after any leave has run out and being an 'illegal entrant'. They may make admissions about their original intentions, believing they are talking about their current situation.

The Home Office has the power to detain people alleged to be illegal entrants pending their removal from the UK and this is frequently done; ▶see chapter 15 for more information on detention. Continued detention may also be used as a threat against people who are being interrogated, to urge them to admit to illegal entry, after which their release will be considered.

Advising alleged illegal entrants

Because the Home Office has powers to remove illegal entrants very quickly, with no right of appeal until after they have left, it is necessary to act promptly; ▶see chapter 12.

It is important to ask the immigration office concerned for a copy of its notes of the person's interview, which may clarify what the person has said and whether the responses have been misunderstood. It may then be possible to write to the Home Office to explain such misunderstandings, or give new evidence, and to urge that the person is not in fact an illegal entrant. The Home Office may accept these arguments. If it does not, it may be possible to refer the person to a solicitor experienced in immigration work to apply to the courts for a judicial review of the decision, showing that the Home Office does not have adequate evidence to support its conclusion. While a judicial review is pending, arrangements for the person's removal will be delayed.

When there are strong compassionate or family reasons why the person should be allowed to remain, representations can be made to the Home Office to treat him or her exceptionally and grant leave to remain, even if there is no way of contesting the illegal entry decision. It is important to give all the relevant details and information to the Home Office as quickly as possible. Representations may also be made through the local Member of Parliament; if an MP takes up a case at this stage, any arrangements for the person's removal will be delayed while the Home Office considers the MP's representations.

Removal

If people alleged to be illegal entrants do not contest this allegation, or their removal, they can be sent away very quickly, because there is no formal right of appeal before removal. The airline or shipping company which brought them to the UK is liable to pay for their return but if negotiations about this appear to be protracted, the Home Office may pay instead. Illegal entrants may be removed either to the country of their nationality, the country which gave them a travel document, the country from which they embarked for the UK, or to any other country where there is reason to believe they will be admitted. There is therefore a wider choice of destinations than for deportees and it may be easier to persuade another country to accept them.

The immigration authorities are likely to hold the person's passport, which they may return as he or she passes through immigration control on exit from the country, or give to the crew of the plane. The Home Office has stated that if a specific request is made for the person to be given the passport on embarkation, this can be done, to avoid the authorities of the country of origin knowing of the basis on which the person is leaving, but it is difficult to verify whether this happens.

Returning to the UK

After a person has been removed as an illegal entrant, there is a right of appeal from abroad, but only on the grounds that the person was not an illegal entrant. As the appellant must be outside the country while the case is being fought and it is always difficult to prove a case in contradiction to the explanatory statement prepared by the immigration service in the UK, such appeals are rare and are very rarely successful.

There are no formal procedures laid down to restrict people who have been removed as illegal entrants applying to return. They may apply immediately, but will have to show that they satisfy the requirements of the immigration law and rules for the category in which they are seeking to return to be successful. Because of their past immigration history in the UK, it is likely that the application will be referred to the Home Office to consider whether any exceptional or compassionate aspects of the case outweigh the illegal entry. Having a spouse and children settled in the UK, who have reasons for being unable to join the removed person abroad, for example, may be strong enough compassionate circumstances. The Home Office is likely to consider the application in great detail, so even if the person is not a visa national it is advisable to apply for entry clearance rather than simply travelling to the UK, in order to minimise the risk of refusal at the airport.

15 Detention

The Home Office and the immigration service have wide powers to detain people for immigration reasons. When people are detained, there is often no right to apply for bail and no time limit laid down for detention. In these circumstances, detention or release is entirely a matter for the discretion of the Home Office and it is not necessary for it to give any substantive reasons for continuing detention. When people detained for immigration reasons are able to apply for bail, often this is to an immigration adjudicator, not to the courts.

Reasons for detention

People may be detained in several different circumstances:

- **People arriving in the UK** may be detained while their application is under consideration or after they have been refused entry and before they have been returned to their country of origin. This includes people seeking asylum in the UK.

- **People who are suspected immigration offenders** can be held by the police while waiting for the immigration service to come to interview them.

- **People who are charged with an immigration offence** to appear before a magistrates' court may be detained either pending the case coming to court or pending Home Office administrative action. They can apply to the court for bail in the normal way, but it is quite common for the police or immigration service to object to bail on the grounds that the person may abscond.

- **People who have been recommended for deportation** by a court will be detained while the Home Office considers the recommendation, even if no custodial sentence was imposed, unless the court also specifically directs that they should be released. It is possible to ask the Home Office to grant temporary release but this is totally discretionary.

- **People who have been sentenced to imprisonment** as well as recommended for deportation may be detained after the sentence is over, while arrangements are made for deportation. They will usually be moved from the prison where they were held either to Haslar prison or to an airport detention centre.

- **People against whom a decision to deport** has been made may be detained on the order of the Home Office or by the immigration service, even if they are appealing against the decision.

- **People against whom a deportation order** has been signed may be detained while travel arrangements are made, or any further representations considered.

- **People alleged to be illegal entrants** may be detained while their case is considered or pending removal from the UK.

Places of detention and visit facilities

Most immigration detainees are held either at Haslar prison, Gosport, Hampshire or in the immigration service detention centres at Harmondsworth, near Heathrow airport, Queens Building at Heathrow airport, or the Beehive at Gatwick. On 1 November 1991, the Home Office announced that it was preparing another 300 immigration detention places, to be used for the detention of asylum-seekers.

Immigration service detention centres were the first privatised prisons in the UK. Detainees at Harmondsworth are guarded by the security company Group 4. The firm has a contract with the Home Office to operate the centre and to escort detainees to immigration interviews and courts. Detainees are able to move around the communal areas of the detention centre during the day and visiting hours are between 2pm and 8pm, with no limit on how long a single visitor may stay. Visitors may be asked to provide proof of identity, and frequently passports, before they are permitted to go in and see people in the visiting area. Legal visits may also take place within this time.

The centres at the airports are intended for short-term detention and people may not be held there for more than five days – they must then be transferred to another centre or prison such as Harmondsworth or Haslar or a local prison.

Haslar prison used to be a young offenders' institution but has held only Immigration Act detainees since July 1989. It is run by the prison service, under the same conditions as those which apply to remand prisoners. It is the main detention centre for men arrested in London and the south-east. There are time limits on legal visits, which must be in the sight, but not the hearing, of a prison officer. The visitor normally has to book in advance, to be sure that one of the limited number of legal visit rooms is available, and will have to show proof of identity on arrival. Family visits are restricted to a quarter of an hour a day for detainees, as for other remand prisoners, and there is no privacy for discussion. Detainees are held in four large dormitories, where they can receive and make telephone calls. The Richmond Citizens Advice Bureau has set up the Latchmere/Haslar Project, which visits Haslar twice a week. It advises on welfare and other problems and can pass on messages from and to other advisers, or collect or deliver documents. The Project has funding only until April 1992.

People arrested in other areas of the country may be held in police station cells or sent to the local remand prison. When there is no room in Haslar, men from London may be sent to Pentonville. Women are normally detained at Harmondsworth detention centre or Holloway prison.

Getting people out of detention

Bail

Some people detained under Immigration Act powers have the right to apply to an adjudicator for bail. They are:

* people who have lodged appeals against a decision to deport or against destination after a deportation order has been signed

* people refused entry to the UK who have a right of appeal before departure (because they had obtained a visa or entry clearance before travelling) and who have appealed

* people seeking entry to the UK, whose cases have been decided after seven days.

There are specific bail application forms which ask for details of where the person would live if granted bail, the amount of money the detainee him or herself could offer as recognisance and of other people prepared to stand as sureties. Bail forms should be returned to the immigration office dealing with the case; it will inform the immigration appeals authorities and the hearing will probably be listed within a few days. Notification of the date is usually by telephone, but in writing.

Large amounts of money are now usually demanded from the sureties; one adjudicator states that he would normally request £5000–£10,000 and £2000 is not uncommon. Anyone may represent a bail application to an adjudicator; it does not have to be a solicitor or barrister. It is necessary for the people standing surety to go to the appeal hearing, with evidence of the money that they are prepared to put up, such as their own bank statements or savings books, and of their standing, such as evidence of their house ownership, or job details. They may also be asked what their connection with the detainee is and what sanctions they can use to ensure that the detainee complies with his or her bail conditions.

Temporary release

It is always possible to ask the Home Office to consider the temporary release of a person detained under Immigration Act powers, even when there is no formal right to appeal or to apply for bail. This includes:

* people detained on arrival in the country, when no decision has been made on their case, for example, asylum-seekers

- people who have been refused entry, but have some time before their removal directions
- people detained as alleged illegal entrants
- people held pending deportation.

It is best to speak on the telephone, if possible to the official dealing with the case (▶see chapter 19 for details of Home Office groups and telephone numbers and ▶chapter 12 for more information on dealing with immigration officials). The Home Office states that the use of detention is reviewed on a weekly basis for all those detained, so it is possible to request temporary admission repeatedly and for it to be reconsidered over a long period of detention. It is usually important that the detainee should have a stable address to go to. New factors, like the distress caused to the detainee and his or her family, and medical evidence of deterioration, may all be useful.

16   The immigration appeals system

An appeals system exists in order that administrative decisions made by the Home Office, the immigration service and British posts abroad can be reviewed by an independent judicial body. The immigration appeals system is separate from the Home Office and independent of it. Its personnel are now appointed by the Lord Chancellor's department but until 1987 they were appointed by the Home Office. The appeals system is set up under the Immigration Acts and the practical details of its operation are laid down in the Immigration Appeals (Procedure) Rules 1984. It is a two-tier system:

- appeals are heard first by an **adjudicator**, who sits alone to decide a case
- the losing side then has the right to apply for leave to appeal to the higher level, the **Immigration Appeal Tribunal**, to review the case. This is a three-person panel, and will grant leave to appeal when it believes that there is a legal point at issue, or if there are other special circumstances which it believes justify a further appeal.

The Asylum Bill, published on 1 November 1991, proposes a separate appeal system for people refused asylum, with special adjudicators to decide on asylum appeals, and different procedure rules. This is not yet in force at the time of writing.

An adjudicator normally only has the power to consider whether a decision made by the Home Office or an entry clearance or immigration officer was in accordance with the immigration rules; an appeal can normally only be successful on those grounds. When the application made to the Home Office was a request to exercise discretion and to deal with a case outside the immigration rules, it is possible for an appeal to be allowed on the grounds that the discretion should have been exercised differently. If the adjudicator or Tribunal believes the decision was correct, but that there are strong compassionate or other reasons why the authorities should have acted differently, in certain circumstances they can make a recommendation to the Home Office to make an exception in this case. Not all adjudicators make recommendations but the Home Office states that it will normally consider them if they are made.

When the system was set up in 1969, it was accompanied by a change in the immigration rules which required people coming to join relatives for settlement to obtain entry clearance from the British high commission or embassy in their country of origin before travelling to the UK. As all appeals were to be heard in the UK (the idea of having them abroad was rejected as too expensive) this means that the people appealing (the appellants) often cannot be present at the appeal to give evidence or to present their own case.

Appeal hearings are open to the public, unless any party to the appeal specifically requests that it should be in private. Tribunal decisions may be quoted by the appellant or the respondent (the representative of the immigration authority which made the decision appealed against) in support of their arguments. Selected decisions of the Tribunal, and of the courts, are published quarterly by HMSO in *Immigration appeals: selected determinations of the Immigration Appeal Tribunal on appeals under the Immigration Act 1971 and selected reports of decisions of the House of Lords, the Court of Appeal and the High Court* (usually cited as Imm AR), known as the 'green books' because of the colour of their covers.

When people can appeal

There are very strict time limits laid down under the Immigration Act 1971 with regard to lodging appeals. This means that the person appealing may have to act very quickly initially, but there are then no time limits within which the Home Office or British post abroad has to respond, or by which the appellate authorities have to act.

Appeals from abroad

When entry clearance is refused by a British embassy or high commission abroad, there is a right of appeal within *three months* of the decision. The forms have to be returned to the entry clearance officers at the British post.

Appeals against refusal of entry

When people are refused entry at a British air- or sea port there is a right of appeal. If the people obtained entry clearance they must appeal within *28 days*, and can remain in the UK while the appeal is under consideration. If they did not have entry clearance, they can only appeal after they have been sent back and the appeal forms must be returned to the immigration service at the port where they were refused, to reach them within *28 days* of the removal.

Appeals against refusal to vary stay in the UK

When the Home Office refuses people permission to stay longer in the UK, or refuses to alter their conditions of stay, there is a right of appeal as long as the application was made in time, before their leave ran out. The appeal forms must be received by the Home Office within *14 days* of the date of refusal.

APPEALS AND TIME LIMITS

Decision	Notes	Time limit to appeal to adjudicator	Time limit to apply to Tribunal
refusal of entry clearance/visa	appellant outside UK	3 months	42 days
refusal of entry to UK	appellant in UK if had visa/entry clearance	28 days	14 days
	appellant outside UK if no visa/entry clearance	28 days	42 days
refusal to vary or extend leave to remain	appellant in UK if applied in time	14 days	14 days
	if applied late/ 'out of time'	no appeal —————	
decision to deport	full appeal if in UK over 7 years	14 days	14 days
	on facts of case only, if in UK less than 7 years	14 days	14 days
– on national security grounds	no appeal – review by panel only ———————		
court recommendation for deportation	appeal through courts system only ———————		
deportation order signed	only against destination	14 days	14 days
removal as illegal entrant	appellant in UK, only on identity grounds	28 days	14 days
	after removal	28 days	42 days
refusal to revoke deportation order	appellant outside UK	28 days	42 days
refusal of asylum	new procedure rules being debated with the Asylum Bill 1991		

Appeals against deportation and removal

When the Home Office makes a decision to deport a person, there is a right of appeal. The appeal forms must be received by the Home Office within *14 days* of the date of the decision. However, if the person has been in the UK for less than seven years at the date of the decision, the appeal is only on whether the facts on which the Home Office made its decision are correct; see pages 185–186 for further details.

When a deportation order has been signed against a person, there is a right of appeal against destination (the country to which the person is to be deported) only. The appeal forms must be received by the Home Office within *14 days* of the date on which the notice was served on the person. The appeal can only be won if it can be shown that another country will accept the deportee.

When a person is alleged to be an illegal entrant, there is a right of appeal only after the person has been removed to his or her country of origin. The appeal forms must be received by the immigration office which dealt with the case within *28 days* of the person's removal.

When an application to revoke a deportation order is refused, an appeal can be made to the authority which refused the application. It must be received within *28 days* of the refusal.

When people can apply to the Tribunal

When an appeal is lost before an adjudicator, there is the right to apply for leave to appeal to the Immigration Appeal Tribunal. If the appellant is in the UK, the appeal forms must be received by the Tribunal within *14 days* of the adjudicator's decision. If the appellant is abroad, the forms must be received within *42 days* of the adjudicator's decision. When the appellant wins the case, the Home Office can apply to the Tribunal.

When there is no right of appeal

People who are late in applying to the Home Office for permission to remain, after their previous permission has run out, have no formal right of appeal against any refusal. It does not matter for how short a time the person had overstayed, or whether he or she knew that the application was late, the right of appeal has still been lost.

The way in which applications are made to the Home Office is important. If people's circumstances change while an application for leave to remain is pending at the Home Office and they write to give new information or explain changes of circumstances, *it is important to stress that this new information is in continuation of the first application*. For example, a woman may apply for an extension of stay as a student, her leave as a student may expire while she is waiting for an answer, but she may marry her British boyfriend during this time. When she applies to remain with her husband she should not withdraw her outstanding student application, as this would leave her without any legal basis for her stay in the country. She should write to the Home Office in continuation of the previous application, explaining her change of circumstances and asking for leave to remain as a wife.

There is no right of appeal if the Home Office makes a decision to deport on national security grounds. The person can ask a three-person panel to review the decision, but is not told the details of the allegations against him or her and the Home Secretary does not have to follow the panel decision.

How to appeal

Forms and time limits

When people are refused by the immigration authorities, they must be given notice in writing of the decision and the reasons for it. This is a standard printed letter, with a space at the top for two or three written lines explaining why the application has been refused. The printed part explains the right of appeal and the time limits for appealing (▶see appendix for example). It may be handed to people who are applying in person at the Home Office or a British high commission or embassy abroad, or will be posted by recorded delivery post (in the UK) or registered post (abroad).

The refusal letter used for people in the UK may be confusing, as it explains that if they do not appeal they have 28 days in which to make arrangements to leave. People sometimes misunderstand this to mean either that they have 28 days in which to appeal, instead of 14, or that they should leave within 28 days even if they appeal. The letter informs people of the possibility of consulting UKIAS (▶see chapter 19) for free advice and representation for the appeal. The authorities also send appeal forms to be filled in and returned, with the address to which they must be sent.

These time limits are extremely important because the right of appeal can be lost if the forms are not received in time. Thus if a person seeks advice on an appeal the first thing to check is the date of refusal, to make sure any appeal is still in time. If it is nearly the end of the period, the appeal forms should be filled in and returned to the Home Office or British post abroad straight away, by fax or telex if it is too late to post them. The section on 'grounds of appeal' does not have to be completed in detail at the time of lodging the appeal. It is sufficient to state 'The decision is not in accordance with the immigration law and rules applicable. Further grounds will follow' in order to lodge a valid appeal, if there is not time to obtain the full facts or to refer the person to a specialist agency. Further grounds can be sent after the person has received more detailed advice.

Grounds of appeal

The appeal can only determine whether the Home Office or other immigration authority has interpreted the law correctly. Thus, in preparing detailed grounds of appeal, it is important to look at the reasons given in the refusal letter, to see whether they can be refuted, or whether further arguments or evidence can be put to show that the reasons are wrong. The decision may be based on a simple factual error – for example, students being told 'You have applied for further leave to remain as a student but the Secretary of State is not satisfied that you are enrolled on or attending a full-time course of studies' when in fact they are attending a full-time course but had not been doing so at the time of the application because they had to wait until the end of the summer holidays before being able to obtain a confirmatory letter from a college, or had not known that they had to send fresh evidence.

If the refusal was made on the basis of wrong or out-of-date information, it is important to lodge a formal appeal and to return the forms in time. A new application should also be made, with the fresh evidence, either together with the appeal forms or afterwards. If the refusal can easily be shown to be wrong, the Home Office may change its mind and decide to grant fresh leave to remain. If the decision is changed, the Home Office will write to state this and will also send another form for the person to withdraw the appeal. Once the Home Office has confirmed that leave will be granted, it is safe to withdraw the appeal.

It may not be possible to argue in detail against the reason for refusal at this stage. For example, a visitor refused entry because the immigration official is 'not satisfied you only intend to remain for this limited period' will have no indication about why the officer was not satisfied. A husband refused entry clearance to come to the UK to join his wife, because the entry clearance officer 'is not satisfied that the marriage was not undertaken primarily to obtain admission to the UK' will not be told fuller reasons for this belief, based on an interview between the officer and the husband, at the time of refusal. Usually all that can be stated on the form is the assertion that the visitor intends to leave within the period of time requested or the marriage was not undertaken primarily to gain admission to the UK. It can be useful to ask the person concerned to write down as much as he or she can recollect about the series of questions and the answers given, as soon as possible after the interview at the British post. There will then be some record to compare with the detailed report prepared later by the entry clearance officer.

Appealing 'out of time'

There are very limited provisions for appealing to an adjudicator after the time limit given. When people have been refused an extension or variation of leave in the UK, they have 14 days in which to lodge an appeal, but are also given 28 days in which to make arrangements to leave the UK if they do not appeal. If they miss the first 14-day deadline, but send an appeal which reaches the Home Office within the 28 days, that appeal may be considered.

The Home Office has to refer the case to the appellate authorities to decide, as a preliminary issue, whether the reasons for the appeal being late are such that it would be just and right to allow it to proceed. The appellant or representative has the chance to write to explain the reasons for lateness. It has been decided that if the notice of refusal was sent to the wrong address, because the appellant had not told the Home Office of any change, or if the Post Office could not deliver the recorded delivery letter and it was not collected in time, these are not strong enough reasons to overlook the appeal being late.

Waiting for an appeal

After an appeal has been lodged, the person appealing will receive an *acknowledgement letter* from the authority appealed against, to confirm that the appeal has been lodged. When the person is in the UK, this acknowledgement is proof of his or her immigration status, and that he or she can remain in the UK while the appeal is under consideration. This letter supersedes the refusal letter, as it shows that the person may stay in the UK beyond the 28 days then stated, for however long it may take until the appeal is heard. During this time, there are no restrictions on an appellant working in the UK; any restrictions on working lapse at the end of the 28 days' leave granted in order to travel.

The Home Office acknowledgement is sufficient evidence for the Benefits Agency that the person is free to work and can therefore be issued a national insurance number. Whether working is advisable or not depends on the person's case. For example, if the appellant is a student who has been refused because the Home Office was not satisfied about financial support without working or recourse to public funds, working during the appeal time could be used by the Home Office in the future to show that there was inadequate support.

The appeals process

The immigration authorities next prepare a detailed statement, known as an *explanatory statement*, amplifying the reasons for the refusal. Any other documents on which the officials have relied are attached to the statement.

If the appeal is against a refusal of an extension of stay, the explanatory statement will go into some detail about the person's immigration history in the UK, from the Home Office point of view. There will be details about the application that has been refused, the checks carried out by the Home Office, the information it has gathered and the reasons why it believes that the person does not qualify. The Home Office will annex any documents in support of its case to the explanatory statement, as well as copies of correspondence. There are frequently delays of several months before the statement is prepared.

If the appeal is against refusal of entry at a port or airport, the explanatory statement is prepared by an immigration officer and is usually much shorter and prepared more quickly.

If the appeal is against refusal of entry clearance, the explanatory statement is normally prepared by an entry clearance officer at the overseas post, probably not the person who made the decision. It frequently includes a report, in question-and-answer form, of the interview between the entry clearance officer and the appellant, and anyone else who was interviewed, and then an explanation of the reasons for the refusal. Many posts have their own forms for asking details of the appellant's family tree in family settlement cases; this is also attached to the statement. The time taken to prepare the statement varies between posts. Where there is little immigration work it may be only a few days or weeks but it may be much longer from countries of the Indian subcontinent, when statements may only be prepared in a few of the less busy months of the year. If the post referred the case to the Home Office for decision, the explanatory statement is written by the Home Office.

If the appellant is in the UK, the statement and documents are sent to the immigration appellate authorities in the UK, normally to the office nearest to the appellant's or representative's address. The appellate authorities then arrange when the case can be listed for hearing before an adjudicator. When this has been fixed, they send copies of the documents to the appellant, or to the representative if one is known, with notification of the date of hearing. Usually about six weeks' notice is given for the hearing date. If the appellant has not yet sought detailed advice about the case it is sensible to do so now, rather than appearing unrepresented.

If the appellant is abroad, the immigration appellate authorities send the papers to the representative in the UK, who may also be the sponsor. No date of hearing is fixed at this stage. The representatives are asked to contact the appellate authorities when they are completely ready to proceed with the case and the appellate authorities will then fix a date.

Appeals listed for 'pre-hearing review'

When a case has been pending for some time, but is still not ready for hearing, the appellate authorities may list it for a 'pre-hearing review' or 'for mention'. This means that the representative is expected to go to the court on that date to explain whether or not the case is ready to proceed. If it is, a date of hearing will be fixed later; if it is not, another pre-hearing review date, usually about three months ahead, will be fixed. The appellate authorities use this procedure when the Home Office is reconsidering a refusal on the basis of further information, so the appeal may not be necessary, or when other evidence, such as a DNA test about the relationship of the appellant to the sponsor (▶see box on page 35), is awaited.

Appeals against refusal of asylum have frequently been listed for pre-hearing review, as asylum cases are particularly complicated and may require detailed evidence, often from abroad, which may take a long time to obtain. The appeal procedures set out in the Asylum Bill, which lay down very strict time limits for asylum appeals, will mean that this process will no longer be used in asylum cases. These procedures are not yet in force at the time of writing; there is more information on the proposals in chapter 5.

How to prepare for an appeal

The appellants or sponsors in the UK should seek specialist advice when they receive the explanatory statement, if they have not done so before.

Although people do not have to be lawyers to represent at immigration appeals, appeals are becoming more specialised and rely on legal precedents, so it is important that the representatives understand and have experience of the system.

The basis of the appeal is the explanatory statement. This is normally accepted by the adjudicator as a statement of fact, rather than as a statement prepared by one of the parties to a case. If it is argued that the statement is not correct, it is important to have evidence to show what actually happened. For example, if it is alleged that a student did not attend her course regularly but the student contends that she did, it is important to have a letter from the course tutor, college registrar or someone else in authority to confirm her attendance. If it is alleged that a husband cannot adequately support his wife it is important to have pay slips, bank statements or other evidence of the financial support available.

It is important that the person concerned has read through the explanatory statement carefully, so that he or she can explain anything that is not correct. If the appellant is abroad, it is also important for the representative in the UK to have received comments on the statement from him or her. This may be a letter or may be in the form of a sworn affidavit. Documents from abroad may be used at the hearing by submitting them in advance, or may be used by the sponsor in the UK to help in giving evidence about the appellant's intentions. Other evidence from abroad, such as letters between a husband and wife or an engaged couple, or other documents to prove a relationship or a situation, will also be helpful. Documents which are not in English should be translated before being sent to the appellate authorities, where the translation will be checked.

At the time of writing, legal aid for advice and assistance (green form) is available for preparation of cases for appeal but not for representation at the hearing. People may therefore receive bills from solicitors for representation at the hearing, who have been acting on legal aid up to this time. People who may have difficulty in paying should obtain an estimate of cost as early as possible, so they will not need to change their representative shortly before the appeal. UKIAS, JCWI, law centres and some other advice centres do not charge for representing at appeals but may not be able to take a case on at very short notice.

Withdrawal of appeals

When people receive the explanatory statement for their appeal and discuss the case with their advisers, they may not wish to continue with it. This may be because they have already spent the time they needed in the UK, because circumstances have changed so much since the appeal was lodged that it is no longer relevant, or because it is clear that an appeal cannot succeed. If the person plans to leave the UK before the date of hearing it is worth writing to the appellate authorities and to the Home

Office just before the person leaves, giving travel details and stating that the appeal is being withdrawn. If the Home Office then checks departure records and sees that the person did indeed leave, this will be recorded in the Home Office file. It will therefore be clear what happened at that time if the person should seek to return to the UK in the future.

If the appellant is in the UK and wants to remain longer but on a different basis from that of the application that has been refused, the person's new situation cannot be considered at the appeal hearing. For example, someone who appealed against a refusal of an extension as a student and who subsequently married a British citizen cannot put that new fact to the appellate authorities. Instead, the person may make a new application to the Home Office for leave to remain as a spouse and ask the appellate authorities to adjourn consideration of the appeal against the previous refusal while the Home Office considers a fresh application.

In order to safeguard the person's position in the UK, this new application should be made before the date of hearing of the appeal. A copy of the application should be sent to the appellate authorities with a request for the appeal to be adjourned while the Home Office considers the new application. Adjudicators may grant an adjournment on those grounds. If the Home Office decides the new application favourably, it will respond to say that further leave has been granted and will ask the person to withdraw the appeal.

If an appeal is simply withdrawn before the Home Office has made any decision to grant fresh leave to remain, the person immediately becomes an overstayer, liable to deportation (▶see chapter 14) and is in the UK without authority. This is a vulnerable position and should be avoided if possible by keeping the appeal pending while any fresh application to the Home Office is under consideration.

Appeals on the papers

The appellant can choose whether to ask for an oral hearing of the appeal, or to request that it be decided on the papers available and any further written representations. Most people want to have an oral hearing, so that they can see what is happening and put their case in their own words. This is usually helpful, particularly when the case depends on the credibility of the persons involved, for example a primary purpose marriage refusal. Sometimes, however, when the case depends purely on points of fact and there is adequate written evidence, or when the person is afraid of speaking out in a formal setting, or when the main point of the appeal is to gain time, it may be better to ask for the appeal to be decided on the basis of written representations. It is still important to go through the explanatory statement with the appellant to check all possible inaccuracies, to write with evidence to correct them, and to give all the arguments on the person's behalf. A letter asking for the appeal to be decided in writing should reach the appellate authorities several days before the date fixed for hearing, to give them time to rearrange other hearings on that date.

An appeal may be lodged mainly in order to enable the person to gain more time in the UK, for example a visitor who applied to remain for longer than six months and has been refused. It is not possible to win such an appeal because the immigration rule is specific about the time allowed, so it is not necessary to argue the case in detail.

Normally nothing will happen on the date that had been designated for the hearing; the adjudicator will send his or her decision in writing some time afterwards. The appeal is still pending, and the person is not an overstayer, while waiting for the decision.

Oral hearings: at the appeal

Appeals are supposed to be an 'informal process' but there are formal operating procedures. The adjudicator sits with a clerk, who is there to carry out any clerical duties such as photocopying required during the appeal. The appellant and representative are on the left side of the room, and the Home Office presenting officer, representing the official who made the decision, is on the right. The case is started by the appellant's representative, who is able to call witnesses (including the appellant if he or she is in the UK) and to go through the case and the evidence with them, asking questions to draw out the information required. It is important for the appellant and any other witnesses to be confident about what they are saying and to have organised their thoughts in advance.

The Home Office representative may then cross-examine the witnesses, and the appellant's representative can ask further questions to clarify any points. At any point the adjudicator may intervene to ask questions of the witnesses. When all the evidence has been heard, the Home Office representative and then the appellant's representative sum up their respective cases. The adjudicator may give a decision orally at the end of the hearing, but it is more common for the decision to be 'reserved' and sent in writing to both the representatives some time later.

Appeals to the Tribunal

With the determination of the case, the losing side also receives an application form to apply for leave to appeal to the Tribunal. The form must be received by the Tribunal within 14 days of the decision being sent out when the appellant is in the UK and within 42 days when the appellant is abroad.

These time limits for applying for leave to appeal to the Tribunal are very strict and the time begins to run from the date of the adjudicator's decision. There are no provisions for an application which is received late to be considered; even when the Home Office made an application which was received late the courts confirmed that the appeal could not be considered. The forms can be returned without detailed grounds of appeal being stated, in order to preserve the right to argue the case further after deciding whether there are grounds to do so. Statements such as: 'the adjudicator erred in law in his decision' or 'the adjudicator failed adequately to consider the evidence about . . . ' are sufficient to lodge a valid application for leave. When the Home Office loses cases, it commonly puts in these brief applications and then later withdraws them after deciding the case is not worth pursuing. The Tribunal will write in a few weeks to state that the application will be decided by a certain date; more detailed grounds must be submitted before then for the application to have any chance of succeeding.

Most applications for leave to appeal to the Tribunal are unsuccessful. While an application to the Tribunal is pending, the person is still in the UK with permission, but once the application is refused, the person becomes an overstayer and is liable to deportation for that reason.

If leave to appeal is granted, it will be some months before a date will be fixed for hearing. A Tribunal hearing is more formal than one before an adjudicator. There is a panel of three members hearing the case; it is based on legal, not factual, arguments and it is rare for the Tribunal to hear witnesses. Fresh evidence can be put before the Tribunal, although it should be identified in the grounds of appeal and preferably submitted at the same time as the grounds. The hearing is usually based on legal argument, first from the appellant and then from the respondent, and the decision will usually be sent out to the representatives in writing some months after the hearing. The person is still in the UK with permission while the Tribunal appeal is pending.

Judicial review

If the Tribunal dismisses the appeal, it is possible to apply to the courts for a judicial review of the decision – but only on legal grounds. This means that the grounds in support of the request for leave to apply for judicial review should identify all the legal points the appellant wishes to raise. At this stage, full legal aid becomes available for representation in the courts. If the case appears to have a new dimension to it, is contesting a Home Office reinterpretation of the rules, or is on a new point which will be of significance to many people other than the appellants involved, this may be worth doing.

While any court proceedings are pending, the person is still in the UK with permission. Once the proceedings are over and any period in which to apply for leave to go to a higher court has lapsed, the person becomes an overstayer and is liable to arrest or deportation. Further representations, outside the immigration rules, can be made to the Home Office even after appeals have been dismissed, urging that a different decision should be made.

When no formal appeal is pending, the person is not legally protected against the Home Office making a decision to deport, or signing a deportation order, just because a fresh application for leave to remain has been made to the Home Office and representations are under consideration. It is possible to request an assurance from the Home Office that if representations are being made, the representative should be informed of their rejection before a deportation order is signed, but no guarantees can be offered in advance.

This is a difficult situation in which to advise, particularly after an appeal against a decision to deport has been lost. The person may wish to wait if there is the slightest chance of a change in the Home Office's decision, but risks a deportation order being signed and therefore being prohibited from return to the UK for a prolonged period until the order has been revoked. Representations can still be made after a deportation order has been signed and before the person has left the UK, but are rarely successful.

17 British nationality

Some information about the historical background to British nationality law and its interrelation with immigration law is essential to understanding the present situation. This chapter gives a brief outline of how the law developed, with an illustrative flowchart on page 213, and then explains the different kinds of British nationality in existence at present.

The historical background

Before 1948

Until 1948, Britain had no citizenship legislation. People born in, or with a connection with, the UK or a British colony or dependency had the status of **British subject**, which described the allegiance of an individual to the British Crown. The status of a British subject born in the UK was identical in UK law to that of a British subject born in India, Hong Kong or the Caribbean: this included the right of entry to the UK itself and the right to vote and hold public office once in the UK. People who were not British subjects were classified as **aliens**, and their right of entry to the UK was restricted during the twentieth century by various Aliens Acts.

In addition to subjects and aliens, there was also a comparatively small group of people called **British Protected Persons**, who were born in or had a connection with a protectorate, protected state or trust territory, rather than with a colony. (Many British territories were protectorates, for example, all the princely states in India, all of Tanzania, part of Kenya, northern Nigeria). Technically, they fall between subjects and aliens; under international law they are British nationals, but in UK law they are treated as aliens.

1948–1962

The British Nationality Act 1948 created the status of **citizen of the United Kingdom and Colonies** (CUKC). This was acquired by people born in, or with a connection with, the United Kingdom itself or any country which was still a colony. The Act also recognised the existence of independent Commonwealth countries with their own citizenships. But it also retained the status of **British subject**, which was held by all citizens of the

THE DEVELOPMENT OF IMMIGRATION & NATIONALITY LAW

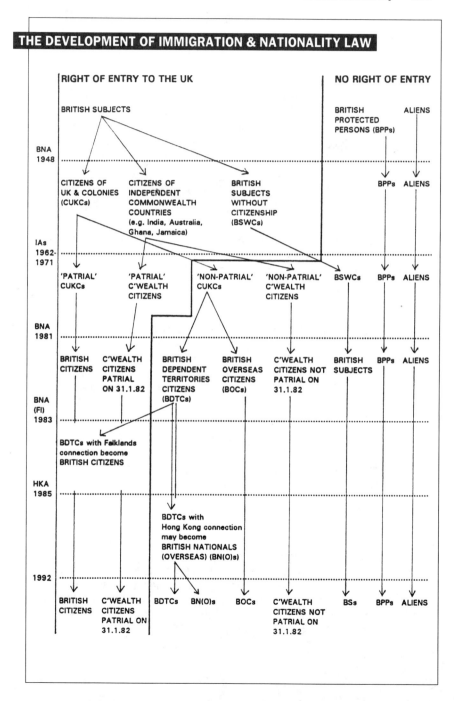

RIGHT OF ENTRY TO THE UK

NO RIGHT OF ENTRY

BRITISH SUBJECTS

BRITISH PROTECTED PERSONS (BPPs) ALIENS

BNA 1948

CITIZENS OF UK & COLONIES (CUKCs)

CITIZENS OF INDEPENDENT COMMONWEALTH COUNTRIES (e.g. India, Australia, Ghana, Jamaica)

BRITISH SUBJECTS WITHOUT CITIZENSHIP (BSWCs)

BPPs ALIENS

IAs 1962-1971

'PATRIAL' CUKCs

'PATRIAL' C'WEALTH CITIZENS

'NON-PATRIAL' CUKCs

'NON-PATRIAL' C'WEALTH CITIZENS

BSWCs BPPs ALIENS

BNA 1981

BRITISH CITIZENS

C'WEALTH CITIZENS PATRIAL ON 31.1.82

BRITISH DEPENDENT TERRITORIES CITIZENS (BDTCs)

BRITISH OVERSEAS CITIZENS (BOCs)

C'WEALTH CITIZENS NOT PATRIAL ON 31.1.82

BRITISH SUBJECTS

BPPs ALIENS

BNA (FI) 1983

BDTCs with Falklands connection become BRITISH CITIZENS

HKA 1985

BDTCs with Hong Kong connection may become BRITISH NATIONALS (OVERSEAS) (BN(O)s)

1992

BRITISH CITIZENS

C'WEALTH CITIZENS PATRIAL ON 31.1.82

BDTCs BN(O)s BOCs

C'WEALTH CITIZENS NOT PATRIAL ON 31.1.82

BSs BPPs ALIENS

UK and Colonies *and* all other Commonwealth citizens – almost like a dual nationality. Once again, all British subjects, whether they were CUKCs or Commonwealth citizens, had the same rights, principally the right of abode in the UK without being subject to any immigration requirements. **British Protected Persons** retained their peculiar in-between status, but were still free from immigration controls.

The 1948 Act also created the status of **British subject without citizenship** for people, mainly from India and Pakistan, who had failed to acquire citizenship of countries which were already independent, but who were not eligible for CUKC status either.

As more colonies became independent after 1948, the normal procedure was for people in those countries to lose their CUKC status, provided that they gained citizenship of the newly independent country, but to retain their status as British subjects. In British nationality and immigration law, they were classified as **Commonwealth citizens** *and* **British subjects**. These two terms had been made interchangeable in the British Nationality Act 1948. As British subjects, they had full rights of entry and abode in the UK.

1962–1981

Between 1962 and 1971, the main corpus of British immigration law was developed, and for the first time restricted the immigration rights of British subjects. Those laws did not do so by distinguishing between British subjects who were CUKCs and British subjects who were citizens of independent Commonwealth countries. Instead, they withdrew the right of abode in the UK from some people in both categories. The right of abode means not being subject to British immigration control. It was also called patriality between 1973–1983 and was developed to differentiate between people with the same nationality status.

CUKCs who had acquired their citizenship in the UK (through birth or by registration or naturalisation), who had a parent or grandparent who had similarly acquired CUKC status in the UK, or who had themselves lived in the UK for five years or more, kept the right of abode in the UK. Other CUKCs, for example people of Asian origin in East Africa and people from existing colonies such as Hong Kong, lost that right. **Commonwealth citizens** who had a parent born in the UK, or who were women married to a man with right of abode, were also able to retain or gain right of abode in the UK; other Commonwealth citizens were not able to do so. It was no longer possible to tell from people's nationality status whether or not they were free from immigration control: CUKC passports were endorsed on page 5 if the holder had right of abode.

The British Nationality Act 1981

The British Nationality Act 1981 came into effect on 1 January 1983. It changed the way people can acquire British nationality, by birth, descent or grant (▶see chapter 18). It also abolished CUKC status and created three new citizenships, which came into existence automatically on 1 January 1983:

- **British citizenship** for people who, at 31 December 1982, were CUKCs with right of abode in the UK
- **British Dependent Territories citizenship** for people who, at 31 December 1982, were CUKCs by virtue of a connection with a country which was still a British dependency (for example Hong Kong)
- **British Overseas citizenship** for other CUKCs, who did not have right of abode or a connection with a British dependency (for example East African Asians).

The citizenship status of Commonwealth citizens was unchanged and those who had the right of abode retained it.

The Act also abolished the status of British subject as a unifying status for British and Commonwealth citizens: citizens of independent Commonwealth countries, together with all kinds of British nationals except British Protected Persons, are now simply known as Commonwealth citizens. It also changed the name of those people defined in the 1948 Act as British subjects without citizenship: confusingly, they are now called **British subjects**. The status of **British Protected Person** survived untouched. (Both these latter categories will die out with their present holders as it is not now possible to acquire them).

Since 1983, there have been two changes to the structure set out in the 1981 Act. People from the Falkland Islands, who were classed as British Dependent Territories citizens, were made into full British citizens after the Falklands war under the British Nationality (Falkland Islands) Act 1983. People from Hong Kong, who are also British Dependent Territories citizens, were given the opportunity to acquire yet another new British status, **British National (Overseas)**, under the Hong Kong Act 1985, to prepare for the return to China in 1997: this status does not carry the right of abode in the UK.

There are now six different groups of people who may hold current British passports:

British citizens	**British subjects**
British Dependent Territories citizens	**British Protected Persons**
British Overseas citizens	**British Nationals (Overseas)**

Only the first category, British citizens, have the right of abode in the UK and are not subject to immigration control. Other kinds of British nationals need to fit in to the immigration rules as described in the other chapters of this book; they may therefore have permission to be in the UK (for example as students, visitors or spouses) but they have no automatic right by virtue of their British nationality – they are treated like any other foreigner applying to enter Britain (except for British Overseas citizens eligible for special quota vouchers: ▶see page 227).

Establishing citizenship

In some cases, the passport will indicate the exact status of the holder. ▶See chapter 13 for examples.

Passports issued before 1 January 1983

Most British passports issued before 1 January 1983 will describe the holder, on page 1, as a 'British subject: citizen of the UK and Colonies'. If this is the case, turn to page 5 of the passport. This usually says 'holder has the right of abode in the UK'. If this is in the passport, and has not been crossed out, it is almost certain that the holder is now a **British citizen**. She or he would automatically have become a British citizen on 1 January 1983 without needing to do anything about it.

If the wording on page 5 has been cancelled, then it is likely that the holder is now a **British Dependent Territories citizen** or a **British Overseas citizen**. This will mean that he or she does not have right of abode in the UK and will need to fit into the immigration rules, or to get a special quota voucher (▶see page 227) to come or stay in the UK. But it is still worth checking the points below in case this status has changed since the passport was issued, or it was issued in error.

The status of **British Protected Person** and **British subject** was not changed by the British Nationality Act 1981. A few British subjects (usually married women) have right of abode in the UK; if this is the case, it will be signalled on page 5 or as a stamp called a certificate of patriality. But the majority of British subjects and all British Protected Persons do not have right of abode in the UK and will need to fit into the immigration rules or get a special quota voucher (▶see page 227) if they wish to come to or stay in the UK.

Points to note

- Check that nothing has happened to change the person's status since the passport was issued. A passport is not proof of present nationality; it is only evidence that a person had that status when the passport was issued. This is particularly relevant for people from Commonwealth countries who hold British passports which were issued before their countries became independent. At independence, most people from that country lost their British nationality and gained nationality of the newly independent country; but their British passports were not recalled and they were usually not even told about their change of nationality. For people born outside the UK, without parents or grandparents born in Britain, it is therefore worth checking the date of issue of the passport against the date of independence of their country of origin (▶see glossary) especially if the passport is no longer current.

People from Caribbean countries which gained their independence from 1981 onwards gain citizenship of the new country but also, if they had lived in the UK for more than five years and were settled before independence, keep their British citizenship. This applies so far to people from Belize, St Kitts-Nevis and Antigua and Barbuda.

• **Some people from Hong Kong** are not any kind of British nationals, though they have travel documents issued by the Hong Kong government or the British Home Office. They are people born in the People's Republic of China, who emigrated to Hong Kong and may subsequently have come to the UK. They travel on brown documents called certificates of identity (or CIs in Hong Kong). They are in effect stateless people and have no special rights in British immigration and nationality law.

Passports issued on or after 1 January 1983

These passports should describe people's nationality status on page 1: 'British citizen', 'British Overseas citizen', 'British Dependent Territories citizen', 'British subject', 'British Protected Person' and, very rarely, 'British National (Overseas)'.

Points to note

• There is now no endorsement on page 5 of British citizen passports stating that the holder has the right of abode: that is automatic because of the holders' status as British citizens. This worries some people, when they get a new passport, in case their right of abode has been withdrawn. They should be reassured that this is not the case.

• No other British nationals have the right of abode in the UK, except for a few British subjects (usually married women). They should have passport endorsements called 'certificates of entitlement to the right of abode', (▶see chapter 13 for examples) which have replaced the old certificates of patriality, issued before 1 January 1983.

• Many new British passports now issued are the uniform EC passports, which are burgundy in colour and are computer-readable. Some people, wrongly, believe that they are of lower status than the old blue passports.

British citizens

Checking for British citizenship

If people have current passports which describe them as 'British citizens', or as 'British subjects: citizens of the UK and Colonies with the right of abode in the UK', then it is clear that they are British citizens. But some people do not have passports (for example, children born in the UK), or may have changed their status since their British or foreign passport was issued. The flowcharts will help to identify other people who are British citizens.

Points to note

1 It is not definite that people are *not* British citizens just because they do not fit into the flowchart; there are other, somewhat rare, ways of acquiring British citizenship.

2 The flowcharts deal only with *British citizens* and not other kinds of British national.

3 'Parent' or 'father' applies to men only if they were legally married to the child's mother. If the parents married after the child's birth it depends on the law of the country where the marriage took place whether the marriage automatically 'legitimates' the child and makes him or her a British citizen, or whether any special procedures have to be followed.

4 British citizens are divided into those who acquired their citizenship 'by descent' (that is, through a parent or grandparent) and those who acquired it 'otherwise than by descent'. (Page 223 explains how to tell, and what difference it makes.)

Children born or adopted in the UK

Before 1983

Prior to 1 January 1983, every child born in the UK or adopted in the UK by a British father was a British citizen. The only exception was the children of diplomats. The British Nationality Act 1981 did not change the status of children born before 1 January 1983; and therefore all children born in the UK before that date (except diplomats' children) are British citizens automatically.

After 1983

One of the major changes in the British Nationality Act 1981 was the provision for acquiring nationality by birth in the UK. Children born in the UK on or after 1 January 1983 become British citizens at birth only if one of their parents *either* is a British citizen *or* is settled (allowed to stay permanently) in the UK at the time of the birth.

WHO IS A BRITISH CITIZEN?   People born before 1 January 1983

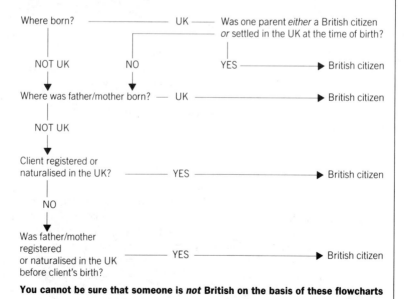

Where born? ——————— UK ————————————▶ British citizen

NOT UK

Where was father born? ——— UK ————————————▶ British citizen

NOT UK

Client registered or
naturalised in the UK? ——————— YES ————————————▶ British citizen

NO

Was father registered or
naturalised in the UK ——————— YES ————————————▶ British citizen
before client's birth?

WHO IS A BRITISH CITIZEN?   People born on or after 1 January 1983

Where born? ——————————— UK ——— Was one parent *either* a British citizen
                                   or settled in the UK at the time of birth?

NOT UK   NO   YES ————————————▶ British citizen

Where was father/mother born? — UK ————————————▶ British citizen

NOT UK

Client registered or
naturalised in the UK? ——————— YES ————————————▶ British citizen

NO

Was father/mother
registered
or naturalised in the UK ——————— YES ————————————▶ British citizen
before client's birth?

You cannot be sure that someone is *not* British on the basis of these flowcharts

Throughout, father = father who is married to mother

Children adopted in the UK become British citizens if either adoptive parent is British at the time of adoption.

Most children born in the UK after 1 January 1983 are still born British, even if their parents are not British, because the vast majority of foreign nationals living in the UK have settled status.

Points to note

- The people whose children are likely *not* to be British are foreign nationals who are in the UK as students, visitors, au pairs, work permit holders during their first four years, refugees within their first four years, and people granted exceptional leave to remain within their first seven years. Children of overstayers and of people treated as illegal entrants are not born British citizens.

- 'parent' in nationality law does not include the father of a non-marital child. In order to gain any benefit from a father's nationality or immigration status, the parents must be married (in the UK, this can be either before or after a child's birth).

- Some children born in the UK after 1 January 1983 are born stateless, if they cannot obtain nationality from their parents' country of origin or if the parents do not want to claim that nationality for them (for example, because they have asylum in the UK). In such cases, the Home Office should provide travel documents (▶see page 239 on passports and travel documents).

- Children born in the UK and not born British do not have any immigration status. They cannot therefore overstay a leave to remain, as they do not have, or need, leave, so long as they remain in the UK. However, if their parents are deported as overstayers, their non-British-citizen children can be deported as part of the family unit. Otherwise, the children (though not necessarily their parents) can remain in the UK indefinitely. However, if they leave the UK, they will not automatically be able to return. If they are travelling with parents who have leave to remain in the UK (for example as students or refugees) the children will usually be readmitted for the same time period and on the same conditions as their parents; they will then be subject to the usual sanctions if they overstay that leave.

If the parents do not become settled their children have no claim to British nationality through birth until they have lived in the UK for ten years. If the parents want to travel and to take the children, the children have no claim to a British passport. They may be entitled to the nationality of either parent, depending on the nationality laws of their country and may be able to get a passport from the relevant high commission or embassy, or a parent may be able to have the children's names inserted on his or her passport. If the children are not able to get a passport, the parent should try to obtain the refusal in writing, or confirmation that the children are not regarded as citizens of the country. It may then be possible for the parent to obtain stateless travel documents for the children from the Home Office.

• Children born in the UK and not born British may be able to register as British citizens after their birth *either* if their parent becomes settled *or* if they live in the UK for ten years. ▶See chapter 18 for further details.

People born overseas

People born before 1 January 1983 with a British parent

Before 1 January 1983, British nationality could pass only through fathers; children born overseas to British mothers and foreign fathers were not born British.

Children born abroad to British fathers automatically became British citizens if their father acquired his British citizenship in the UK in one of the following ways:

1 by being born, or being adopted by a UK citizen father, in the UK

2 by being registered or naturalised in the UK before the child was born.

Both conditions are very important. Registration outside the UK would give the father (and possibly the child) some other kind of British nationality (see above) and not British citizenship. If the father became British after a child's birth, this did not retrospectively confer British nationality on the child.

It is also important to remember that *father* in British nationality law applies only to men who were legally married to the child's mother; marriage certificates or some very clear proof of marriage will be required in order to prove the citizenship of people born overseas. The authorities are likely to demand a higher standard of proof than that required in family reunion cases.

Children born outside the UK before 1983 to British *mothers* could not inherit their mother's citizenship. However the Home Office has stated that if British-born mothers apply for their minor children born outside the UK to be registered to become British citizens, this will be granted, provided the father (if the parents are still married) has no well-founded objection and provided that the child is still under 18 at the time of application. There is no special provision for people who are now adults born abroad to British mothers to become British citizens.

There are some circumstances in which a British *grandfather* could confer British citizenship on a child born overseas before 1 January 1983. This only applies if:

• the grandfather in question is the father's father *and*

• the grandfather acquired his British citizenship in the UK by birth, registration or naturalisation *and*

- the child was born in a non-Commonwealth country (▶see list in glossary for Commonwealth countries) *and*
- the child's birth was registered at a British consulate within a year of the birth.

People born on or after 1 January 1983 with a British parent

Since 1 January 1983, women as well as men have been able to pass on British nationality to children born overseas. Children born abroad on or after 1 January 1983 are therefore British citizens automatically if either their father or mother is a British citizen who acquired citizenship in the UK as in (1) or (2) above. Once again, the father's status only counts if he was married to the mother and can prove this to be the case.

This provision is not retrospective: in other words, there will be families of British women living overseas where some children (born before 1 January 1983) are not British citizens while their siblings born after 1 January 1983 are British citizens.

From 1 January 1983, any British citizen who acquired his or her citizenship *otherwise than by descent* (see below) is able to pass on that citizenship to children born abroad. Thus there is a further category of people whose children born abroad from 1983 onwards are British citizens: people who had gained the right of abode by living in the UK, as a UK and Colonies citizen, for five years or more, and being settled in the UK, before 1 January 1983 and before the child's birth. The parent must have been British during the five-year period and must have remained so at least until the child's birth. If the child was born before 1983, he or she will not be a British citizen. Thus there are families in, for example, Hong Kong, where the parents are British citizens because they lived in the UK for more than five years before 1983. Their older children born in Hong Kong before 1983 are British Dependent Territories citizens and their younger children, born after 1983, are British citizens and British Dependent Territories citizens.

The provisions for acquiring British citizenship for subsequent generations are set out in the flowchart on page 224.

People without a British parent

People born overseas who do not have a British parent or grandparent can usually only obtain British citizenship by living in the UK and meeting the residence and other requirements for registration or naturalisation (▶see chapter 18).

British citizenship by descent

People born overseas who acquire British citizenship only because one or both of their parents is a British citizen are classified as **British citizens by descent**.

People who acquire British citizenship by birth in the UK, by registration/ naturalisation in the UK or by being UK and Colonies citizens with five years' residence and settlement in the UK before 1 January 1983 are classified as **British citizens otherwise than by descent**.

The only difference between the two kinds of British citizens is that those who are citizens by descent cannot automatically pass on citizenship to their children born abroad.

Before 1 January 1983 British men who had children in *non-Commonwealth countries* could pass on British nationality through numerous generations, provided that the children's births were registered at a British consulate. This would not usually make the children full British citizens after the second generation born abroad (that is, if they did not have a grandfather born, registered or naturalised in the UK). Such children would not fulfil the requirements for patriality under the Immigration Act 1971 (▶see glossary for definition of patriality) and would therefore normally have become British Overseas citizens on 1 January 1983. Children born in *Commonwealth countries* did not acquire any form of British nationality if their father was British by descent.

After 1 January 1983 the British Nationality Act 1981 removed the difference between Commonwealth and non-Commonwealth countries but restricted the automatic transmission of British nationality to one generation. Children born abroad to a parent who is a British citizen otherwise than by descent are automatically born British. However, if the British citizen parent is a citizen by descent, a child born abroad will not be born British. This means that British citizenship can now pass automatically only for one generation to a child born abroad to British parents. However, the Act included provisions for some second-generation children to be registered abroad as British citizens.

These provisions allow a child born overseas to be registered at the British consulate as a British citizen within a year of the birth provided that:

- one of the parents is a British citizen by descent
- the British parent has a parent who is or was British otherwise than by descent
- the British parent had at some time before the child's birth lived in the UK for a continuous period of three years, not being absent for more than 270 days in that period.

In those circumstances, the child has a right to become a British citizen by registration provided that an application is made within one year of the birth. A registration form (MN1) must be completed and a fee is payable. The child will become a **British citizen by descent**.

If the child and its parents do not fulfil all the above requirements, it is not possible for the child to be registered as a British citizen overseas. A third-

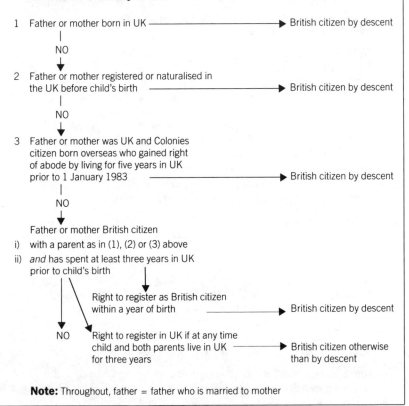

CITIZENSHIP BY DESCENT

For children born outside the UK to a British parent on or after 1 January 1983

1 Father or mother born in UK ──────────▶ British citizen by descent

   |
   NO
   ↓

2 Father or mother registered or naturalised in the UK before child's birth ──────────▶ British citizen by descent

   |
   NO
   ↓

3 Father or mother was UK and Colonies citizen born overseas who gained right of abode by living for five years in UK prior to 1 January 1983 ──────────▶ British citizen by descent

   |
   NO
   ↓

Father or mother British citizen
i) with a parent as in (1), (2) or (3) above
ii) *and* has spent at least three years in UK prior to child's birth

Right to register as British citizen within a year of birth ──────────▶ British citizen by descent

NO   Right to register in UK if at any time child and both parents live in UK for three years ──────────▶ British citizen otherwise than by descent

Note: Throughout, father = father who is married to mother

generation child born overseas will never have a right to registration under the provisions above, because she or he will never be able to fulfil the second requirement (▶see chart above). The only exception to this is if a parent is in 'designated service' (see below).

However, there is a fallback provision if the child and *both* its parents return to live in the UK. Any child born overseas to a British citizen by descent parent has a right to be registered as a British citizen in the UK provided that the child and both parents (unless they are divorced or one is dead) live in the UK for a continuous period of three years. In that case, the child will have a right to register as a British citizen and moreover will become a **British citizen otherwise than by descent**.

It is possible to use this last provision as an alternative to registration abroad; for example, if the parents have missed the one-year deadline or if they would rather wait and register the child in the UK so that the child will be able to pass on its own British nationality at a later date without any problems. Once a child has been registered abroad as a citizen by descent, it is not possible to alter this to become a citizen otherwise than by descent, even if the family comes to live in the UK for more than three years.

There are further details about other registration and naturalisation provisions in chapter 18.

Citizenship through Crown or designated service

There are special citizenship provisions for people doing certain government service jobs abroad. The work must be either Crown service (that is, working at a British embassy or high commission abroad, or serving in the British armed forces abroad) or designated service (working outside the UK in a defined list of jobs for the British government, for example working for the British Council, the British Tourist Authority or the Medical Research Council, or working abroad for an EC or international institution, for example the United Nations). People in these jobs are considered as working in the UK for the purpose of passing on citizenship. A child born outside the UK to a parent who is a British citizen (by descent or otherwise than by descent) working in Crown or designated service at the time of the birth will be born a British citizen otherwise than by descent.

British nationals who are not British citizens

British Overseas citizens, British Dependent Territories citizens, British Protected Persons and British Nationals (Overseas) do not have the right of abode in the UK. Nor do British subjects, except for a very few who had a UK-born mother and a very small number of women who were married before 1 January 1983 to men who had the right of abode in the UK. Pages 215–217 explain how to identify these categories of people.

For these people, their British status amounts to little more than a travel document facility. It does not give them the right to live anywhere. Most British Dependent Territories citizens, however, will have the right to live in the territory where they or their parents were born, but this will depend on the immigration ordinance or regulations of that territory. If the territory becomes independent, they can expect to be granted citizenship of the newly independent country.

Right of readmission

British Overseas citizens who have been admitted for settlement to the UK have a right to be readmitted for settlement at any time. They may obtain an endorsement from the Home Office, 'Holder has the right of readmission to the UK' on page 5 of their passports. This means that even if they stay away from the UK for more than two years at a time they cannot be refused indefinite leave to remain when they return. They are not, therefore, subject to the requirements of the returning residents rule (▶see page 154).

Passing on nationality to children

British Overseas citizens, British Protected Persons, British subjects and British Nationals (Overseas) cannot normally pass on their citizenship to their children. Apart from the special provisions for Hong Kong, it is no longer possible to acquire BOC, BPP or BS status, so these nationalities will die out with their present holders.

British Dependent Territories citizens (BDTCs) can pass on their status to their children in exactly the same way as British citizens. Children born in a dependent territory will become BDTCs at birth automatically provided that they have one parent who is either a BDTC or is settled in the territory (▶see glossary for list of dependent territories). Children born in a dependency who do not automatically become BDTCs at birth will have a right to register as BDTCs if either of their parents become settled in the territory or if the children remain in the territory for ten years.

A BDTC parent who has a child born outside a dependency is able to pass on his or her BDTC status in exactly the same way as a British citizen parent can pass on British citizenship to a child born abroad (see above for details).

There are some provisions to protect the children of British nationals who would otherwise be **stateless**, but these are very restrictive. Children born to a British national, other than a British Protected Person, in the UK or a dependency have a right to acquire their parent's status by registration if they would otherwise be stateless. Children born outside the UK or a dependency to such a British national parent only have a right to registration if they become settled in the UK or a dependency and have lived there for three years.

There are general discretionary provisions for the Home Secretary to register minors as British subjects (s32), British Overseas citizens (s27(1)) and British Dependent Territories citizens (s17(1)). The qualifications for this are not defined and the provisions are very rarely used.

British nationals with an East African connection
The special quota voucher scheme

In the late 1960s, British nationals living in East and Central Africa, most of whose families originated from the Indian subcontinent, faced pressure to leave some of the newly independent countries, particularly Uganda and Kenya. It was because of this pressure, and the fear that such British nationals might come to the UK, that the Commonwealth Immigrants Act 1968 was passed. This prevented the entry of citizens of the UK and Colonies (as they were then called) who had not acquired their citizenship in the UK, or who did not have a parent or grandparent who had acquired citizenship in the UK.

At the time the 1968 Act was passed, the UK government announced the creation of the special quota voucher scheme to admit a small number of these British nationals who were under pressure to leave the countries where they were living. In 1972 there was a large-scale expulsion of British nationals of Asian origin from Uganda. The people concerned found it difficult or impossible to enter the UK and many sought temporary refuge in India to wait for a voucher under this scheme. Some people made complaints to the European Commission of Human Rights, which found the UK guilty of 'inhuman and degrading treatment' of its own nationals. As a result, it agreed to increase the number of vouchers issued every year; the nominal annual quota is now 5000.

However, people in India found that they were waiting longer and longer for vouchers to be issued. The British government refused to say how many of the 5000 'global quota' were allocated to India, and how many to East Africa (where demand and supply soon met, because most of the people who needed to leave had already done so). In 1982, it emerged that only 600 of the 5000 vouchers were allocated to India, and most of the rest of the notional quota remained unallocated. As a result, in the mid-1980s the queue for issue of a voucher in India reached eight years. In 1991 it was still nearly two years, though only 920 vouchers were issued in total in 1990 and there were only 1600 people in the queue.

Qualifications for obtaining a special quota voucher

The voucher scheme is completely outside the immigration rules and is administered at the discretion of the Home Secretary. Vouchers are issued only to British nationals, with no other nationality, who are:

- under pressure to leave the country in which they are living
- *and* who are heads of households.

British nationals with no other nationality: this includes British protected persons and British subjects as well as people who are now British Overseas citizens, but not British Dependent Territories citizens. However, it does not apply to any of these people if they have access to another nationality, even if they do not want to take up that nationality. This means, for example, that most people whose families originate from Pakistan will not be considered eligible for vouchers, because Pakistan allows dual nationality (whereas India does not).

Under pressure to leave: this means people living in the countries of East and Central Africa (Uganda, Kenya, Tanzania, Malawi, Zambia) and people who left those countries to go to India and wait for admission to the UK. Vouchers are not normally issued to people from East Africa who went to live in other countries (for example to work in the Gulf States) or to British nationals living in other countries in the world, even if their immigration or other status is very insecure.

Heads of households: under the voucher scheme, married women are not regarded as 'heads of households'. Therefore, British national women married to Indian men, for example, cannot qualify for vouchers unless they can show that their husband is physically or mentally incapacitated and cannot be considered the 'head of household'. Divorced or widowed women are eligible for vouchers if they fulfil the other requirements.

Admission of dependants

Voucher-holders' immediate family may qualify to accompany or join them in the UK. This includes spouses and dependent children up to the age of 25 (this upper age limit was introduced because the eight-year queue in India meant that children who were nearly 18 when their parents applied would reach 25 before the application was considered). In order to remain dependent, however, children must be unmarried and financially dependent on their parents (that is, not working). Young men who take up employment or marry will normally be able to apply for a voucher in their own right once they reach 18, if they are also British nationals. However, young women who marry non-British men will cease to be eligible for a voucher as they will not be considered heads of households.

A voucher-holder does not have to fulfil the public funds requirement (▶see box on page 124). However, the dependants of a voucher-holder do have to fulfil this requirement. Either they will have to have a sponsor in the UK who promises to support and accommodate them until the family can be self-supporting, or the voucher-holder himself will have to go first to the UK to find accommodation and a job to support his family.

How to apply for a voucher

Applications for special quota vouchers are made to the nearest British high commission. There is no special form for the voucher applicant, but his or her dependants will have to fill in the usual forms for people seeking settlement in the UK, IM2A and IM2B. Voucher applicants do not have to pay a fee, but their dependants have to pay the usual settlement fee at the time they apply.

Voucher applicants and their dependants then wait for an interview. In East Africa, the interview will take place within a few weeks. However, in India, applicants were still waiting nearly two years before interview in mid-1991. If there are young adult children, particularly daughters, decisions on their applications may be held up after interview, pending further enquiries to check whether or not they are married.

If a voucher is issued, the voucher-holder has to travel to the UK within six months and will be admitted for an indefinite period (settlement). If entry clearance is issued to his or her dependants, this also has to be used within six months of issue and they will be admitted for a year initially.

British nationals from Malaysia

The other country where there are many British Overseas citizens is Malaysia. Three areas of Malaya – Penang, Melaka and Singapore – were ruled directly by Britain as the Straits Settlements and Malayan independence law provided that people who were born or whose father had been born in those areas before independence (31 August 1957) would retain their citizenship of the UK and Colonies. When Singapore became independent separately from Malaysia, this provision was lost for Singaporeans, but it still exists for people from Penang and Melaka. Because they have no connection with East Africa, they do not qualify for special quota vouchers. Malaysia does not permit people to gain any advantage from holding another nationality without forfeiting their Malaysian nationality and many Malaysians do not know that they may be entitled to British nationality. People with this connection with Penang or Melaka who wish to claim their British nationality should obtain specialist advice.

British nationals from Hong Kong

Most British nationals from Hong Kong lost the right to live in the UK under the Commonwealth Immigrants Act 1962. The only citizens of the UK and Colonies (as they then were) from Hong Kong who retained the right of abode, and who still have the right of abode now, are:

- people who were born, registered or naturalised in the UK
- people who had at any time before 1983 spent five years continuously and legally in the UK and were settled in the UK at the end of that period
- people with a parent or grandparent who was born, registered or naturalised in the UK
- women married to a man who fulfilled any of these conditions.

These conditions meant that most people of Chinese or other Asian origin in Hong Kong lost the right of abode in the UK. However, a number of these people spent time in the UK as students or workers in the 1950s or 1960s. At that time, people from Hong Kong and other Commonwealth countries were technically 'settled' in the UK, because no conditions could be put on their stay if they were admitted. It is therefore worth checking whether and when any Hong Kong British nationals have lived in the UK. If they lived in the UK for more than five years, before 1983, and had no time limit on their stay at the end of that five year period, they gained the right of abode and are therefore British citizens now.

British Nationals (Overseas): the Hong Kong Act 1985

In 1985, Britain and China signed an agreement for the return of Hong Kong to China on 1 July 1997. They agreed that the status of British Dependent Territories citizen would no longer apply to people from Hong Kong after that date. Instead, it was agreed that they would be able to apply for a new status, called British National (Overseas). This does not carry the right of abode in the UK. The Chinese authorities do not regard this as a citizenship, merely as a travel document facility.

BDTCs from Hong Kong can apply for British National (Overseas) passports at any time up to 30 June 1997. Children born between 1 January and 30 June 1997 can apply up to the end of that year. Anyone who has not applied before those dates will lose British nationality altogether when Hong Kong returns to China.

Most BDTCs from Hong Kong are also considered by the Chinese authorities to be Chinese citizens and will have Chinese citizenship after 30 June 1997. People who are not of Chinese ethnic origin may not be Chinese citizens, for example people of Indian origin who have lived in Hong Kong for many years or generations. If they have no other nationality, they may apply to become British Overseas citizens after 30 June 1997.

British citizenship: the British Nationality (Hong Kong) Act 1990

After the events in Tiananmen Square in June 1989, people in Hong Kong became very alarmed about their future and the emigration rate from the territory increased. There was great concern that this might endanger the financial and social stability of Hong Kong. After representations from the Hong Kong government and others, the UK government agreed to provide up to 50,000 full British citizen passports for BDTCs from Hong Kong in certain specified categories.

Applications are decided on a points system, based on the so-called 'emigrateability rate' of the groups of people concerned (their age, qualifications and the actual emigration rates of people in their profession). There are also special categories for people in 'sensitive services' (for example key civil servants or people in the security services), for 'disciplined services' (for example police, immigration and prison officers) and for a small number of 'key entrepreneurs'. Applications for the first tranche of 43,000 places had to be returned by 28 February 1991. There were fewer than anticipated – only 65,623 compared with the hundreds of thousands which had been predicted, and some categories were under-subscribed. Few decisions had been made at the time of writing. The remainder of the 50,000 places under the scheme will be made available in 1996.

This scheme provides the only route to right of abode in the UK for most Hong Kong BDTCs.

People from Hong Kong who are living in the UK

The following checklist will help to decide the status of someone from Hong Kong who is living in the UK:

- **Does the person have a (brown) certificate of identity?**

  If so, the person is not a British national of any kind. He or she was born in mainland China and is probably entitled to Chinese citizenship. He or she may be able to obtain British citizenship by naturalisation if he or she fulfils the requirements; ▶see chapter 18.

- **Does the person have a British passport?**

  – does the passport state 'holder has the right of abode in the UK' on page 5, or 'British citizen' on page 1? If so, the person is a British citizen, with the right of abode in the UK.

  – did the person, at any time before 1 January 1983, live legally in the UK for at least five years, without any conditions on his or her stay at the end of the period? If so, and provided that the person can prove this, he or she is a British citizen with the right of abode in the UK.

  – was the person born in the UK before 1 January 1983? was the person born in the UK on or after 1 January 1983 with a parent who was British or was settled in the UK at the time of the birth? If so, the person is a British citizen with the right of abode in the UK.

If none of these apply, check the immigration stamp on the passport (▶see chapter 13 for examples of different passport stamps). This will show under what conditions, if any, the person has been admitted or allowed to remain. Only people with indefinite leave can apply for British citizenship (▶see chapter 18 for details of the requirements and how to apply). Students, visitors and work permit holders cannot apply and should not do so as this may prejudice future applications to remain here or return here. Some students who have been in the UK for ten years or more may be able to obtain indefinite leave (▶see page 160 for details).

18 How to become British

There are two ways in which people of other nationalities can obtain British citizenship:

- **naturalisation** is the way almost all adults (people aged 18 and over) can become British. It is always discretionary and can be refused with no reason given. There is no right of appeal against a refusal of citizenship.

- **registration** is the way all children (people under 18) and a very small number of adults (see below) can become British. It is sometimes a right which cannot be refused, but in most cases is discretionary, without the need to give reasons and without a right of appeal.

Points to note

- All adults applying for British citizenship *must* be settled (have indefinite leave to remain) in the UK at the date of application. Sometimes people who are in the UK for a limited period (for example as students) mistakenly believe that an application for citizenship will be a means of being able to stay in the UK permanently. Quite the reverse is true: they do not qualify for citizenship, and the Home Office is likely to interpret a citizenship application as evidence that they do not intend to leave the UK at the end of their studies and therefore may refuse an extension of leave as a student.

- Applications for citizenship will probably lead to an investigation of the whole family's immigration status. If there is any irregularity in the applicant's status or that of a close family member (for example if they are overstayers) they should seek advice about regularising their status before making a citizenship application.

- The Home Office now retains most of a citizenship fee, even if the application is unsuccessful (▶see appendix). It is therefore very important for people to check *before* applying that they at least fulfil the objective criteria (that is, residence, language) rather than risk losing money.

Naturalisation

Requirements for naturalisation

- residence and settlement in the UK
- language
- good character
- intention to live in the UK

The requirements (and the fees) are slightly different for people who are married to British citizens and people who are not married to British citizens. The former will usually find that it is easier and cheaper for them to become British.

The requirement of marriage is a requirement at the time of application. However, if a couple separate or divorce after the application is made but before it is granted, and if the Home Office is aware of the state of the marriage, it is likely that the application will be refused. The person may be asked whether he or she wants to apply instead on the basis of residence, by paying the extra amount of money.

Residence and settlement

People who are not married to British citizens must have been living legally in the UK for five years continuously, and must have been physically present in the UK on the date five years before they apply. They must not have been absent for more than 450 days in total and not more than 90 days in the year immediately before they apply. They must have been settled (have had indefinite leave to remain in the UK) for at least a year before they apply.

People who are married to British citizens must have been living legally in the UK for three years continuously, and must have been physically present in the UK on the date three years before they apply. They must not have been absent for more than 270 days in total and not more than 90 days in the year immediately before they apply. They must be settled (have indefinite leave to remain in the UK) at the time they apply.

Language

People who are not married to British citizens must show that they have a 'sufficient knowledge' of English, Welsh or Gaelic. They do not need to be literate in the language, but should be able to converse in it. This test is assessed by the immigration service in London and by police forces in other areas. It is usually done by means of a visit or an interview, occasionally by a telephone call to the applicant. It is very unsatisfactory as the people making the assessment are not trained to do so and the people being assessed may be shocked by the arrival of a police officer, or have difficulties with telephone conversations. In theory, elderly or infirm applicants can be excused the language test, but this is at the discretion of the Home Office.

People who are married to British citizens do not need to pass a language test.

Good character

All applicants must show that they are of 'good character'. This is very ill-defined. Unspent criminal convictions are taken into account (applicants have to list these on the application form). Checks are also usually made on financial solvency. The Special Branch is also usually asked to comment on any alleged security risk. In addition, the local police force (or, in London, the immigration service) may be asked to run checks on the applicant, which may include an interview. This is the most subjective of the tests and the one where the Home Office is least likely to give the reasons why it has refused.

Intention to live in the UK

People who are not married to British citizens have to show that they intend to continue to live in the UK if the application is granted. Ministers have said that they want to be sure that applicants are really committed to the UK and do not simply want 'the convenience of a British passport'. It is therefore unwise, for example, to seek to speed up the processing of an application because there is likely to be a prolonged absence abroad.

Technically, applicants can travel overseas for as long as they like after the application has been submitted (the residence requirements refer to the period before the application was made). However, if it is clear that an applicant is no longer living permanently in the UK while the application is being considered (for example, if it is impossible for a police interview to be arranged) the Home Office may consider this as evidence of a lack of intention to live permanently in the UK. It may then require evidence that the stay abroad is only a temporary one (for example, contractual employment, study or caring for a sick relative). People who have submitted naturalisation applications remain in any case subject to the returning residents rule (▶see page 154) and will need to return within two years to secure their settled status in the UK.

People who are married to British citizens do not have to show that they intend to continue to live in the UK.

The process of application

Applicants have to fill in Form AN, available from the Home Office Nationality Division (▶address in chapter 19). They need to send the fee (▶see appendix) at the same time as the application. A married couple applying together pay only one fee between them. Since March 1991, the Home Office retains most of the fee if the application is unsuccessful.

Naturalisation applications have been taking a very long time to process. In June 1991, the average waiting period was 36 months. The Home Office has stated that it will consider representations to expedite consideration in particular cases when there are exceptional circumstances.

Applicants do not need to send their passports with the application form, because it takes so long to deal with applications. The Home Office will ask to see the passport when it is needed.

Refusals of applications

The Home Office is not obliged to give reasons for refusal. If the refusal is because of a technicality (for example, a failure to meet the residence requirements, an assessment that the applicant's language skills are inadequate) the Home Office will usually indicate this. In other cases, an MP may be able to elicit more information about the reasons for the refusal. If the Home Office refuses to give any details, this is usually because the refusal has been made under the 'good character' test and may well be connected with political activity or allegations of financial impropriety.

Although there is no right of appeal against refusal, it is sometimes possible to challenge refusals which are manifestly wrong. This should be done through the applicant's MP. JCWI has successfully challenged refusals on language grounds where it has been perfectly obvious that the applicant can communicate effectively in English. It is also possible to argue against a Home Office assumption that an applicant who has spent long periods abroad since applying does not intend to make his or her home in the UK.

Crown service

A person who is not British but who is working in Crown service overseas may apply for naturalisation on the ground of a period of work rather than of residence in the UK. Crown service involves working for the British government abroad, but no length of service is stipulated. The other requirements for naturalisation must be met, including the intention to continue in the service of the British government, rather than to live in the UK. It is rare for naturalisation to be granted on this basis.

Registration

Registration of adults

There are two small groups of adults who are able to obtain British citizenship by registration and whose applications cannot be refused:

a) British nationals who are not British citizens

British nationals who are not British citizens (British Overseas citizens, British Dependent Territories citizens, British Protected Persons, British subjects and British Nationals (Overseas) ▶see chapter 17 for definitions) have a right to obtain British citizenship by registration if they gain settlement rights in the UK. It is very difficult for most of these people to gain settlement rights in the UK as they are subject to immigration control.

They have to fulfil the following requirements:

• they must have lived in the UK legally for at least five years, and have been physically present in the UK on the date five years before they apply, and not have been absent for more than 450 days, not more than 90 of those days in the year immediately before applying

• they must have been settled (have had indefinite leave to remain in the UK) for at least one year.

b) Some Commonwealth citizens who were under 18 on 1 January 1983

A very small number of young Commonwealth citizens have a right to register as British citizens. They must:

• have been settled (have had indefinite leave to remain) in the UK before 1 January 1973

• have been under 18 on 1 January 1983

• have remained ordinarily resident in the UK

• apply within five years of their 18th birthday, that is, be aged between 18 and 23 on the date of application. This provision will therefore become obsolete by the end of 1995.

The process of application

Applicants who are British nationals have to fill in Form B. Applicants who are young Commonwealth citizens have to fill in Form R. Both forms are available from the Home Office Nationality Division (▶address in chapter 19). Applicants need to send the fee (▶see appendix) at the same time as the application.

Registration of children
Children with a right to register

Children under 18 always obtain British citizenship by registration. Two groups of children have a *right* to register as British citizens. They are:

a) Children born in the UK since 1 January 1983 and not born British

Children who were born in the UK but who did not acquire British citizenship at birth because neither of their parents was a British citizen or settled in the UK have a right to register as British citizens if:

- one of their parents becomes settled (is given indefinite leave to remain) in the UK or
- the children remain in the UK for the first 10 years of their life and are not outside the UK for more than 90 days in any of those years.

b) Children born overseas to parents who are British citizens by descent

Children who are born overseas to a parent who is a British citizen by descent do not acquire British citizenship automatically. Some of these children have a right to register overseas within a year of their birth, while others will acquire a right to register if they and their parents live for three years in the UK. For details of the requirements, ▶see the section on British citizens by descent in chapter 17.

Children who can apply to register at discretion

All other children can register only at the discretion of the Home Secretary. There are no specific qualifications in the British Nationality Act 1981, which simply says (s3(1)) that the Home Secretary can register a minor child as a British citizen. In theory, this means that any child, anywhere, could be registered as British. In practice, it is rare for registration to be granted to a child living outside the UK (except those children with a right to register, described above). The Home Office has also stated that children born outside the UK before 1983 to British-born mothers (who would have automatically been born British by descent if they had been born after 1 January 1983) will be registered if the mother applies for this before the children are 18, and, if the parents are still married, if the father has no well-founded objection.

In other cases, if children are living in the UK, there are no specific residence or other requirements. The Home Office has given little guidance on the factors it examines, only that 'consideration is given to' the following:

- the child's connections with the UK (for example, whether the child is settled)

- where the child's future is likely to lie
- the views of the parents
- the nationality of the parents.

In the case of 'older children, particularly those approaching 18', the Home Office will also take into consideration:

- whether the child is of good character (▶see above for definition of this)
- the length of time the child has lived in the UK.

Because the qualifications are so unclear, it is very difficult to be sure whether a child's registration application will succeed. In practice, if one or both parent(s) is or are British or applying to become British, the Home Office will usually register young children, and older children who have lived in the UK for some time (this is undefined, but would certainly include children who have been living in the UK for five years or more). If neither parent is British, or intending to become British, there may be some difficulty in fulfilling the requirements. The Home Office would not normally register a child whose parents were not settled in the UK, unless the child had been taken into local authority care and it was clear that there was no prospect of the parents regaining custody.

The process of application

Parents or guardians normally apply on behalf of a child. If an older child makes an application him or herself, the reasons for this should be explained to the Home Office. When an application is made for children on their own, whether they are applying as of right or at discretion, it is on form MN1, available from the Home Office Nationality Division (▶address in chapter 19). Parents who are applying for registration for their children at the same time as for naturalisation or registration for themselves may list the children on their own naturalisation or registration form. A single fee covers all the children in the same family if they apply at the same time either on their own or with their parent(s). If the application is unsuccessful, the Home Office retains most of the fee.

Registration applications usually do not take so long to process as naturalisations. However, there are still substantial delays. In early 1991, registrations were taking 23 months to process.

Passports and travel documents

When the Home Office grants an application for British citizenship, it sends the person a certificate to confirm the grant of citizenship. This certificate is then evidence of the person's citizenship status.

In order to obtain a British passport, people need to apply to the Passport Office nearest to where they live (▶see chapter 19 for addresses). They can get application forms for British passports from any large Post Office; there are separate forms for adults and children. The forms must be filled in and sent together with the citizenship certificate, any other documents requested and the fee (▶see appendix) to the Passport Office. At present, the time this takes varies with the season, summer being the slowest. The Passport Office now has agency status and its target time for issuing passports is a few days at any time of year. Some Passport Offices are now issuing the uniform EC machine-readable burgundy-coloured British passports, rather than the old blue British ones; the colour of the passport makes no difference to the person's status and rights.

Stateless people living in the UK, for example some children born in the UK but not born British, apply to the Home Office Travel Documents Section for travel documents. They fill in a form TD112 and return it to the Home Office with the fee (▶see appendix). The Home Office normally requires evidence that the person cannot get a travel document from any other country which might be expected to provide it, for example, a letter from the embassy of their parents' country confirming that the child does not have that nationality, before issuing a travel document. When it is hard to obtain this evidence, or when the parents are not prepared to contact the embassy, for example if they have been granted exceptional leave to remain, this should be explained to the Home Office and the application submitted anyway. In August 1991 the Home Office was advising people to allow at least 16–18 weeks for the issue of a travel document.

19 Useful addresses and telephone numbers

**Home Office Immigration and
Nationality Department**
Lunar House, Wellesley Road
Croydon CR9 2BY

Main telephone number: 081 686 0688,
fax 081 760 8689/1181

Direct telephone lines to the groups dealing
with individual cases are organised initially
by the last two numbers of the Home Office
reference for the case. They all start 081
760, followed by the direct number.

Group	Reference	Extension	Room
1	01–04	2191	511
2	05–08	2188	507
3	09–12	2271	510
4	13–16	2266	508
5	17–20	2280	504
6	21–24	2284	501
7	25–28	2330	502
8	29–32	2173	513
9	33–36	1348	728
10	37–40	2157	512
11	41–44	2683	516
12	45–48	2615	519
13	49–52	2154	524
14	53–56	2296	528
15	57–60	2080	529
16	61–64	2631	715
17	65–68	2546	707
18	69–72	2759	730
19	73–76	2727	701
20	77–80	2397	703
21	81–84	2035	721
22	85–88	2038	728
23	89–92	2066	734
24	93–96	2030	733
25	97–00	2785	741

Illegal entry groups 2605, 2456
Settlement groups 2038, 1196, 2955

Home Office, *continued*
BOCs group 2641
DNA section 1414
EC section 2604, 2364

Asylum

Most asylum cases are dealt with at Quest
House, Wellesley Road, Croydon, CR9 2BY
and are divided by the geographical region
from which the asylum-seeker comes.
Numbers all start 081 760. The general
registry for Quest House is 4964.

Section A
    Eastern Europe, China, the Americas
    2255, 2070
Section B
    Middle East, Turkey, North Africa
    4986, 4823
Section C1
    Africa north of the Equator
    4815, 4912, 4826
Section C2
    Africa south of the Equator
    4882, 4974
Section D
    Asia, Far East 2561, 2526

Nationality

During 1991, the Home Office Nationality
Division moved to Liverpool. All nationality
work will be done there from 1992.

Nationality Division, Home Office
3rd floor, India Buildings, Water Street
Liverpool L2 0QN
tel. 051 236 4723

Home Office regional Public Enquiry Offices

Belfast
Olivetree House, Fountain Street
Belfast BT1 5ER
tel. 0232 322547/232951

Glasgow
Admin Block D, Glasgow Airport
Abbotsinch, Paisley
Renfrewshire PA3 2TD
tel. 041 887 2255

Harwich
Parkestone Quay, Harwich
Essex CO12 4SX
tel. 0255 504371

Liverpool
Graeme House, Derby Square
Liverpool L2 7SF
tel. 051 236 8974

Norwich
Norwich Airport, New Terminal Building
Norwich NR6 6EP
tel. 0603 408859

Southampton (only in winter)
Town Quay, Southampton
tel. 0703 631756

Ports of entry
Immigration service and detention areas

London Heathrow
Terminal 1
  casework: 081 897 2731,
  arrivals control 081 897 1282,
  fax 081 897 3623
Terminal 2
  general: 081 897 3129,
  casework 081 897 1033,
  fax 081 897 3620
Terminal 3: 081 897 7651,
  switchboard 081 897 9631,
  fax 081 759 5042
Terminal 4: switchboard 081 897 7261,
  fax 081 759 5376
Queens Building detention centre
  081 564 9727/081 897 1849
  (detainees)
  081 745 6484 (Group 4)
Harmondsworth Detention Centre
  Building JA 081 564 7790/7686
  Building DA 081 897 8040 (detainees)
  081 759 9727 (Group 4)

Belfast city office 0232 322547,
  fax 0232 244939,
  airport 08494 2200,
  switchboard 0894 22888
Birmingham International Airport
  021 782 4321,
  fax 021 782 0006
Midland Enquiry Unit,
  021 782 0771,
  fax 021 782 2901
Bristol 027587 2843,
  fax at Avonmouth 0272 820 469
Cardiff 0222 481080,
  fax 0222 494979,
  airport 0446 710485
City Airport (London) immigration
  071 474 1395
Dover East immigration 0304 240123,
  fax 0304 213594
Detention (Dover police station)
  0304 206260
Dover West immigration 0304 201913,
  fax 0304 240558,
  detention (Sealink) 0304 203203
  ex 3308
Dover Hoverport 0304 240246,
  fax 0304 215343
East Midlands Airport 0332 850167
Edinburgh 031 344 3330,
  fax 031 335 3197
Folkestone immigration 0303 850541,
  fax 0303 50233,
  detention 0303 54202
Gatwick South switchboard 0293 502019,
  casework 0293 502654,
  fax 0293 553643
Gatwick North switchboard 0293 567303,
  casework 0293 567282,
  fax 0293 567349
Detention holding room 0293 502640,
  Beehive 0293 502631
Glasgow 041 887 4115,
  fax 041 887 1566
Gravesend 0474 352308,
  fax 0474 534731
Harwich immigration 0255 504371,
  fax 0255 240233,
  detention 0255 241326/252176
Hull 0482 223017,
  fax 0482 219034

Ports of entry *continued*
Leeds 0532 502931,
CIO 0532 502328,
fax 0532 505716

Liverpool 051 236 8974,
fax 051 236 4656

Luton 0582 421891,
fax 0582 405215

Manchester Ringway 061 437 2402,
CIO 061 437 0168,
fax 061 499 0879

Newcastle 091 286 9469,
fax 091 214 0143

Prestwick 0292 78675,
fax 0292 671459

Ramsgate 0843 594716,
fax 0843 587605

Sheerness 07956 67733,
fax 07956 661509,
interviews 07956 667591

Stansted 0279 680118/680692/813654,
fax 0279 680041

H.M. Prison Haslar 0705 580381,
fax 0705 504432,
fax to IOs 0705 528631
Dormitories
A 0705 528604, B 0705 510653,
C 0705 510599, D 0705 510 362

Immigration service offices

Isis House 071 928 6824,
casework 071 928 3350,
fax 071 928 0015

Harmondsworth 081 897 0771,
casework 081 759 4908,
fax 081 564 7316

Immigration appeals offices

Thanet House, 231 The Strand
London WC2R 1DA
tel. 071 353 8060,
fax 071 583 1976
All Immigration Appeal Tribunal cases are
heard at Thanet House.

Government Buildings, Clay Lane, Yardley
Birmingham B26 1EA
tel. 021 706 4382/9741

Oxford House, The Hayes
Cardiff CF1 2DR.
Part-time hearing centre, administered
from Harmondsworth.

Government Buildings, Colnbrook Bypass
Harmondsworth, West Drayton
Middlesex UB7 0HB
tel. 081 897 9641

4th floor, Coronet House, Queen Street
Leeds LS1 2SH
tel. 0532 449898

3rd floor, Aldine House
New Bailey Street
Manchester M3 5EU
tel. 061 832 9571, ext. 322/328

The Merchant House, 7 George Street
Glasgow G2 1BA
tel. 041 221 6779

Home Office presenting officers

19–29 Woburn Place
London WC1H 0JH tel 071 278 4678,
fax 071 278 5472

Outside London:
addresses as Immigration Appeals
offices

Birmingham 021 706 9741
Harmondsworth 081 897 2919
Leeds 0532 603245
Manchester 061 832 9571
ext. 284/5/6/7/8

Passport offices

Clive House, Petty France
London SW1H 9HD
tel. 071 279 4000
(recorded message 071 279 3434)

Hampton House, 47–53 High St
Belfast BT1 2QS
tel. 0232 232371

3 Northgate, 96 Milton Street
Cowcaddens, Glasgow G4 0BT
tel. 041 332 0271

5th floor, India Buildings
Water Street
Liverpool L2 0QZ
tel. 051 237 3010

Olympia House, Upper Dock Street
Newport, Gwent NP9 1XA
tel. 0633 244500/244292

Aragon Court, Northminster Road
Peterborough PE1 1QG
tel. 0733 555688

Some other government departments

Aliens Registration Office
10 Lamb's Conduit Street
London WC1X 3MX
tel. 071 725 2451

Employment Department
Overseas Labour Section
Caxton House, Tothill Street
London SW1H 9NF
tel. 071 273 5336/5337

Department of Social Security
Benefits Agency Overseas Branch
Benton Park Road, Longbenton
Newcastle-upon-Tyne NE98 1YX
tel. 091 213 5000

Foreign and Commonwealth Office
Migration and Visa Department and
Nationality and Treaty Department
Clive House, Petty France
London SW1H 9HD
tel. 071 270 3000

Home Office (Minister's private office)
Queen Anne's Gate
London SW1H 9AT
tel. 071 273 4604

Training and Employment Agency
Netherleigh, Massey Avenue
Belfast BT4 2JP
tel. 0232 63244

Treasury Solicitor
Queen Anne's Chambers, 28 Broadway
London SW1H 9JS
tel. 071 210 3000, fax 071 222 6006

Members of Parliament

Write to them at the House of Commons
London SW1A 0AA, tel. 071 219 3000
or House of Lords
London SW1A 0PW, tel. 071 219 3000

Some British high commissions and embassies abroad

Bangladesh
British High Commission
Immigration Section
House 42, Road 135, Gulshan, Dhaka 12
tel. 600224/8, fax 880 2 412544
office hours GMT 01.30–08.00

Barbados
British High Commission
Lower Collymore Rock, P.O. Box 676
Bridgetown
tel. 436 6694, fax 809 426 7916
office hours GMT 12.00–20.00.
For Anguilla, Antigua and Barbuda,
Dominica, Grenada, Montserrat,
St Christopher and Nevis, St Vincent and
the Grenadines: all apply at Barbados.

China
11 Guang Hua Lu, Jian Guo Men Wai
Beijing
tel. 861 5321 961/5, fax 861 5321 939

Cyprus
British High Commission
Alexander Pallis Street, P.O. Box 1978
Nicosia
tel. 0 2 473131/7, fax 357 2 367198
office hours GMT 04.30–11.00
except Tuesdays, 04.30–10.00 and
    11.00–14.30.

France
35 rue du Faubourg St Honoré
75008 Paris
tel. 331 42 669142, fax 331 42 669590

Ghana
British High Commission, Osu Link
off Gamel Abdul Nasser Avenue
P.O. Box 296, Accra
tel. 221665, 221715, 221738
office hours GMT 07.45–14.45.

Guyana
British High Commission
44 Main Street, P.O. Box 10849
Georgetown
tel. 65881/2/3/4, fax 592 253555
office hours GMT 11.00–15.00 and
    16.00–19.00.

Hong Kong
Immigration Department
61 Mody Road, Kowloon
tel. 852 5 8293333, fax 852 5 8452870

India
British High Commission
Immigration Section, Chanakyapuri
New Delhi 1100–21
tel. 601371, fax 91 11 6872882
office hours GMT 04.00–08.00 and
    09.00–12.00

India *continued*

Office of the British Deputy High
  Commissioner, Immigration Section
Maker Chambers IV
222 Jamnalal Bajaj Road
P.O. Box 11714, Nariman Point
Bombay 400 021
tel. 91 22 230517
fax 91 22 274959/2027940
office hours GMT 02.30–07.30
  08.30–10.30.

Office of the British Deputy High
  Commissioner, Immigration Section
1 Ho Chi Minh Sarani, Calcutta 700 071
tel. 44 5171, fax 283458

Office of the British Deputy High
  Commissioner in Southern India
24 Anderson Road, Madras 600 006
tel. 473136, fax 91 44 869004
office hours GMT 03.00–07.30
  and 08.00–10.30.

Jamaica
British High Commission
P.O. Box 575, Trafalgar Road
Kingston 10
tel. 926 9050, fax 1 809 92 97869
office hours GMT 13.30–18.00 and
  19.00–21.30.

Jordan
British Embassy, The Third Circle
Jebel, Amman
tel. 962 6823100, fax 962 6813759

Kenya
British High Commission
P.O. Box 30465, Bruce House
Standard Street, Nairobi
tel. 335944, fax 254 2333196
office hours GMT 05.15–09.30
  and 10.30–13.30

Malawi
British High Commission
Lingadzi House, P.O. Box 30042
Lilongwe 3
tel. 731544, fax 265 734163
office hours GMT 05.30–10.00
  and 11.30–14.00.

Morocco
British Embassy
17 boulevard de la Tour Hassan
(B.P. 45), Rabat
tel. 209 05/6, 314 03/4
office hours GMT
  winter 08.00–12.30, 14.30–17.30
  summer 07.00–13.00

Nigeria
British High Commission
Private Mail Box 12136, 11 Eleke Crescent
Victoria Island, Lagos
tel. 619531/619537/619541/6195443/
  619566
fax 234 1 666909
office hours GMT 07.00–14.00
Visa Section, Chellaram Building
54 Marina, Lagos
tel. 667061/666413/666510/666313

Pakistan
British High Commission
Diplomatic Enclave, Ramna 5
P.O. Box 1122, Islamabad
tel. 822131/5, fax 92 51 823439

Office of the British Deputy High
  Commissioner
Shahrah-e-Iran, Clifton, Karachi 6
tel. 532041–6
office hours GMT
  Sun , Wed 03.00–08.30
  Mon, Tues, Thurs, 03.00–12.00

Philippines
British Embassy
15–17 Floor, L. V. Locsin Building
6752 Ayala Corner, Makati
Metro Manila 3116
P.O. Box 1970 MCC
tel. 632 816–7116, fax 63 2 819 7206
office hours GMT 00.00–08.30

Sierra Leone
Standard Bank Sierra Leone Buildings
Lightfoot, Boston Street, Freetown
tel. 232 22223961/5

Sri Lanka
British High Commission
Galle Road, Kollupitiya, P.O. Box 1433
Colombo 3
tel. 27611/19, fax 941 587079
office hours GMT 03.00–11.00
  Visa Office 03.00–05.00

Tanzania
British High Commission
Hifadhi House, Samora Avenue
P.O. Box 9200, Dar-es-Salaam
tel. 29601, fax 255 51 30365

Trinidad and Tobago
British High Commission
3rd and 4th floor, Furness House
90 Independence Square
P. O. Box 778, Port of Spain, Trinidad
tel. 62–52861–6, fax 1 809 623 0621

Turkey
British Embassy
Sehit Ersan Caddesi 46/A
Cankaya, Ankara
tel. 127 43 10/15, fax 90 4 168 3214

British Consulate-General
Mesrutiyet Caddesi no. 34
Tepebasi, Beyoglu, PK 33, Istanbul
tel. 144 75 40, 144 75 45/9
fax 90 1 145 4989
office hours GMT
  summer 05.30–10.00, 10.45–13.45
  winter 06.30–11.00 and 11.45–14.45

Zambia
British High Commission
Independence Avenue, P.O. Box 50050
Lusaka
tel. 228955, fax 2601 253421
office hours GMT 06.00–10.30
  and 12.00–14.30

Some agencies working on immigration and nationality matters
Joint Council for the Welfare of Immigrants
115 Old Street
London EC1V 9JR
tel. 071 251 8706, fax 071 253 3832

Independent Immigration Support Agency
  (formerly JCWI West Midlands)
3rd Floor, Spencer House, Digbeth
Birmingham B5 6DD
tel. and fax 021 622 7353

African Churches Council for Immigration
  and Social Justice (ACCIS)
Unit 6–7, 321 Essex Road
London N1 3PS
tel. 071 704 2331

Amnesty International British Section
99–119 Rosebery Avenue
London EC1R 4RE
tel. 071 278 6000, fax 071 833 1510

Asylum Aid
244 Upper Street
London N1 1RU
tel. 071 359 4026

Avon Immigration and Nationality Advice
  Centre
118 Church Street
Bristol BS5 9HH
tel. 0272 551149

British Agencies for Adoption and Fostering
11 Southwark Street
London SE1 1RQ
tel. 071 407 8800

Cellmark Diagnostics
Blacklands Way, Abingdon Business Park
Abingdon, Oxon, OX14 1DY
tel. 0235 28609

CHAT (Counselling, help and advice
  together)
Royal College of Nursing, Henrietta Place
London W1M 0AB
tel. 071 629 6441, 071 580 2646

Children's Legal Centre
20 Compton Terrace
London N1 2UN
tel. 071 359 9392, fax 071 354 9963

Commission for Racial Equality
Elliot House, 10–12 Allington Street
London SW1E 5EH
tel. 071 828 7022

Educational Grants Advisory Service
501–505 Kingsland Road
London E8 4AU

European Commission London office
8 Storey's Gate
London SW1P 3AT
tel. 071 222 8122

European Commission and Court of
  Human Rights
67006 Strasbourg Cedex, France
tel. 88 614961

Greater Manchester Immigration Aid Unit
400 Cheetham Hill Road
Manchester M8 7EL
tel. 061 740 7722

Immigration Law Practitioners' Association
115 Old Street
London EC1V 9JR
tel. 071 250 1671

Institute of Race Relations
2–6 Leeke Street
London WC1H 8LS
tel. 071 837 0041

Interights
5–15 Cromer Street
London WC1H 8LS
tel. 071 278 3230, fax 071 278 4334

International Social Service of Great Britain
Cranmer House, 39 Brixton Road
London SW9 6DD
tel. 071 735 8941

Kalayaan
c/o Commission for Filipino Migrant Workers
St Francis Centre, Pottery Lane
London W11 4NQ
tel. 071 221 0356

Law Centres Federation
Duchess House, 18–19 Warren Street
London W1P 5DB
tel. 071 387 8570

Legal Action Group
242–244 Pentonville Road
London N1 9UN
tel. 071 833 2931, fax 071 837 6094

Liberty-NCCL
21 Tabard Street
London SE1 4LA
tel. 071 403 3888, fax 071 407 5354

Medical Foundation for the Care of
Victims of Torture
96–98 Grafton Road
London NW5 3EJ
tel. 071 284 4321, fax 071 284 4265

Merseyside Immigration Advice Unit
34 Princes Road
Liverpool L8 1TH
tel. 051 571 1437

National Association of Citizens'
Advice Bureaux
Myddleton House
115–123 Pentonville Road
London N1 9LZ
tel. 071 863 2181

National Union of Students
461 Holloway Road
London N7 6LJ
tel. 071 272 8900

North East Refugee Service
John Haswell House
8–9 Gladstone Terrace
Gateshead, Tyne and Wear NE8 4DY
tel. 091 490 0314, fax 091 477 1260

Phil Powell
1 Horton Road
London E8
for digests of immigration appeal decisions
in family cases

Some racial equality councils, contact
National Association of Racial Equality
Councils
8–16 Coronet Street
London N1 6HD
tel. 071 739 6658 for details of local RECs

Refugee Arrivals Project
Room 2005, 2nd floor, Queen's Building
Heathrow Airport TW6 1DL
tel. 081 759 5740, fax 081 759 7058

Refugee Council
Bondway House, 3–9 Bondway
London SW8 1SJ
tel. 071 582 6922

Refugee Forum
54 Tavistock Place
London WC1H 9RG
tel. 071 482 3829, 071 388 7313

Refugee Legal Group
c/o North Islington Law Centre
161 Hornsey Road
London N7 6DU
tel. 071 607 2461, fax 071 700 0072

Rights and Justice
24 St Ann's Terrace
London NW8
tel. 071 586 4656

Runnymede Trust
11 Princelet Street
London E1 6QH
tel. 071 375 1496

Standing Conference on Racial Equality in
Europe
Brixton Enterprise Centre
444 Brixton Road
London SW9 8EJ
tel. 071 274 4000 ext. 303

United Kingdom Council for Overseas
Student Affairs
60 Westbourne Grove
London W2 5SH
tel. 071 229 9268, fax 071 229 3000

United Kingdom Immigrants Advisory
Service
County House, 190 Great Dover Street
London SE1 4YB
tel. 071 357 6917

Refugee Unit, same address
tel. 071 357 7421, fax 071 378 1979

Government Buildings
Clay Lane, Yardley
Birmingham B26 1DX
tel. 021 706 9765/4256

Room 3049, 3rd floor
Terminal Office Block, Gatwick Airport
Horley, Surrey, RH6 0NN
tel. 0293 33385

Government Buildings
Colnbrook Bypass
Harmondsworth, Middlesex UB7 0HG
tel. 081 897 9167/1514

Room 0001A, Queen's Building
Heathrow Airport
Hounslow, Middlesex TW6 1DF
tel. 081 759 9234

UKIAS *continued*
14 Eldon Terrace, Woodhouse Lane
Leeds LS2 9AB
tel. 0532 442460

Elliot House, 2 Jackson's Row
Manchester M2 5WD
tel. 061 834 9942

115 Wellington Street
Glasgow G2 2XT
tel. 041 248 2956

Unit 8, Williams Court, Trade Street
Cardiff CF1 5DQ
tel. 0222 223321

United Nations High Commission for
Refugees
7 Westminster Palace Gardens
Artillery Row
London SW1P 1RR
tel. 071 222 3065

University Diagnostics
University College
London, Gower Street
London WC1E 6BT
tel. 071 387 1413, fax 071 383 4061

World University Service
20 Compton Terrace
London N1 2UN
Tel. 071 226 6747

Glossary

Ad Hoc Group on Immigration: This is a grouping of civil servants and ministers responsible for immigration, from all the EC countries. It meets six-monthly, at the same time and place as the *Trevi group* (see below) to decide Europe-wide immigration and refugee policies.

Adjudicator: The person who hears and decides an immigration appeal at first instance. Adjudicators sit on their own, in centres around the country, to decide cases. It is possible to apply for leave to appeal to the Immigration Appeal Tribunal against an adjudicator's decision.

Asylum: Another word for *refugee* status (see below).

Asylum-seeker: A person requesting asylum or refugee status in the UK, whose application has not yet been decided.

Benefits Agency: The administrative branch of the Department of Social Security (DSS), which makes benefits payments.

British citizens

There are two kinds of British citizens: British citizens **otherwise than by descent** and British citizens **by descent**. The only difference is that the first group can pass British citizenship on automatically to their children born outside the UK and the second cannot.

British citizens otherwise than by descent are people who acquired their citizenship in the UK, either because they were born in the UK, or because they registered or naturalised in the UK, or because they are people who would have become British Dependent Territories citizens or British Overseas citizens but had been settled and had spent more than five years in the UK before 1983.

British citizens by descent are people born outside the UK who became British automatically at birth because their father, or in some circumstances their paternal grandfather, or (after 1 January 1983) their mother or father was a British citizen. A British citizen by descent can never change his or her status to become a British citizen otherwise than by descent.

British Dependent Territories citizens: These are people who are British because of their connection with a place that is still a British colony. They may have been born, adopted, registered or naturalised in that colony and can retain British Dependent Territories citizenship as long as the colony continues. When the colony gains independence or ceases to exist, people from that territory lose British Dependent Territories citizenship as the dependent territory no longer exists.

British Nationals (Overseas): This status has been created for British Dependent Territories citizens from Hong Kong who will be able to keep this British nationality status when Hong Kong reverts to China in 1997.

British Overseas citizens: These are people who were born in a place that used to be a British colony but who did not qualify for citizenship under the law of the new independent country or of any other country and therefore retained their British nationality.

British protected persons: These are people who are from a country which used to be a British protectorate, protected state or trust territory rather than a colony, but who did not gain the citizenship of the new independent country or of any other country.

British subjects: These are people who are from a country which used to be a British colony, who never became citizens of the UK and Colonies under the British Nationality Act 1948 and who did not gain citizenship of the new independent country or of any other country. Before 1983, the term 'British subject' meant exactly the same as 'Commonwealth citizen' but it is now only used for this small group of people.

Carriers' Liability Act: The legislation which allows the Home Office to fine airlines £2000 for each person they bring to the UK who does not have valid entry documents.

Colony: A country which is not yet independent. The largest British colony is Hong Kong, which will return to China on 1 July 1997. The others are Anguilla, Bermuda, British Antarctica, British Indian Ocean Territory, Cayman Islands, Falkland Islands, Gibraltar, Montserrat, Pitcairn Island, St Helena, Turks and Caicos Islands, Virgin Islands, Cyprus sovereign base areas.

Commonwealth citizens: All kinds of British nationals, except British protected persons, are Commonwealth citizens. So are citizens of the following countries, with their dates of independence in brackets:

Antigua and Barbuda (1 November 1981), Australia (1 January 1901), Bahamas (10 July 1973), Bangladesh (26 March 1971, as East Pakistan 15 August 1947), Barbados (30 November 1966), Belize (21 September 1981), Botswana (30 September 1966), Canada (1 July 1867), Cyprus (16 August 1960, joined 13 March 1961), Dominica (3 November 1978), Gambia (18 February 1965), Ghana (6 March 1957), Grenada (7 February 1974), Guyana (26 May 1966), India (15 August 1947), Jamaica (6 August 1962), Kenya (12 December 1963), Kiribati (12 July 1979), Lesotho (4 October 1966), Malawi (6 July 1964), Malaysia (31 August 1957), Malta (21 September 1964), Mauritius (12 March 1968), Namibia (joined 21 March 1990), Nauru (31 January 1968, joined 31 January 1980), Nevis (19 September 1983), New Zealand (26 September 1907), Nigeria (1 October 1960), Pakistan (15 August 1947), Papua New Guinea (16 September 1975), St Kitts (19 September 1983), St Lucia (22 February 1979), St Vincent and the Grenadines (27 October 1979), Seychelles (29 June 1976), Sierra Leone (27 April 1961), Singapore (3 June 1959, was part of Malaysia from 16 September 1963 until 8 August 1965), Solomon Islands (7 July 1978), Sri Lanka (4 February 1948), Swaziland (6 September 1968), Tanzania (9 December 1961), Tonga (4 June 1970), Trinidad and Tobago (31 August 1962), Tuvalu (1 October 1978), Uganda (9 October 1962), Vanuatu (30 July 1980), Western Samoa (1 January 1962, joined 28 August 1970), Zambia (24 October 1964), Zimbabwe (18 April 1980).

Deportation means sending a person out of the UK under an order signed by the Home Secretary, after the person has remained illegally in the UK, or has been convicted of a serious criminal offence, or because the Home Secretary has decided on public policy or national security grounds that the person's presence is 'not conducive to the public good'. The person cannot return unless the order has first been revoked.

Domicile means the country to which people feel they belong and in which they intend to spend the rest of their life. Normally people are considered to have a 'domicile of origin', usually the country in which they were born and grew up. This can only be changed by a conscious decision to settle and stay in another country and thus acquire a 'domicile of choice'. Questions asked to determine the domicile of people who have left their countries of origin often include where they hope to die and be buried/cremated. Domicile is important in deciding which countries' laws affect a particular person, for example in deciding whether a person is capable of contracting a polygamous marriage, or of adopting a child in a particular country. People's immigration status has no direct connection with their domicile.

EC: The European Community, which the UK joined on 1 January 1973. The other member states are Belgium, Denmark, France, Germany, Greece, Ireland, Italy, Luxembourg, the Netherlands, Portugal, Spain.

Entry clearance officers: Officials at British posts overseas who deal with immigration applications there. In a visa country, they may be known as visa officers, in a non-visa Commonwealth country as entry certificate officers.

Exceptional leave to remain: People who apply for refugee status in the UK and are refused, but the Home Office does not think it is safe for them to return for the time being, may be granted exceptional leave to remain in the UK. So may other people who have strong compassionate reasons for needing to remain. It is entirely outside the immigration rules, at the discretion of the Home Office.

Green books: The popular name for the Immigration Appeals Reports (Imm AR).

Illegal entrant means a person who immigration officers believe has entered the UK illegally, either by bypassing immigration control altogether, or by deception as to his or her identity or reasons for coming to the UK, or by entering in breach of a current deportation order.

IM2: The application forms, obtainable from British posts overseas, to apply for entry clearance to the UK. The basic form, filled in by all who apply for entry clearance, is IM2A; those applying for settlement for the first time also fill in IM2B, those who have the right of abode IM2C, those coming for work IM2D, those who have previously been refused entry IM2E.

Imm AR: The Immigration Appeals reports, published quarterly, but with page numbers continuing throughout a year. They contain selected decisions of the High Court, Court of Appeal, House of Lords and of the Immigration Appeal Tribunal. They are also known as the 'green books'. Cases are usually cited by their name, year and page, for example, *Wirdestedt*, Imm AR 1990, 20.

Immigration Appeal Tribunal: The second tier of the immigration appeals system. The Tribunal will grant leave to appeal if it decides there is an arguable point of law in a case, or other arguments which should be heard. It is a three-person body. It is possible to apply for leave to appeal from its decision through the judicial review process.

Immigration officer: An official at a British port of entry dealing with immigration applications who decides on granting and refusing leave to enter, and on what conditions.

Immigration rules: The rules of practice, published by the Home Office, on how immigration officials should implement the Immigration Acts. They have the force of law and are interpreted by the Home Office and through decisions of the Immigration Appeal Tribunal.

Indefinite leave: Leave to enter or remain in the UK without any time limit. If there is no time limit, no other conditions can be put on the person's stay either. A person who has indefinite leave to enter or remain is 'settled' (see below) in the UK.

Leave to enter/remain: Permission given by immigration officials to people to enter or remain in the UK. It may be indefinite or limited.

Limited leave: Permission to enter or remain in the UK which has a time limit, and may have other conditions attached to it.

Naturalisation: A process of applying for British nationality. The application is at the discretion of the Home Office and can be made on the basis of residence in the UK, marriage to a British partner or Crown service. Naturalisation and registration (see below) are both ways of gaining British citizenship; the citizenship obtained is the same whichever process is used.

Ordinary residence: This has been defined in the courts as the place where someone is normally living for the time being. People can be ordinarily resident in the UK without being settled here – for example, the UK is the normal place of residence for students, work permit holders and au pairs. It is not an immigration status and has no direct connection to this; the term is also used in other areas of law, including the National Health Service and benefits regulations. People stop being ordinarily resident in the UK if they change their normal place of residence to another country; the Home Office could argue that several months residence abroad, particularly if the person had taken a job there or given up a home in the UK, had broken ordinary residence in the UK. However, it is possible to be ordinarily resident in more than one country at a time, so such decisions can be challenged.

Overstayer means a person who was allowed in to the UK for a limited period but who has remained longer than the time allowed without permission from the Home Office.

Patriality is another word for *right of abode*. It was first used in the Immigration Act 1971 but was replaced by the term 'right of abode' in the British Nationality Act 1981.

Permanent stay: Another phrase meaning *settled* (see below).

Permit-free employment: A list of jobs which people may come to the UK to do without the employers needing to get work permits from the Employment Department. Permission is obtained direct from the Home Office or through the British post in the worker's country of origin.

Person from abroad: A term used by the Department of Social Security Benefits Agency meaning a person who is not eligible to claim income support at the normal rate.

Police registration certificate: The certificate given by the police to those non-Commonwealth, non-EC citizens who are required to register details with them.

Political asylum: Another word for *refugee* status (see below).

Public funds: Public funds for immigration purposes are income support, housing benefit, family credit and housing under Part III of the Housing Act 1985, Part II of the Housing (Scotland) Act 1987 and Part II of the Housing (Northern Ireland) Order 1988 (the homelessness provisions) *only*.

Quota voucher see Special quota voucher.

Re-entry visa: These were abolished from 16 May 1991. Previously, a visa national normally required a visa on every entry to the UK. When visa nationals had been granted leave to remain in the UK and wished to travel and return within that period, they needed a re-entry visa. For most visa nationals, this was obtained from one of the British passport offices, and was valid until one month before any limited leave expired, and for any number of entries within two years for settled people. Citizens of Algeria, Bangladesh, Ghana, India, Morocco, Nigeria, Pakistan, Sri Lanka, Tunisia and Uganda obtained re-entry visas from the Home Office. Since 16 May 1991, visa nationals granted leave to remain for more than six months have been exempt from requiring visas if they travel within that period, but there are no longer any passport stamps to show this.

Refugee: The United Nations Convention relating to the Status of Refugees defines a refugee as a person who, 'owing to a well-founded fear of being persecuted for reasons of race, religion, nationality, membership of a particular social group or political opinion is outside the country of his nationality and is unable, or owing to such fear, is unwilling to avail himself of the protection of that country; or who, not having a nationality and being outside the country of his former habitual residence . . . is unable or, owing to such a fear, is unwilling to return to it.' When people have been recognised as refugees, they have been granted asylum.

Registration: There are three distinct immigration/nationality law uses of this term.

1 A process of applying for British nationality. The word is now used for any child applying for British nationality and for a person who holds any other kind of British nationality applying to become a British citizen. Registration and *naturalisation* (see above) are both ways of gaining British nationality; the nationality obtained through either process is the same.

2 Registering the birth of a child at a British post overseas. A child born outside the UK to a British citizen parent who was not him or herself born in the UK may be registered within one year of birth to become a British citizen by descent.

3 Registering with the police. People who are not Commonwealth or EC citizens, who are over 16 and who have been allowed to remain in the UK for more than six months but are not settled may be required to register with the police. This means going to the local police station, or the Aliens Registration Office in London, with the passport, two passport-sized photos and details of address and occupation, registering these details with the police and paying a fee (see appendix).

Removal means the procedure for sending a person refused entry, or a person being treated as an illegal entrant, away from the UK. People have no right of appeal against removal until they have left the UK. There is no formal order made against them so they are able to apply to return, but will have to fit into the immigration rules.

Returning residents are people who are settled in the UK and are returning to the UK within two years of departure. They should be admitted for an indefinite period, provided the immigration officers are satisfied that they intend to return for settlement.

Right of abode means being free of immigration control and able to enter the UK freely at any time, after no matter how long an absence. It is more than simply having the right to live in the UK, or the right to stay indefinitely. All British citizens have the right of abode. So do some Commonwealth citizens – people who were born before 1 January 1983 and had a parent born in the UK and Commonwealth-citizen women married before 1 January 1983 to a man who was born, registered or naturalised in the UK, or who is a Commonwealth citizen with a parent born in the UK.

Schengen group: A group of EC countries which includes Belgium, Luxembourg, the Netherlands, France, Germany, Italy, Spain and Portugal. The intention of the group is to work towards a common immigration policy and common border controls.

Settled means someone who is legally in the UK, without any conditions (for example, they have no limit on the time they can remain, and no restrictions on working or the sort of work they can do while in the UK). Other terms used for this are 'permanent stay' or 'indefinite leave'. People who have lived in the UK for a long time, or who came with their parents are likely to be settled (as long as they are in the country legally). Most (but not all) settled people have a stamp in their passports saying that they have 'indefinite leave to remain in the UK'.

Special quota voucher: The permission granted to certain British nationals, who are not British citizens, to come to settle in the UK. The system was set up in 1968, after the Commonwealth Immigrants Act 1968 removed the rights of British people without a connection by birth or descent with Britain itself to come to Britain. In order to qualify under the scheme, people must have no other nationality but British, be heads of households, have some connection with East Africa and be under pressure to leave the country in which they are currently living.

Sponsorship: The act of supporting financially people who are applying to come to the UK. Sponsors may be requested to sign a formal *undertaking* (see below).

Temporary admission: A kind of limbo state, used as an alternative to detention. While immigration officers are considering whether to allow someone in at a port of entry, or after refusal of entry and before removal, or when a person is being treated as an illegal entrant, he or she may either be detained or released on temporary admission. If released, the person has not been granted formal leave to enter the UK, and can be recalled and detained at any time.

Trevi group: The Interior or Justice Ministers of all 12 EC countries, meeting together to discuss issues of border controls and control of terrorists, drug traffickers and other criminals. When it meets, at the same time and place there is also a meeting of the *Ad Hoc Group on Immigration* (see above) discussing immigration issues within the EC.

Undertaking: A formal statement signed by a person living in the UK that he or she will support another person, usually a relative, who is applying to come to or to remain in the UK. It gives the DSS power to reclaim from the signer any income support paid to the person whose support was guaranteed.

Visa exemption stamps: Before 16 May 1991, visa nationals (see below) from particular countries who were exempt from requiring visas in certain circumstances could get this exemption confirmed by a passport endorsement, either from the Home Office or from an immigration officer when they left the country. This was useful as confirmation for airline staff and others that they were eligible to return without a visa. From 16 May 1991, all visa nationals have been exempt from requiring visas if they have been granted leave to remain for more than six months and are returning within that time or if they are returning residents, and visa exemption stamps are no longer used.

Visa nationals are people who always need to get entry clearance in advance of travelling to the UK, for whatever purpose.* Countries whose citizens are visa nationals in January 1992 are:
Afghanistan, Albania, Algeria, Angola, Armenia, Azerbaijan, Bangladesh, Belarus, Benin, Bhutan, Bulgaria, Burkina Faso, Burma, Burundi, Cambodia, Cameroon, Cape Verde, Central African Republic, Chad, China, Comoros, Congo, Cuba, Djibouti, Egypt, Equatorial Guinea, Ethiopia, Gabon, Georgia, Ghana, Guinea, Guinea-Bissau, Haiti, India, Indonesia, Iran, Iraq, Jordan, Kazakhstan, Kirgizstan, Korea (North), Laos, Lebanon, Liberia, Libya, Madagascar, Mali, Mauritania, Moldòva, Mongolia, Morocco, Mozambique, Nepal, Nigeria, Oman, Pakistan, Philippines, Poland, Romania, Russia, Rwanda, Sao Tome e Principe, Saudi Arabia, Senegal, Somalia, Soviet Union, Sri Lanka, Sudan, Syria, Taiwan, Tajikistan, Thailand, Togo, Tunisia, Turkey, Turkmenistan, Uganda, Ukraine, Uzbekistan, Vietnam, Yemen, Zaire.

* people do **not** need visas if they are returning residents or are returning within a period of earlier leave granted for more than six months.

Work permits: The permission gained by employers to employ a worker from overseas who does not otherwise qualify to come to live in the UK. The Employment Department issues permits to employers, not to workers, to employ a named person in a specific job. Any change of job means the new employers must apply for a new permit.

Appendices

1 RELEVANT ACTS AND RULES

Immigration Act 1971

British Nationality Act 1981

Immigration (Carriers' Liability) Act 1987

Immigration Act 1988

Immigration rules in force at January 1992

HC 251	Statement of changes in immigration rules, 23 March 1990, in effect from 1 May 1990. The full rules, as referred to in the text.
HC 454, June 1990.	Abolished visas for citizens of Argentina and the then German Democratic Republic.
Cm 1220, September 1990.	Abolished visas for citizens of Czechoslovakia and Hungary.
HC 320, March 1991.	Introduction of visas for Ugandan citizens.
HC 356, April 1991.	Abolition of re-entry visas.
Cm 1672, September 1991.	Applications for extensions of stay in order to obtain or extend work permits to be made direct to the Employment Department, not to the Home Office.
HC 670, October 1991.	Czechoslovakian and Hungarian women may become au pairs.
HC 175, January 1992.	Added the new countries from the USSR to the list of visa countries, except for Estonia, Latvia and Lithuania and abolished visas for the US Pacific Trust Territories.

2 SELECTED FEES, as at January 1992

The Home Office or Foreign and Commonwealth Office may raise fees at very short notice. It is rare for these rises to receive much publicity unless they are unusually steep.

Applying for entry clearance

All entry clearance fees are non-refundable.

Visitor, single-entry £20

  under 25, single entry £10

  six-month multiple entry £30

  two-year multiple entry £40

  five-year multiple entry £85

Student, single entry £20

  under 25, single entry £10

  multiple entry £40

Transit visa £20

Work permit or permit-free employment or self-employed or sole representative, 6 months or under £20

  over 6 months £60

Business or independent means £60

Family members of any of these people accompanying them or coming to join them pay the same fee as their sponsor.

Commonwealth citizens with UK-born grandparent £60

Working holidaymaker £20

  under 25 £10

Settlement (to accompany or join a relative already settled in the UK) £80

Returning resident £20

  under 25 £10

Certificate of entitlement (from abroad) £80

Other fees in the UK

Fee for a police registration certificate £27.50

Fee for DNA testing through Cellmark Diagnostics £140 plus VAT per sample of blood tested, £1.50 plus VAT for transport of each sample to the UK.

Fee for DNA testing through University Diagnostics £447.67 for up to 3 samples tested, £100 plus VAT for each additional sample.

Fee for a certificate of entitlement of the right of abode from the Home Office £12.50

British passport (standard) £15

British passport (jumbo) £22.50

Home Office travel document £15

Applying for British citizenship

Registration (for children under 18 and other kinds of British nationals applying for British citizenship) £85 (£25 refunded if application is refused)

Naturalisation on the grounds of marriage to a British citizen £135 (£5 refunded if application is refused)

Naturalisation on the grounds of residence in the UK £170 (£35 refunded if application is refused)

Renunciation of British citizenship £15

Resumption of British citizenship after renunciation £15

3 DELAYS

Entry clearance applications

In July 1991 the waiting times for interviews for settlement entry clearance were:

Philippines	ten weeks
Ghana	one week
Jamaica	six weeks
Nigeria	one day
Morocco	ten days

In the countries of the Indian subcontinent there are separate queues. In July 1991 the delays (in months) were:

	Q1	Q2	Q3	Q4
Islamabad	3	4	6	10
Karachi	3	3	4	6
Dhaka	3	5	6	11
New Delhi	1	4	7	10
Bombay	0	5	10	11
Madras	1.5	1.5	1.5	1.5
Calcutta (days)	10	10	10	10

Q1 People with a claim to the right of abode, dependent relatives over 70 years old, special compassionate cases (not defined further)

Q2 All spouses, and all children under 18

Q3 Fiancé(e)s and other relatives applying for the first time

Q4 Reapplicants

Applications for citizenship

Applications for naturalisation completed in October 1991 had taken 31 months on average. Applications for registration completed in October 1991 had taken 22 months on average. There were still nearly 9,000 applications for registration made before the 31 December 1987 deadline under consideration. The Home Office believes it may have lost touch with some applicants and therefore asks **anyone who applied for registration before 31 December 1987 and who has not yet received a decision** to write to the Home Office.

4 STANDARD FORMS

ENTRY CLEARANCE APPLICATION FORM   for all applicants (IM2 A)

- Please complete the form in black ink and
- ☑ tick the boxes which apply.
- Short stay applicants must complete all the questions on this form.
- Long stay applicants must complete questions 1-19 and any additional forms stated below.

THIS FORM IS SUPPLIED FREE   IM2A (Revised 12/90)

Application for United Kingdom entry clearance

This form incorporates the questions contained in the EC standard application forms for short stay and transit visas, approved by EC Ministers in December 1989.

Please send with this form -
- the correct fee *(entry clearance fees will not be refunded)*
- two passport-sized photographs *(not more than six months old)* and
- your current passport

A separate form should be completed by every person intending to travel *unless* you are a dependant under 16 included on your parent's Passport.

➡ **All applicants must sign this form on page 3**

---

1 Reason for travelling to the UK *(please tick appropriate boxes)*

Short stay: Visitor ☐   *(please specify)*
Private ☐ Official ☐ Business ☐ Student ☐ Other ☐ [   ]

Type of entry clearance required   Transit ☐   Single entry ☐   Double entry ☐   Multiple entry ☐

Long stay: Settlement as: spouse/fiance(e)/other relative ☐   *Please also complete form IM2B*

Permit free employment/work permit holder/or to establish a business ☐   *Please also complete form IM2C*

Certificate of entitlement, UK ancestry ☐   *Please also complete form IM2D*

Returning resident ☐

2 Full name *(as written in your passport, please write in both styles if two scripts have been used)*

3 Other names used now or in the past *(eg name before marriage)*

4 Date of birth day   month year   **5** Sex M ☐ F ☐   **6** Town and country of birth

7 Your father's full name

8 Your mother's full name

9 Passport or travel document details   Issuing government/authority   Number   Nationality as shown in passport

Document type *(eg ordinary passport)*   Place of issue   Date of issue day month year   Valid until day month year

If you are not travelling on your own passport give the following details:
Name of passport holder   Your relationship to passport holder

Only complete this section if dependants included on your passport are travelling with you.

Full name of dependent	Place of birth	Date of birth	Relationship to yourself	Nationality

ENTRY CLEARANCE APPLICATION FORM for all applicants (IM2 A)

10 What is your present job?

11 Where do you work? *(Give name and address of company/organisation)*

What date did you start this job?
day month year

What is your annual income?

12 What is your present address?

13 Please give your permanent address if different from above

14 Are you? Married ☐ Single ☐ Divorced ☐ Widowed ☐ Separated ☐

15 If married, please give details of spouse:

Full name of spouse

Date of birth
day month year

Where is your spouse now?

Where is your spouse normally resident?

16 How many children under 16 years old do you have?

17 Have you applied to go to the UK before? If so, please give dates and places of application

18 Have you visited the UK before? If so, please give dates and and lengths of each stay

19

a Have you ever been refused a visa or entry clearance at a UK diplomatic mission or Post? [no] [yes] *If yes complete form IM2E*

b Have you ever been refused leave to enter on arrival in the UK? [no] [yes] *If yes complete form IM2E*

c Have you ever been deported, removed or otherwise required to leave the UK? [no] [yes]

If yes name country

d Have you ever been refused a visa for another country? [no] [yes]

If yes name country

e Have you ever been deported from another country? [no] [yes]

➡ **Answer questions 20-33 ONLY if you are applying for a short stay in the UK**

20 Country of normal residence

Residence Permit number *(if any)*

Date of issue
day month year

Valid until
day month year

21 Re-entry visa *(if applicable)*

Visa number

Date of issue
day month year

Valid until
day month year

22 How long do you intend to stay in the UK?

23 What is your proposed date of arrival in the UK?
day month year

24 How will you travel to the UK?

25 Have you bought your ticket already? [yes] *If yes what kind of ticket do you have?* [no] *If no what kind of ticket do you intend to buy?*

single

open dated

return confirmed

☐ ☐ ☐

26 How much money is available to you during your stay? *(Evidence of this may be required.)*

a From your own resources

b From other sources

ENTRY CLEARANCE APPLICATION FORM for all applicants (IM2 A)

27 Where will you stay in the UK? *Please give details of host/sponsor/contact address.*
☛ If you are staying in a hotel give its name and address.
(It is not enough to say c/o Embassy or High commission.)

Full name of sponsor/contact address/hotel | Nationality of sponsor

Address

Telephone number | Resident in UK since: | Occupation | Relationship to you:

28 Is your visit for business or official reasons? *If so, give name of UK company/organisation to be visited*

➡ This section to be answered by transit applicants only

29 Are you are travelling to another country BEFORE the UK? *If so, please give details:* Name of country | *Please tick appropriate boxes* Do you have permission to enter that country? no | yes | not needed

Do you have a visa or resident permit for that country? *If so, please give details:* Number | Valid until day month year | Issuing Authority

30 To which country are you travelling AFTER the UK? Name of country | *Please tick appropriate boxes* Do you have permission to enter that country? no | yes | not needed

Do you have a visa or resident permit for that country? *If so, please give details:* Number | Valid until day month year | Issuing Authority

➡ This section to be answered by students only

31 Please give name and address of school/ university at which you will study

32 What technical or educational certificates do you hold? *(Any relevant diplomas or certificates should be submitted.)*

33 Describe fully the course you wish to follow *Please submit evidence of acceptance for a course of study, and evidence of accommodation.*

34 Who will pay for the course?

➡ This section must be read and signed by all applicants

☛ An entry clearance can be a Visa, Entry Certificate or a Letter of Consent.

☛ Even if you hold a valid entry clearance you can still be refused entry into the United Kingdom by an Immigration Officer if he is satisfied that:

a your entry clearance was obtained by false representations or by concealment of relevant facts, whether or not you knew of these actions; or

b a change in circumstances between the date of your application and your arrival in the UK invalidates your entry clearance; or a refusal is justified on the grounds of restricted returnability, medical grounds, criminal record, because you are subject to a deportation order, or your exclusion would be conducive to the public good.

☛ An immigration Officer can ask anyone to be medically examined on arrival in the UK, if he considers it necessary. If you intend to stay in the UK longer than six months you may be required to have a medical examination before your entry clearance is issued.

Please attach your photograph here ➡

DECLARATION
☛ I have read and understood the notes above.
☛ I declare that the information given in this application is correct to the best of my knowledge and belief.

Signed

Date

Page 3

FORMAL UNDERTAKING OF SUPPORT (RON 112)

RON 112

IMMIGRATION ACT 1971

Undertaking given in pursuance of Immigration Rules

Please complete this form in block capitals

1. I, ... (name), of

   .... (address),

   Home Office reference number ....

   hereby declare that my date of birth is ....

* and that I am employed as .... (occupation)

* at .... (address).

* My National Insurance number is ....

2. I hereby undertake that if .... (name of sponsored person) who was born in .... on .... (place and date of birth of sponsored person) is granted leave to enter or remain in the United Kingdom I shall be responsible for his/her maintenance and accommodation in the United Kingdom, throughout the period of that leave and any variation of it.

3. I understand that this undertaking shall be made available to the Department of Health and Social Security in the United Kingdom who may take appropriate steps to recover from me the cost of any supplementary benefit paid to or in respect of the person who is the subject of this undertaking.

Signed:

Date:

*To be completed only if sponsor
is resident in the United Kingdom

FOR OFFICIAL USE ONLY

Certificate

I certify that this document, apart from this certificate, is an undertaking given in pursuance of immigration rules within the meaning of the Immigration Act 1971.

Signed by   , being a person authorised to make this certificate
on behalf of the Secretary of State.

Signature:

Personalised Date Stamp:

Print date: September 1987   **RON 112**

NOTIFICATION OF TEMPORARY ADMISSION (IS 96)

HOME OFFICE

ind

IMMIGRATION SERVICE

Port Reference:

Home Office Reference:

IS 96

HM IMMIGRATION OFFICE

Telephone:

IMMIGRATION ACT 1971 – NOTIFICATION OF TEMPORARY ADMISSION TO A PERSON WHO IS LIABLE TO BE DETAINED

To ....

LIABILITY TO DETENTION

A. You are a person who is liable to be detained*

TEMPORARY ADMISSION/ RESTRICTIONS

B. I hereby authorise your (further) temporary admission to the United Kingdom subject to the following restrictions**:-

- You must reside at:- ....
....
.... Telephone: ....
- You may not enter employment, paid or unpaid, or engage in any business or profession.
- You must report to

Tick ☑ as appropriate

☐ an Immigration Officer at ....
☐ the Police
☐ on .... 19 .... at .... hrs.
☐ each .... day at .... hrs. until further notice.
☐ on a day and at a time to be notified to you in writing
☐ ....

ANY CHANGE OF RESTRICTION

If these restrictions are to be changed, an Immigration Officer will write to you.

- Although you have been temporarily admitted, you remain liable to be detained
- You have NOT been given leave to enter the United Kingdom within the meaning of the Immigration Act 1971.

Date

Immigration Officer

* Paragraph 16 of Schedule 2 to the Act
** Paragraph 21 of Schedule 2 to the Act

(IS 96 Temporary Admission)
Printed in the UK for HMSO 10/90 Dd 8255950 C180 CCN 56294

REFUSAL OF LEAVE TO REMAIN with right of appeal (APP 101A)

Reference: APP 101A

Home Office Immigration and Nationality Department

IMMIGRATION ACT 1971 - NOTICE OF REFUSAL TO VARY LEAVE

(Paragraph/s   )

To:

The Secretary of State therefore refuses your application.

Under the Immigration (Variation of Leave) Order 1976, your stay has been
extended to 28 days after the date of this notice. If you do not wish to
appeal, you should leave the United Kingdom by that date.

RIGHT OF   You are entitled to appeal against this decision under
APPEAL   Section 14(1) of the Immigration Act 1971 to the appellate
                  authorities.

HOW TO   If you wish to appeal you should complete the attached form
APPEAL   (APP 1) and return it to the Appeals Section, Home Office,
                  Lunar House, Wellesley Road, Croydon, CR9 2BY. An envelope
                  is provided for this purpose but you will need to affix a
                  postage stamp and you may wish to return it by recorded
                  delivery.

TIME LIMIT   The completed appeal form must be returned to arrive at
FOR APPEALING   Lunar House not later than 14 days after the date of this
                  notice.

ASSISTANCE   Please turn over.
AND ADVICE

                                        Signed:
                                        On behalf of the Secretary of State

                                        Date:

LH2.8

REFUSAL OF LEAVE TO REMAIN without right of appeal (RON 110)

Home Office Reference: RON 110

IMMIGRATION ACT 1971

Refusal to grant leave to remain or to vary leave to enter

To:

The Secretary of State therefore refuses your application.

Under section 14(1) of the Immigration Act 1971 an entitlement to appeal against a refusal to vary a limited leave is conferred only on a person whose limited leave to enter or remain has not expired.

Your application was made on   but your limited leave expired on   . You therefore have no right of appeal against the Secretary of State's decision.

I have to remind you that because your limited leave to enter or remain has expired you should leave the United Kingdom without delay. If you fail to leave you may be prosecuted for an offence under the Immigration Act, the penalty for which is a fine of up to £1,000 and up to 6 months imprisonment, and you will also be liable to deportation.

Signed:

On behalf of the Secretary of State

Date:

Home Office
Immigration and Nationality Department

GRANT OF EXCEPTIONAL LEAVE TO REMAIN (GEN 19)

Immigration and Nationality Department

Lunar House 40 Wellesley Road
Croydon CR9 2BY
Telephone 081-760

Exceptional-Grant
GEN 19

Your reference

Our reference

Date

Dear

Your application for refugee status in the United Kingdom has been carefully considered but I have to tell you that it has been refused. It has been decided, however, that although you do not qualify for refugee status it would be right to give you exceptional leave to remain in the United Kingdom until .... The grant of exceptional leave to remain has been given under the .... exceptional policy*/because of the particular circumstances of your case.

You should, however, fully understand that if during your stay in the United Kingdom you take part in activities involving, for example, the support or encouragement of violence, or conspiracy to cause violence, whether in the United Kingdom or abroad, the Secretary of State may curtail your stay or deport you.

POLICE REGISTRATION

* you must now register with the police: please take this letter to your local police station as soon as possible.

* I enclose your police registration certificate which has been suitably endorsed.

* please send (or take) your police registration certificate, your passport and this letter to your local police registration officer so that the certificate can be endorsed.

If you change your address or any other details of your registration you should tell your local police registration officer (either in person or by letter) within 7 days. Ask your local police station if you do not know how to contact your police registration officer.

EMPLOYMENT

You do not need the permission of the Department of Employment or the Home Office before taking a job. The Manpower Services Commission can help you find a job or train for work - any job

LH1.5

GRANT OF EXCEPTIONAL LEAVE TO REMAIN (GEN 19)

centre or employment office will be able to help you and you can apply for a place on a government sponsored training scheme if you meet the normal conlitions for these schemes. You are free to set up in business or any professional activity within the general regulations that apply to that business or profession.

If you want to live or work in the Isle of Man or one of the Channel Islands you must first ask the Island's immigration authorities.

HEALTH AND SOCIAL SERVICES

You are free to use the National Health Service and the social services and other help provided by local authorities as you need them. You will be able to get Social Security Benefit (including Supplementary Benefit) if you meet the ordinary conditions. If you need any of these services, take this letter with you and show it if there is any question about your entitlement to the service. Your local Social Security Office will give you advice on social security benefits, the British Refugee Council Bondway House, 3-9 Bondway, London SW8 1SJ: telephone 071-582 6922) can advise you on other welfare services, and your local Citizens Advice Bureau will help you with general questions.

TRAVEL ABROAD

You should keep your present passport valid. If however, your national authorities will not renew or replace your passport, or you can show that it would be unreasonable to expect you to approach your Embassy or Consulate here, you can apply for a Home Office travel document from the Travel Document Section (telephone 081-760 2345) at the Home Office, Lunar House, Croydon, CR9 2BY.

FURTHER LEAVE TO REMAIN

Your passport is enclosed, endorsed with leave to remain until   Any application you make for further leave to remain will be carefully considered.

                                        Yours sincerely

Encs

* Delete as appropriate

LH1.5

for one year initially (RON 124)

Immigration and
Nationality Department

Lunar House 40 Wellesley Road
Croydon CR9 2BY

RON 124

Telephone 081-760

Your reference

Our reference

Date

Dear

I am writing about your application to remain in the United Kingdom
following your marriage.

A person who marries someone settled in this country may be allowed
to stay here for an initial period of up to 12 months, provided
that the requirements of the Immigration Rules are met. You may
now stay in the United Kingdom until   and
may set up a business or take employment without a work permit.

During this period you will be expected not to rely on public funds
to support yourself, although there is no objection to your spouse
receiving any assistance to which he or she is entitled in his or
her own right. Public funds means housing under Part III of the
Housing Act 1985 and income support, family credit and housing
benefit under Part II of the Social Security Act 1986.

You may apply for the time limit attached to your stay in this
country to be removed shortly before your leave expires. It is
important that this application is made before then and you should
enclose your passport and the birth certificate or passport of your
spouse for identification purposes with it.

For the application to be granted, we will need to be satisfied
that your marriage has not ended and that you and your spouse both
still intend living permanently with each other as husband and
wife. If you provide a statement to this effect, signed by you
both, this will assist us in considering your application.

We shall also need to ask if you have received any of the public
funds described above since the date of this letter, and any
information you can provide about this could again save further
enquiry on our part. Short term assistance from public funds in an
emergency will not lead to a refusal of your application, but if
you have received substantial help from public funds, and in
particular it is clear that you are unable to maintain and
accommodate yourself without further help, your application may be
refused under the general considerations in paragraph 100 of the
Immigration Rules.

LH2.11

GRANT OF LEAVE TO REMAIN AS A SPOUSE
for one year initially (RON 124)

If, when you make your further application, you are no longer living with your spouse, your continued stay in this country (including the question of continuing in employment or in business) will normally be subject to your qualifying for further leave in some other capacity under the Immigration Rules. You should therefore explain your current circumstances and make an application accordingly.

* You are no longer required to register with the police, and your police registration certificate has been endorsed to this effect.

The requirements of the Immigration Rules covering those who wish to stay in this country on the basis of their marriage to someone permanently resident here are set out in full in the 'Statement of Changes in Immigration Rules', House of Commons Paper 251 which came into effect on 1 May 1990. This publication also sets out the requirements for those who wish to stay here in most other categories. Copies are available from Her Majesty's Stationery Office or through booksellers.

If you have any questions about this letter, please write to us at the above address, quoting our reference number.

Yours sincerely

* delete as appropriate

LH2.11

GRANT OF INDEFINITE LEAVE TO REMAIN (RON 60)

RON 60

Immigration and Nationality Department

Lunar House 40 Wellesley Road
Croydon CR9 2BY
Telephone 01-760

Your reference

Our reference

Date

Dear

I am writing to say that there are no longer any restrictions on the period for which you may remain in the United Kingdom. Your passport, which is enclosed, has been stamped to show this.

You can now remain indefinitely in the United Kingdom. You do not need permission from a Government Department to take or change employment and you may engage in business or a profession as long as you comply with any general regulations for the business or professional activity.

*As a visa national, you still need a visa every time you enter the United Kingdom and you may be refused entry if you do not have one. You may get a re-entry visa at any British Passport Office in the United Kingdom or at a British Embassy, High Commission or Consulate abroad.

If you are thinking of going to live or work in the Isle of Man or one of the Channel Islands, you should first consult the Immigration authorities in the Island concerned.

If you leave the United Kingdom, you will normally be re-admitted at any time within 2 years of your departure.

If you obtain a new passport, you may ask us to stamp it to show your immigration status before you travel. You should send or bring it to this Department at the address at the top of this letter, or take it to one of our local Public Enquiry Offices. You should also bring or send the enclosed passport and this letter. If you send your passport by post, you should do so at least 2 months before you intend to travel. If you do not have your passport stamped before you travel, when you return to the United Kingdom you will have to satisfy the immigration officer that you had indefinite leave to remain when you left. To do this, you will need to produce either the enclosed passport and other documentary evidence such as bank statements, notices of income tax coding, school or employment records etc relating to the earlier years of your residence in the United Kingdom. It may also be helpful to carry this letter with you.

A child already born to you in the United Kingdom since 1 January 1983, and who is not a British citizen, is now entitled to be registered as such a citizen. More information about British citizenship by birth in the United Kingdom and an application form for registration are available from the Nationality Division of the Home Office at the address at the top of this letter. Any child born to you in the United Kingdom while you remain settled here (or while your husband/wife is settled here) will be a British citizen automatically at birth.

*You no longer need to report changes of address or other particulars to the police. Your police registration certificate, which is enclosed, has been stamped to show this.

Yours

Immigration Division

*Delete as appropriate

ENC

Feb 1986

STANDARD LETTER AFTER AN APPEAL HAS BEEN LOST (RON 67)

RON 67

Immigration and Nationality Department

Lunar House 40 Wellesley Road
Croydon CR9 2BY
Telephone 081-760

	Your reference
	Our reference
	Date

Dear

Your appeal against the Secretary of State's decision of
was dismissed/withdrawn* on

You therefore have no basis of stay in this country and must now
leave the United Kingdom immediately.

If you fail to leave you may be liable to prosecution for an offence
under the Immigration Act 1971. You are also liable to deportation.

*Delete as appropriate.

DECISION TO MAKE A DEPORTATION ORDER (APP 104)

Reference: APP 104

Home Office Immigration and Nationality Department

IMMIGRATION ACTS 1971 AND 1988 - DECISION TO MAKE A DEPORTATION ORDER

To:

The Secretary of State has therefore decided to make an order by virtue of
Section 3(5) of the Immigration Act 1971 requiring you to leave the United
Kingdom and prohibiting you from re-entering while the order is in force.
He proposes to give directions for your removal to   , the
country of which you are a national or which most recently provided you
with a travel document.

RIGHT OF
APPEAL

You are entitled to appeal against this decision under
Section 15(1)(a) of the Immigration Act 1971 (as amended by
the Immigration Act 1988) to the appellate authorities and
you are entitled under Section 17(3) of the Immigration Act
1971 to object to your removal to the country specified
above in your appeal. If you wish to appeal against the
direction for removal you must state the name of the country
to which you claim you ought to be removed. You should
attach to the form a statement of the reasons why you object
to removal to the country specified in the direction. You
should also produce evidence which demonstrates or tends to
show that that country or territory so identified would
admit you if removed there. It is for you to satisfy the
appellate authorities that the government of the country of
your choice will admit you on deportation from the United
Kingdom.

HOW TO
APPEAL

If you wish to appeal you should complete the attached form
(APP 11) and return it to the Appeals Section, Home Office,
Lunar House, Wellesley Road, Croydon, CR9 2BY. An envelope
is provided for this purpose, but you will need to affix a
postage stamp and you may wish to return it by recorded
delivery.

TIME LIMIT
FOR
APPEALING

The completed appeal form must be returned to arrive at
Lunar House not later than 14 days after the date of this
notice.

ASSISTANCE
AND ADVICE

Please turn over.

Signed:
On behalf of the Secretary of State

Date:

Index